KEY CONCEPTS IN HUMAN RESOURCE MANAGEMENT

Palgrave Key Concepts

Palgrave Key Concepts provide an accessible and comprehensive range of subject glossaries at undergraduate level. They are the ideal companion to a standard textbook, making them invaluable reading to students throughout their course of study, and especially useful as a revision aid.

The key concepts are arranged alphabetically so you can quickly find terms or entries of immediate interest. All major theories, concepts, terms and theorists are incorporated and cross-referenced. Additional reading or website research opportunities are included. With hundreds of key terms defined, **Palgrave Key Concepts** represent a comprehensive must-have reference for undergraduates.

Published

Key Concepts in Accounting and Finance
Key Concepts in Business Practice
Key Concepts in Human Resource Management
Key Concepts in International Business
Key Concepts in Management
Key Concepts in Marketing
Key Concepts in Operations Management
Key Concepts in Politics
Key Concepts in Strategic Management
Linguistic Terms and Concepts
Literary Terms and Criticism (*third edition*)

Further titles are in preparation

www.palgravekeyconcepts.com

Palgrave Key Concepts
Series Standing Order ISBN 1–4039–3210–7
(*outside North America only*)

You can receive future titles in this series as they are published by placing a standing order. Please contact your bookseller or, in case of difficulty, write to us at the address below with your name and address, the title of the series, and the ISBN quoted above.

Customer Services Department, Macmillan Distribution Ltd,
Houndmills, Basingstoke, Hampshire RG21 6XS, England

Key Concepts in Human Resource Management

Jonathan Sutherland and Diane Canwell

First published 2004 by
PALGRAVE MACMILLAN
Houndmills, Basingstoke, Hampshire RG21 6XS and
175 Fifth Avenue, New York, N.Y. 10010
Companies and representatives throughout the world

PALGRAVE MACMILLAN is the global academic imprint of the Palgrave Macmillan division of St. Martin's Press, LLC and of Palgrave Macmillan Ltd. Macmillan® is a registered trademark in the United States, United Kingdom and other countries. Palgrave is a registered trademark in the European Union and other countries.

ISBN 1–4039–1528–8 paperback

This book is printed on paper suitable for recycling and made from fully managed and sustained forest sources.

A catalogue record for this book is available from the British Library.

A catalog record for this book is available from the Library of Congress.

10 9 8 7 6 5 4 3 2 1
13 12 11 10 09 08 07 06 05 04

Printed in China

Contents

Introduction

Human resource management, formerly known as personnel management, has gradually become something of a science in recent years, bound by ever stricter controls and checks against abuse and inequality. The management of people in the workplace, whether managers, supervisors or the rank and file of the organization, has developed considerably, underpinned by theory and regulated by legislation.

The sheer complexity of human resource management (HRM) and the implications related to its provision and scope have given rise to a new discipline which requires the systematic training of personnel professionals. Coping with the profusion of terms, jargon, legislation and procedures can be an onerous task for practitioners and an even greater challenge for those studying the discipline.

Human resource management encompasses a far wider field of responsibilities and areas of importance than simply managing the workforce, dealing with pay, conditions, discipline and grievances; it is increasingly concerned with the development and the retention of key employees. To this end, new developments seek to identify and fulfil the requirements of these employees in terms of their training, their attitudes to work and the organization, and their understanding of the part their job role plays in the wider context.

In all areas of human resource management, systems have been developed not only to streamline processes, but to ensure that the increasingly complex legislative framework is adhered to and that mechanisms are put in place to ensure that employees have more extensive opportunities to participate and become involved in their own development and prospects.

The structure of the glossary

Every attempt has been made to include all of the key concepts in this discipline, taking into account currently used terminology and jargon common throughout human resource management in organizations around the world. There are notable differences in legislation and procedure when we compare employer and employee relationships and responsibilities in the United Kingdom, Europe, the United States and Japan. Increasingly in Europe, for example, there is a harmonization process in train which is gradually seeking to standardize regulations and procedures.

The key concepts have been arranged alphabetically in order to ensure that the reader can quickly find the term or entry of immediate interest. It is normally the case that a brief description of the term is presented, followed by a more expansive explanation.

The majority of the key concepts have the following in common:

- They may have a reference within the text to another key concept identified by a word or phrase that is in **bold type** – this should enable readers to investigate a directly implicated key concept should they require clarification of the definition at that point.
- They may have a series of related key concepts which are listed at the end of the definition – this allows readers to continue their research and investigate subsidiary or allied key concepts.
- They may feature book or journal references – a vital feature for the reader to undertake follow-up research for more expansive explanations, often written by the originator or a leading writer in that particular field of study.
- They may include website references – it is notoriously difficult to ensure that websites are still running at the time of going to print, let alone several months beyond that time, but in the majority of cases long-established websites have been selected or government websites that are unlikely to be closed or have a major address change.

Glossary terms – a guide

Whilst the majority of the key concepts have an international flavour, readers are cautioned to ensure that they have accessed the legislation, in particular, which refers to their native country or the country in which they are working. It was not possible to include the legislation of all countries and as a result the slant is very much towards the UK, Europe and the USA.

It is also often the case that there are terms which have no currency in a particular country as they may be allied to specific legislation of another country. In these cases readers should check whether or not the description includes a specific reference to such law and should not assume that the key concept is a generic one and that it can be applied universally to HRM.

In all cases, references to other books, journals and websites are based on the latest available information. It was not always possible to ensure that the key text or printed reference is in print, but the majority of well-stocked college or university libraries should have access to the original materials. In the majority of cases, when generic human resource books have been referenced, these are, in the view of the writers, the best and most readily available additional reading texts.

Absenteeism

Strictly speaking, 'absenteeism' refers to chronic absence from work. In effect, this is deliberate absence. A business can calculate the level of absenteeism within its workforce (excluding ill-health and genuine absences) by using the following formula:

$$\text{Absentee rate} = \frac{\text{number of staff absent} \times 100}{\text{Staff total}}$$

Absenteeism can drastically affect the production and profitability of a business and, obviously, may require a business to reschedule projects, miss deadlines, and ensure that any vital duties carried out by the absent individual are covered. There are, of course, a number of reasons why absenteeism could creep into the habits of an employee, such as:

- *The nature of the job* – physical conditions may be poor, working hours inconvenient, the job may be stressful or boring, or the employee may not have good inter-personal relations, or may feel **alienation**. These problems could be overcome by offering more flexible ways of working, or perhaps considering **job enrichment** or **job rotation** systems.
- *Characteristics of the individual* – it has been suggested that both age and gender can have an impact on absenteeism. Certainly, longer-serving employees are less prone. Other factors may include health, family responsibilities or travelling difficulties. Again, these problems could be overcome by a more flexible approach to staffing and by closer supervision.
- *Motivating factors* – whilst **bonuses** or **non-financial incentives** can have an impact on absenteeism, the availability of **statutory sick pay** has the reverse effect. Ultimately, in terms of motivation, reducing absenteeism relies on managers' ability to persuade employees to come to work, and, perhaps, the readiness of the business itself to institute **disciplinary procedures** in the correct places.

Most businesses will tend to develop an attendance policy, which addresses the following issues:

- What is an allowable absence?
- Will days be paid if missed immediately before and after a holiday?
- What are the attitudes towards excused and unexcused absences?
- The setting up of a system which alerts managers to patterns of absences or lateness.

Frayne, Collette A., *Reducing Employee Absenteeism through Self-Management Training.* Westport, CT: Quorum Books, 1991.

Tylczak, Lynn and Hicks Tony, *Attacking Absenteeism.* Los Altos, CA: Crisp Publications, 1990.

ACAS

See **Advisory Conciliation and Arbitration Service.**

Accreditation of prior learning (APEL and APL)

Accreditation of prior learning (APL) and accreditation of prior experiential learning (APEL) are terms which have been more closely associated with education and training development. APL seeks to identify either uncompleted or non-associated educational courses or programmes of study which can either lead to the individual being accepted on a particular educational training programme, or allow them to trade these elements towards part of a qualification. APEL, on the other hand, does not necessarily assume that the individual has undertaken or partially undertaken a prior educational programme. The individual has instead learned certain skills and can display an ability in these skills from practical experience.

In both cases, educational institutions will employ strict regulations as to the relevance and value of particular APL or APEL claims. Certainly in the case of APEL, evidence should be provided to suggest a level of underpinning knowledge or that their experience replicates a learning equivalent.

See also **experiential learning model.**

Nyatanga, Lovemore, Forman, Dawn and Fox, Jane, *Good Practice in the Accreditation of Prior Learning.* New York: Continuum, 1997.

Administrative Procedure Act (US)

This is a piece of US legislation originally introduced on 6 September 1966 and variously amended over the years. The Act's specific applica-

A

tion to human resource management is the association with the Privacy Act of 1974, which prohibits the disclosure of records that identify an individual, except on the written request of the individual to whom the record belongs. All Federal agencies to whom the Administrative Procedure Act applies must ensure that their records are accurate before disclosure and that individuals are accorded the right to review and amend their records. Equally, only relevant and necessary information can be stored and when information is gathered from an individual he or she is informed of the purpose of the data collection exercise.

Advisory Conciliation and Arbitration Service (ACAS) (UK)

ACAS can trace its history back to 1896. Some 80 years later in 1976, after several changes of name, the organization was finally put on a statutory footing. ACAS operates as a mediator during problems or disputes between employers and employees. Its primary role is to encourage good working relationships between employers and employees and to help set up structures and systems to this end, as well as taking a practical part in the settling of disputes. ACAS has been inextricably involved in most of the major industrial or labour disputes in Britain, particularly since the 1970s.

ACAS not only deals with broader industrial disputes, but also focuses on individual complaints which have been referred to employment tribunals (**industrial tribunals**). On average it settles around 75 per cent of cases which have been referred to an employment tribunal, obviating the need for the tribunal to consider the case. In summation, ACAS is involved in four main areas of activity – these are:

- the providing of impartial information and help (on average, the helpline takes 750,000 calls a year);
- prevention and resolution of problems between employers and employees (ACAS is successful in over 90 per cent of cases);
- settlement of complaints about employees' rights (around 70 per cent of potential employment tribunal cases referred to ACAS are resolved by ACAS);
- fostering effective working relationships through seminars and workshops. Small businesses in particular are targeted, as well as those without clearly identified human resource management departments.

www.acas.org.uk

A

Affirmative action (US)

The term 'affirmative action' is most closely associated with various legislative moves in the United States regarding the elimination of discrimination against employees or **applicants** for employment.

The concept goes somewhat further than requiring an employer not to discriminate on the grounds of race, creed, colour or national origin, as it requires an employer to take positive steps to ensure that those who are chosen for employment, and those who are in employment, are treated without regard to their race and other considerations. In effect, the associated legislation calls for equality in employment.

In the United States, the fundamental rights of an individual are enshrined in the 13th, 14th and 15th Amendments of the US Constitution. However, in 1961 President John F. Kennedy issued Executive Order 10925, which established the President's Committee on Equal Employment Opportunity. This, in turn, led to the Civil Rights Act of 1964. Amongst other things, the Act stated:

> No person in the United States shall, on the ground of race, color or national origin, be excluded from participation in, be denied the benefits of, or be subjected to discrimination under any program or activity receiving Federal financial assistance.

Indeed, this approach, beginning with Federal employees or those working for organizations employed by Federal governments, is often the way that the US seeks to impose fundamental changes in perceptions. Following the Civil Rights Act of 1964, President Johnson issued Executive Order 11246, which prohibited discrimination and introduced the concept of affirmative action: 'through a positive, continuing program in each department and agency.' Shortly after this the Executive Order was amended to include discrimination on the basis of gender.

Affirmative action, therefore, not only enshrines anti-discrimination policy during recruitment and employment, but also promotes active measures to encourage and aid those who had hitherto been discriminated against.

Curry, George E. (ed.), *The Affirmative Action Debate*. Reading, MA: Addison-Wesley, 1996.

AFL–CIO (US)

See **American Federation of Labor – Congress of Industrial Organizations.**

Age Discrimination in Employment Act 1967 (US)

The Age Discrimination in Employment Act (1967), or the ADEA, is specifically designed to protect individuals who are over 40 years of age. The Act encompasses both recruitment and employment, stating that it is illegal to discriminate against an individual in respect of age. The law makes it illegal to include age preferences or limitations in job advertisements, but does not prevent an employer from asking an applicant's age or date of birth.

In 1990 the Older Workers' Benefit Protection Act amended the ADEA by prohibiting employers from denying benefits to older employees. In other words, they should be accorded the same benefits as younger workers.

O'Meara, Daniel P., *Protecting the Growing Number of Older Workers: The Age Discrimination in Employment Act*. Philadelphia, PA: University of Pennsylvania, 1989.

Ageism

The term 'ageism' was arguably coined by Robert Butler in 1969. He was the first director of the National Institute on Ageing and he linked the concept of ageism to racism and sexism. In effect, he defined 'ageism' as being both a stereotyping and discrimination against individuals because they were old. The term is now more broadly defined as prejudice or discrimination against a particular age group.

As with many stereotypes, ageism exhibits the following characteristics:

- age characteristics are exaggerated;
- most stereotypes have no basis in fact;
- the stereotypes are negative;
- the stereotypes leave little opportunity to prove that the facts are different or that individuals vary.

Nelson, Todd D. (ed.), *Ageism: Stereotyping and Prejudice against Older Persons*. Cambridge, MA: MIT Press, 2002.

Palmore, Erdman Ballagh, *Ageism: Negative and Positive*. New York: Springer Publishing, 1999.

Alderfer, Clayton P.

In the 1970s Alderfer identified three categories of human needs which influenced an employee's behaviour. In essence his theory aimed to address some of the limitations of **Maslow**'s hierarchy of needs.

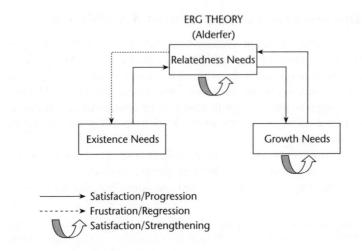

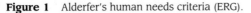

Figure 1 Alderfer's human needs criteria (ERG).

Alderfer's three criteria (ERG) were:

- *existence needs* – which incorporated Maslow's first and second levels and are physiological and safety needs;
- *relatedness needs* – which accord with Maslow's third and fourth needs and include social and external esteem;
- *growth needs* – which are also in line with Maslow's fourth and fifth levels and are needs for internal esteem and self-actualization.

Alderfer did not consider these three criteria to be stepped in any way, as opposed to Maslow's idea that access to the higher-level needs required satisfaction in the lower-level needs.

In effect, the ERG theory recognizes the fact that the order of importance of the three areas may be different for different individuals. Alderfer does, however, recognize that if a particular need remains unfulfilled, then an individual will suffer dissatisfactions, regressions and frustrations. ERG theory is very flexible as it can explain individuals who are perfectly prepared to work under poor circumstances, for limited pay, in employment from which they receive a great deal of personal satisfaction, and those who receive recognition for their work and high pay, yet are frustrated by limitations and boredom.

Alderfer, Clayton P., *Existence, Relatedness and Growth: Human Needs in Organisational Settings*. New York: Free Press, 1973.

Alienation

The term 'alienation' implies a form of estrangement, which may also imply a feeling of powerlessness, meaninglessness, normlessness, isolation, self-estrangement or social isolation.

In a work situation, individuals may feel alienated, or distanced from their work and colleagues, for a number of reasons. One of the most common reasons is feeling that there is a gap between what is going on in the business and what they are told, or that they do not understand their function as part of the organization's whole.

Alienation clearly presents problems within the workplace, as individuals are unlikely to be as productive or content with their work if they feel this distance and lack of connectivity with their colleagues and their surroundings.

Blauner, Robert, *Alienation and Freedom*. Chiago, IL: University of Chicago Press, 1964.

Schmitt, Richard, *Alienation and Freedom*. Boulder, CO: Westview Press, 2002.

Alternative work arrangements

Increasingly, management has looked for ways in which productivity, lower levels of sick leave and family leave, and improved morale, **recruitment** and **employee retention** can be achieved. One such way is to introduce alternative work arrangements. The system, when applied to situations where employers still require their workforce to attend work at a specific location, helps reduce traffic and parking pressures, as well as extending hours of cover and service to customers or clients.

Typically, there has been a shift from standard working hours, with fixed arrival and departure times, to a more flexible approach (*see* **flexitime**). Alternatively, employees can work longer shifts for up to four days a week under **compressed working week** systems.

Clearly there is also an opportunity here within the scope of alternative working arrangements to offer employees the opportunity to work at home, perhaps engaged in **telecommuting** or **tele-work**.

The normal procedure in setting up alternative working arrangements requires the cooperation of both the employees and their immediate manager. Normally decisions will be based on the job function for which the individual is responsible, taking into account staffing needs, budgetary considerations and the availability of space in the office. Work schedules still need to be maintained and there needs to be a degree of supervision in all cases of alternative working arrangements. The introduction of alternative working arrangements needs to be advantageous both to the business and to the employees in question and should be

A

viewed in consideration of any associated advantages and disadvantages to both parties.

Estess, Patricia Schiff, *Work Concepts for the Future: Managing Alternative Work Arrangements*. Los Altos, CA: Crisp Publications, 1996.

American Arbitration Association (AAA)

The function of the American Arbitration Association is somewhat more complex than that of **ACAS**, as it has to encompass specific variations in arbitration rules and procedures in the various US states.

The AAA is recognized as being one of the leaders in a number of arbitration areas, which include employer–employee relations, grievance issues and contractual issues.

www.adr.org

American Federation of Labor – Congress of Industrial Organizations (AFL–CIO)

The AFL–CIO is the federation of America's labour unions, which represent some 13 million members. The AFL–CIO works with several different autonomous and independent organizations including state federations and central labour councils.

The AFL–CIO has a four-yearly conference at which federation members are represented by elected delegates; the conference frames the policies, goals and objectives for the next four-year period, which will be carried out by the elected officers. The elected officers form the Executive Council, which is responsible for the day-to-day work of the AFL–CIO.

A General Board deals with matters referred to it by the Executive Council, and at state level, the 51 state federations coordinate with local unions. There are also some 570 central labour councils operating at city, town and county level.

www.aflcio.org

Americans with Disabilities Act 1990 (US)

This US act, administered by the **Equal Employment Opportunity Commission** (EEOC), prohibits discrimination against individuals with disabilities on account of these disabilities.

The Act attempts to set criteria which seek to evaluate how an employer has selected candidates on the basis of their ability to perform.

Given the fact that many employees with disabilities are equally loyal and diligent as others, there is an opportunity implicit in the Act and in the way that the EEOC applies its analytical framework, which recognizes that employers who employ disabled workers receive a higher degree of diligence and loyalty as a result.

Enshrined within the Act itself are key considerations which need to be appreciated by an employer, including the provision of suitable accommodation, large computer screens, modified work schedules or frequent short rest breaks.

Stefan, Susan, *Unequal Rights: Discrimination against People with Mental Disabilities and the Americans with Disabilities Act.* Washington, DC: American Psychological Association, 2001.

Amsterdam Treaty June 1997 (EU)

The Amsterdam Treaty was finally signed on 2 October 1997, after two years of discussion. In relation to human resource management, part of the treaty was directly related to the globalization of the economy and its impact on jobs, as well as, more specifically, setting up a system by which citizens of the European Union would be entitled to free movement in terms of both accommodation and jobs within the Member States. The treaty also underpins the concepts of equality between men and women, non-discrimination, and the right to data privacy. In addition the treaty called for the establishment of common strategies for employment and the tackling of social exclusion.

Monr, Yorg and Wessels, Wolfgang (eds), *The European Union after the Treaty of Amsterdam.* New York: Continuum International, 2001.

Annualized hours

An annualized hours scheme is an agreement between an employer and an employee to establish the total number of hours worked by that employee within a given year. The system is often applied to industries which have recognizable seasonal peaks and troughs in terms of demand. It can be seen as a way of obviating the need for overtime and has increasingly become prevalent in banking and financial services, as they have moved towards call-centre-based operations. The system itself is fairly straightforward in as much as a calculation is made as to the total number of annual hours, based on an agreed number of hours per week. This figure is then amended, taking into account public holidays and annual leave. The remaining number of hours is then scheduled as a pattern throughout the year.

A

In other industries, such as offshore drilling operations, annualized hours schemes accommodate an intensive two-week period onsite and a two-week 'off on leave' pattern. As far as businesses operating in Europe are concerned, there is a requirement to adhere to the **Working Time Regulations**. These state that the number of hours worked per week should not exceed 48 hours and that there must be minimum rest periods incorporated into the system.

The gradual introduction of annualized hours has caused considerable difficulties and trade unions have been keen to ensure that intensive working does not undermine health and safety, overtime opportunities and other fundamental rights. Annualized hours can also be applied to **part-time workers**, where the system is applied on a pro-rata basis.

Grant-Garwood, Carole and Michael Grisenthwaite, *Tolley's Practical Guide to the Working Time Directive and Regulations*. Oxford: Tolley Publishing, 1998.

APEL/APL

See **Accreditation of prior learning**.

Applicant

The term 'applicant' can be applied to both internal and external recruitment. Essentially an applicant is an individual who has expressed interest or desire in fulfilling a vacant position in a business. Internal applicants are existing workers in the firm, who are applying for an alternative or more senior post. External candidates are hitherto unknown individuals who believe that their skills, experience and education match the requirement of an advertised post.

Applicant tracking system

An applicant tracking system is usually proprietary software which enables a business to streamline and eliminate a great deal of paperwork associated with the application process, or a recruitment drive. Typical applicant tracking systems involve a specifically designed software package that can enable a personnel department or recruiter to identify and track the progress of specific applications and generate automated responses (such as acknowledgements, rejection letters and offers of work). Many businesses are now shifting over to a web-based applicant tracking system. This enables the business to post and update

A

job opportunities on its website (and remove them when they have been filled). Candidates are encouraged to complete online applications, such as CVs or résumés, which can then be responded to by an automated system. The software also allows the sending of automated e-mails to schedule interviews, meetings or appointments. In effect, the system accommodates what is often an onerous task of tracking candidates' status and history at each stage of the recruitment process. Clearly there are considerable economies to be made by essentially shifting the focus from a paper-based recruitment exercise.

Application blank

An application blank is a non-job-specific generic application form which is routinely sent out by a business as a result of a potential **applicant** applying for a post. Normally application blanks will require the applicant to provide basic information, including name, address, telephone number, email address, summary of education and employment, reasons for application, and where they saw the advertisement for the position. Application blanks can be used in the early stages of a recruitment drive in order to filter out unsuitable candidates, or simply to store information on suitable, available employees for future recruitment drives.

Applications

The term 'applications' applies to the number of individuals who have expressed a specific desire to be considered for an available position in a business as a result of recruitment advertising. Many businesses will be particularly concerned with the volume and quality of applications which they receive for any given position and will be interested in statistical information related to the source of each application, the geographical location of the candidate, how the candidate heard of the position, along with age spread, gender, ethnicity, qualifications and other criteria which can suggest to the business how effective their advertisement was in attracting a representative spread of the most suitable candidates.

Appraisal

Appraisals are, in effect, a form of judging an employee's performance in a given job. The performance appraisal considers more than productivity, but is often used as the basis upon which increases in wages or salaries are considered. Whilst managers and colleagues constantly form and reform opinions of those who work for them or with them, a formal appraisal meeting puts these considerations into a more formal context.

The basic functions of an appraisal system are:

- to determine the short-, medium- and long-term future of the employee;
- to identify possible training needs;
- to motivate the employee;
- to assist management in deciding what levels of pay increases will be accorded to that individual.

Typically, appraisals will take the form of a performance review, a potential review or a rewards review. There are, of course, a number of different ways in which appraisal schemes are organized, which include the **ranking method**, **the 360-degree performance appraisal**, **the rating scale** and **behaviourally anchored rating scales (BARS)**.

Appraisals rely on being able to provide positive criticism to individuals, and the setting of realistic standards which require the employee to give maximum effort in order to achieve the set goals. Appraisal systems need to have clearly defined rules and expectations and, above all, the appraiser (the individual delivering the appraisal) and the appraisee (the individual being appraised) need to be speaking the same language. This implies, therefore, that a degree of training for both parties needs to be instituted prior to the running of an appraisal system. This not only sets the pattern and nature of the appraisal, but also allows for the unscheduled reviewing of factors which have been brought up during the appraisal interviews. Clear documentation needs to be drawn up, as well as a log to note performance deficiencies and performance improvements.

Maddux, Robert B., *Effective Performance Appraisals*. Los Altos, CA: Crisp Publications, 2000.

Neal, James E., *Effective Phrases for Performance Appraisals: A Guide to Successful Evaluations*. Perrysburg, OH: Neal Publications, 2003.

Neal, James E., *The #1 Guide to Performance Appraisals: Doing it Right!* Perrysburg, OH: Neal Publications, 2001.

Apprenticeship

Apprenticeships have been in operation for centuries and were originally considered to be the ideal way in which an individual concerned with learning the intricacies of a particular job role (in many cases a specific craft) could learn from the experience of someone who had been fulfilling the role for a number of years. Apprentices would be attached to experienced individuals and, in effect, would not only contribute by delegation, but would also shadow that individual in order to learn their 'tools of the trade'.

Apprenticeships have become somewhat more formalized in recent years and in the UK, for example, there are several schemes sponsored by the government, which aim to structure apprenticeships. As far as the UK is concerned, much of the apprenticeship system is based not only on the acquisition of specific knowledge and skills, but also on the gaining of qualifications. The underlying principle also incorporates the fact that the apprentice is earning a wage whilst training. There are, in the UK, three levels of Modern Apprenticeships – Foundation (FMA), Advanced (AMA) and Graduate.

Apprenticeships are seen as providing considerable benefits to employers, as well as the associated benefits attached to employees. These include:

- the training of individuals with a direct relevance to the given business and industry;
- the ability of the business and the individual to deal with new technologies and new markets;
- the specific tackling of skills shortages;
- assistance in recruitment and staff retention by the provision of apprenticeships;
- an increase in staff morale and other tangible benefits to the business.

In the US there are clear Federal legal requirements with regard to an Apprenticeship Program. Individuals need to be 16 years of age or older, with a clear schedule of work that incorporates at least 2000 hours of work experience. Apprentices should be paid, given organized instructions (in the form of formal or applied education) for at least 144 hours per year, and the business must provide adequate on-the-job supervision. Inherent in both the US and the UK systems there is a requirement to provide evaluation and record keeping, and a recognition of successful completion of the qualification. It is important that discrimination does not occur, either in selection, employment or training.

A

Smits, Wendy and Stromback, Thorsten, *The Economics of the Apprenticeship System*. London: Edward Elgar, 2001.
Boud, David and Solomon, Nicky (eds), *Work-based Learning*. Milton Keynes: Open University Press, 2001.

Aptitude test

Aptitude tests are used as a means by which a business can identify specific skills and characteristics inherent in an individual amongst a group of otherwise very similar potential **applicants** for a given post or training programme. Aptitude tests tend to fall into one of three categories:

- *Verbal tests* – which investigate the applicant's ability to understand the meaning of written passages, words, and relationships of words, as well as their inferences on information that can be drawn from specific passages or statements.
- *Numerical tests* – which require the candidate to carry out calculations, interpretation of data (often as tables or graphs), and to undertake numerically based problem solving.
- *Logic tests* – which present the applicant with shapes and figures and ask them to draw out specific information, particularly regarding the relationships between numbers, objects and other data.

Many of the aptitude tests are multiple-choice in format in order to facilitate the more efficient marking of the tests as an integral part of a recruitment process.

Aptitude tests have moved on from simple IQ tests, which have, in the past, been a popular discriminator but have largely been superseded as a result of their inherent cultural bias.

Hoffman, Edward, *Psychological Testing at Work: How to Use, Interpret and Get the Most Out of the Newest Tests in Personality, Learning Styles, Aptitudes, Interest and More!* New York: McGraw-Hill Education, 2001.

Arbitration

See **Advisory Conciliation and Arbitration Service (ACAS)** *and* **American Arbitration Association (AAA)**.

Argyris, Chris

Argyris has contributed much to the understanding of the relationship between people and organizations, as well as organizational learning itself. Argyris wrote that bureaucratic organizations lead to mistrustful relationships, and that the creation of an environment which incorporates trust leads to greater personal confidence, cooperation and flexibility. Employees desire to be treated like human beings and their complex needs must be recognized by an organization. Businesses should provide opportunities for employees to influence the way in which they work and the way in which the business is structured.

Pyramid or bureaucratic organizational structures still dominate the majority of businesses and these structures have an impact upon the

Table 1 Bureaucratic versus humanistic organizations

Bureaucratic/Pyramidal	Humanistic/Democratic
The crucial human relationships are those which relate to the meeting of the business's objectives.	The crucial human relationships are not only those related to meeting the objectives of the business but also those that maintain the business's internal systems and adapt to environmental issues.
Effectiveness in relationships increases as behaviour becomes more rational, logical, and clearly communicated.	Human relationships increase in effectiveness as all the relevant behaviour becomes conscious, discussed and controlled.
Effectiveness decreases as behaviour becomes more emotional.	
Human relationships are effectively motivated by defined direction, authority, and control. This is in addition to appropriate rewards and penalties that emphasize rational behaviour and the achievement of objectives.	In addition to direction, human relationships are most effectively influenced through control, rewards and penalties, authentic working relationships, internal commitment, psychological success and the use of the process of confirmation.

Immaturity	Maturity
Passiveness	Active
Dependence	Independence
Behaves predominantly in the same ways	Behaves in a variety of different ways
Erratic and shallow interests	Has deep and strong interest
Has short-term perspectives	Has long-term perspectives of both the past and the future
Usually holds subordinate position	Usually holds an equal or subordinate position
Lack of self-awareness	Has self-awareness and self-control

Figure 2 Immaturity–maturity continuum

way in which individuals within an organization behave, and their personal growth characteristics. (See Table 1 for the differences between the two types of organization.) Argyris created the immaturity/maturity continuum, which sought to identify the way in which healthy personalities can be developed within an organization which allows career and personal development. This is best summed up as in Figure 2.

The theory postulates that the organization's culture either inhibits or allows an expression of the growth of an individual who works within that organization. Argyris argued that, at the time he was writing, very few organizations had reached maturity in their approach.

Argyris, Chris, *Personality and Organization*. New York: HarperCollins, 1957.
Argyris, Chris, *Knowledge for Action: A Guide to Overcoming Barriers to Organizational Change*. San Francisco, CA: Jossey Bass, 1993.

Assessment centre

An assessment centre is invariably an outsourced facility which administers either national qualification tests or **aptitude tests** and **attitude surveys**.

Attitude survey

Attitude surveys aim to discover employees' opinions. However, attitude surveys are only useful to a business if they are an integral part of its planning cycle and help determine its objectives, goals and budgets. Scheduled attitude surveys are ideally undertaken prior to the setting of goals and budget planning sessions.

There are a number of key aspects related to the use of attitude surveys which are summarized in Table 2.

Cully, Mark, Woodland, Stephen, O'Reilly, Andrew and Dix, Gill, *Britain at Work: As Depicted by the 1998 Workplace Employee Relations Survey*. London: Routledge, 1999.
Edwards, Jack E., Thomas, Marie D., Rosenfeld, Paul, and Booth-Kewley, Stephanie, *How to Conduct Organizational Surveys: A Step-by-Step Guide*. London: Sage Publications, 1996.

Attrition

'Attrition' is an alternative means of describing **labour turnover**.

Table 2 Use of attitude surveys

Consideration	Description and implications
Creating and communicating specific actions	Employees who will be involved in the attitude survey need to be clear about the planning, data collection and implementation plans. Organizational confusion will reduce not only the effectiveness of the survey but also the chance of being able to carry one out in the future. A clear process means that employees will expect attitude surveys to take place and they will be more inclined to provide useful information which can later be acted upon.
Looking for what is not already known	Most of management may feel that they actually understand problems, but it is unlikely that they appreciate opinions and perceptions across the range of the organization. In this respect, the business needs to be open-minded about what it discovers and not to eliminate areas of investigation which they feel are fully understood and are under control. Attitude surveys can identify potential problems and suggest potential solutions. Attitude surveys which incorporate open-ended questions provide a richer source of information. Although they are more difficult to analyse, the comments are usually more valuable than those obtained in surveys restricted to the allocation of numerical values.
Anonymity	Confidentiality and anonymity are crucial in order to increase the accuracy of the data. These aspects need to be clearly communicated and the parameters for which the information will be used should be made unequivocal.
Analysis	It is advisable to consider how the data will be analysed, prior to the framing of any attitude survey questionnaire. What may have seemed to be an ideal way of approaching a particular subject may prove to be impossible or extremely time-consuming in terms of analysis.
Sampling plan	Businesses may choose to have a rolling programme of attitude surveys, which are presented to each functional area of the business. This not only enables the business to analyse the specific feelings of a given department, but also allows all of the data to be aggregated on a rolling yearly basis. This can highlight new causes for concern almost as soon as the issue has arisen.

A

⇒

Table 2 Use of attitude surveys (*continued*)

Consideration	Description and implications
Key employee involvement	In order to engage employees in the attitude survey process, it is often desirable for the business to involve them in the framing of the survey and enlist their assistance in the distribution, analysis, recommendations and implementation of the results.
Determination to act	When employees feel that they have been specifically asked for their opinions, yet nothing has been done to implement solutions to their concerns, there is a strong possibility that they may become demoralized and will be unprepared to involve themselves in such an activity in the future. The views expressed in an attitude survey will inevitably be the subject of **grapevine communication** and if the management has not taken steps to implement solutions, then expectations will have been dashed.
Reliability and validity	In framing an attitude survey it is also desirable to include at least three, possibly five, questions on each topic. This enables cross-tabulation of results, in order to ensure that the information provided was consistent. Where simply asking a single question on a particular topic, it may be foolhardy to rely on the information which has been provided.

Audit of corporate strategy

An audit of corporate strategy is an assessment of a business's strategy and fit in terms of its objectives and mission. It has a particular focus on human resource policies and practices.

Bristow, Nigel and Sandberg, Sarah J., *The Corporate Culture Audit*. Harlow, Essex: Financial Times Prentice-Hall, 1999.

Audit of employee satisfaction

This is an assessment of employee satisfaction in a variety of work-related areas. The audit is designed to identify human resource implications in terms of established practices and systems.

Audit of human resource system

Essentially, an audit of the human resource system or function involves

Table 3 Stages in assessing human resource systems

Audit process	Description and implications
Data collection	This involves the gathering of information, including recruitment statistics, **labour turnover**, employee benefits, **exit interviews**, employee complaints, promotion opportunities, human resource budgets and expenditures. This is a vital stage as it allows the **audit team** to identify discrepancies between policy and practice.
Interviews	Interviews begin by collecting information from employees regarding their human resource needs. The interview process is then widened to include management. The information required, which forms the basis of the interviews, includes how the business is perceived, the strengths and weaknesses of management, along with perceptions of that management, relations with colleagues, subordinates and managers, career support and an identification of how human resource functions could be improved.
Regulatory compliance	As part of the audit, personnel files and other record-keeping activities should be examined in order to ensure regulatory compliance. Other areas would include **equal pay**, **job descriptions**, **equal opportunities**, **compensation** and attitudes towards leave, whether authorized or unauthorized.
Summarization	Practices differ at this stage, but the process now needs to adapt the information which has been collected into specific recommendations. The **audit team** need to justify their recommendations and determine how improvements or changes will be measured.
Approval	Clearly any recommendations need to obtain the backing of senior management. A focus here is to highlight how the recommendations will support and further the needs of the organization. It is only then that the final results and recommendations should be implemented.
Implementation	It is often advisable to begin the implementation of any of the recommendations by piloting the new procedures first. This will enable the business to monitor and measure their impact and see whether they have provided meaningful improvements. Once this process has been completed, the business is able to focus on the specific improvements and perhaps modify the programme in the light of what has been discovered.

A

assessing the systems and activities of human resources in order to ascertain how they contribute to employee and organizational goals and objectives.

Alternatively the audit may focus upon the effectiveness of the human resource function to ensure regulatory compliance. The process has six clear stages, which are summarized in Table 3.

Fitz-Enz, Jac, *How to Measure Human Resources Management*. New York: McGraw-Hill Education, 2002.

McConnell, John H., *Auditing your Human Resources Department: A Step-by-step Guide*. New York: Amacom, 2002.

Audit of managerial compliance

An audit of managerial compliance is either a sub-function of a full **audit report** or a specific audit carried out by an **audit team**. The audit seeks to identify and review how managers within an organization comply with human resource practices, policies and procedures. The audit also considers the management's compliance with current employment legislation and seeks to identify whether the business's own policies and procedures are at variance with that employment legislation.

Audit report

An audit report in human resource management terms involves a detailed identification and description of all activities undertaken by the functional area. The audit will typically include recommendations for improvements of policies, processes and practices which are ineffective or flawed, as well as congratulating or highlighting areas of excellence.

See also **audit team.**

A

Audit team

An audit team, in the human resource field, is a group of individuals who have been tasked by a business with the responsibility of carrying out an **audit report** or **audit of employee satisfaction**. They will assess the effectiveness of all aspects of the human resource function within the business.

Autonomy

Autonomy is a measure of an individual's independence within their job role. Autonomy implies that within the context of work, an individual has a degree of control over what they do, the order in which they do it and the processes involved in carrying it out. Autonomy also suggests that aside from not requiring close supervision or management in order to carry out the function, the individual may have a larger influence over their own working environment. Truly autonomous workers, therefore, are those who are enabled by being offered **alternative work arrangements** or a form of remote working, such as **telecommuting** or **telework**.

Awareness training

Awareness training is concerned with allowing managers and supervisors to understand the value of diversity within the workforce. The diversity encompasses not only ethnic or national issues but also gender and age, as well as background. Awareness training also incorporates ways of managing diversity within the workplace.

Kohls, L. Robert, *Developing Intercultural Awareness: A Cross-Cultural Training Handbook.* Yarmouth, ME: Intercultural Press, 1994.

A

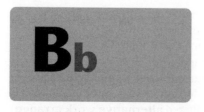

Bb

Balanced scorecard

A balanced scorecard is an integrated means of measuring organizational performance. Aside from looking at the organization's ability to innovate, manage finances and deal with customers, it also addresses internal operations, including human resource management.

Very few organizations are able to effectively align their strategies so as to be able to operate at maximum efficiency. Using the concept of a balanced scorecard, a business can seek to understand, all the way down to individuals within the organization, the exact nature of the key performance indicators that need to be controlled, and facilitate the understanding of relationships within the organization. Whilst the deployment of a balanced scorecard system can help in this understanding, its true value is in enabling a business to implement and track key initiatives. This means providing across the length and breadth of the business a greater vision and utilization of resources.

Kaplan, Robert S., Lowes, Arthur and Norton, David P., *Balanced Scorecard: Translating Strategy into Action*. Cambridge, MA: Harvard Business School Press, 1996.

Kaplan, Robert S. and Norton, David P., *Strategy-focussed Organization: How Balanced Scorecard Companies Thrive in the New Business Environment*. Cambridge, MA: Harvard Business School Press, 2000.

Behavioural interview

Behavioural interviewing is specifically used to screen prospective candidates before a short-listing exercise. Behavioural interviewing requires the preparation of a series of behaviour-provoking questions in order to discover attitudes, opinions and behaviours. It is believed that behavioural interviews can provide a better insight into the candidate than a standard interview does. Experienced interviewers will be able to pick up on not only verbal responses but also body language, which can help unravel true behavioural traits. It is, therefore, possible to recognize whether the individual is fabricating responses or trying to hide true behavioural impulses. Many of the questions used in a behavioural interview are inter-related, which allows the interviewer to cross-check them.

Hersen, Michel (ed.), *Diagnostic Interviewing.* New York: Kluwer Academic/Plenum Publishers, 1994.

Behaviourally anchored rating scales (BARS)

This system utilizes critical incidents to evaluate performance, which focus performance appraisal on employee behaviours that can be changed. Thus, a BARS system describes examples of 'good' or 'bad' behaviour. These examples are 'anchored', or measured, against a scale of performance levels. What constitutes various levels of performance is clearly defined in the figure. Spelling out the behaviour associated with each level of performance helps minimize some of the problems noted earlier.

The construction of BARS begins with the identification of important job dimensions, which are the most important performance factors in an employee's description. Short statements are developed that describe both desirable and undesirable behaviours (anchors). Then they are 'retranslated' or assigned to one of the job dimensions. This task is usually a group project and the assignment is for 60–70 per cent of the group to agree the dimensions. The group, consisting of individuals familiar with the job, then assigns each 'anchor' a number, which represents how 'good' or 'bad' the behaviour is. When numbered, these anchors are fitted to a scale (as shown in Figure 3).

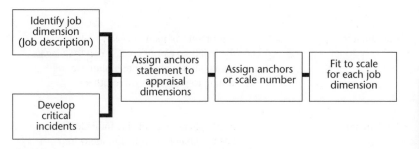

Figure 3 A flow diagram of the BARS construction process

Behaviourally anchored rating scales require extensive time and effort to develop and maintain, and separate BARS forms are necessary to accommodate different types of jobs in an organization.

Aiken, Lewis R., *Rating Scales and Checklists: Evaluating Attitudes, Behavior, and Personality.* Chichester: John Wiley, 1996

Belbin, Meredith

Belbin suggested that the most effective teams include 5–7 individuals who have a specific blend of team roles. He identified nine team-role types, which implies that an individual has the capacity to perform more than one role in the team (see Table 4).

Belbin also created four categories to identify the different types of teams:

- *Stable extroverts*, who excel in roles which place a focus on liaison and cooperation. These are ideal human resource managers.
- *Anxious extroverts*, who tend to work at a higher pace than others and exert pressure on other people. They are typified by a sales manager.

Table 4   Meredith Belbin's team-role types

Team role type	Characteristics and contribution
Completer/finisher	An individual who attempts to finish tasks on time whilst seeking out any errors or omissions. Tends to take a conscientious approach to work. They prefer to carry out the work themselves rather than delegate.
Coordinator	A promoter of joint decision-making with the ability to clarify goals. Keen to delegate but is often seen as manipulative and willing to pass work on to others.
Implementer	A disciplined and reliable individual who has the ability to transform ideas into practical solutions. Is often seen as slow to adopt new ways of working due to their inflexibility.
Monitor/evaluator	Has the ability to take a wider view and assess all available options. Not considered to be a great motivator and often appears to lack essential drive.

$\Rightarrow$

- *Stable introverts*, who work well with a small, stable team, where relationships are high on priorities. They are ideal local government officials.
- *Anxious introverts*, who rely on self-direction and persistence and are often committed to the longer term. The majority of creative individuals fall into this category.

Belbin, R. Meredith, *Team Roles at Work*. Oxford: Butterworth-Heinemann, 1995.
Belbin, R. Meredith, *Management Teams: Why They Succeed or Fail*. Oxford: Butterworth-Heinemann, 1996.
Belbin, R. Meredith, *Beyond the Team*. Oxford: Butterworth-Heinemann, 2000.

www.belbin.com/meredith.html

Table 4   Meredith Belbin's team-role types (*continued*)

Team role type	Characteristics and contribution
Plant	Essentially a problem solver who is both imaginative and creative. Is more preoccupied with communication than the detail of a task.
Resource investigator	Highly communicative and usually able to identify and deploy useful resources and contacts. Since their contribution is based on their enthusiasm for progress, they can be over optimistic and lose interest if little progress is being made.
Shaper	Able to deal with pressure and to overcome obstacles. They tend to be rather abrasive individuals who can often offend.
Specialist	Has access to specialist information and is often single-minded. They tend to only be able to contribute to certain aspects of a task and are quite technically focused.
Team worker	Cooperative and diplomatic listeners who wish to avoid conflict. They tend to be indecisive and lack the ability to contribute under pressure.

B

Benchmarking

A benchmark is a predetermined set of standards against which future performance or activities are measured. Usually, benchmarking involves the discovery of the best practice for the activity, either within or outside the business, in an effort to identify the ideal processes and prosecution of an activity.

The purpose of benchmarking is to ensure that future performance and activities conform with the benchmarked ideal in order to improve overall performance. Increased efficiency is key to the benchmarking process as, in human resource management terms, improved efficiency, reliability of data and effectiveness of activities will lead to a more competitive edge and ultimately greater profitability.

Damelio, Robert, *The Basics of Benchmarking*. New York: Productivity Press, 1995.

Benefit audit

A benefit audit is an activity carried out by an **audit team** in order to investigate the efficiency of an employee benefit programme.

Black Lung Act (US)

The Black Lung Act was formally incorporated into Title 4 of the Federal Coalmine Health and Safety Act (1969) in a series of amendments between 1972 and 1981.

The provision addresses benefits for disability or death due to respiratory illnesses, or Black Lung Disease, most closely associated with coalmining operations.

Barth, Peter S., *Tragedy of Black Lung: Federal Compensation for Occupational Disease*. Storrs, CT: University of Connecticut Press, 1987.

B

Blake and Mouton

Robert Blake and Jane Mouton developed a grid, strongly reminiscent of that of **Likert**. The grid provides an opportunity to identify styles adopted by managers in specific situations. The managers complete a questionnaire, and their people- or task-related scores are then tallied and cross-referenced to discover to what degree they accord with the four broad types of manager identified on the grid. An example is shown in Figure 4.

The *Country Club* manager is typified by an individual who tries to avoid problems and considers productivity to be subservient to staff contentment. Anything which disturbs the balance is avoided.

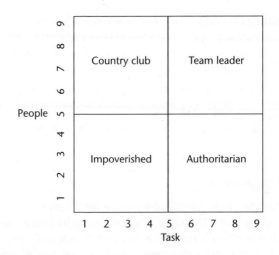

Figure 4 An example of the Blake and Mouton grid.

A *Team Leader* or Team Manager manages to maintain a high simultaneous concern for both productivity and employees. The focus is upon providing the employees with the means by which they can achieve organizational objectives. Employees are encouraged to participate, state their opinions, not avoid conflict (as this is seen as a means by which problems can be resolved), and to approach all working relationships with honesty.

An *Impoverished Manager* is not interested in productivity or employee relations. The manager does not encourage creativity or initiative, seeks to avoid conflict and does not seem to wish to contribute. This is an individual who is just concerned with survival.

An *Authoritarian* is, essentially, a task-orientated autocrat who shows little concern for employees. All issues are subservient to productivity, conflict is suppressed and social aspects of work discouraged.

At the very centre of the grid is a mid-point which illustrates that managers could, at various times, adopt the characteristics of any of the four categories. Typically, this point describes the manager as being 'middle of the road', where there is equal concern for productivity and for employees. Conflicts usually end in compromise and creativity is encouraged, provided it is not too revolutionary.

Blake and Mouton consider management leadership within the context of the type of organization in which the manager operates (clearly there would be differences if the business was a bureaucracy

B

rather than some other organizational structure). The theory also takes into account the manager's own values and personal history, which tend to colour the way in which a manager operates, as they will invariably refer to past similar situations.

Blake, Robert R. and McCanse, Anne Adams, *Leadership Dilemmas: Grid Solutions* (The Blake/Mouton Grid Management and Organization Development Series). Houston, TX: Gulf Publishing, 1991.

Blake, Robert R. and Mouton, Jane S., *The Managerial Grid*. Houston, TX: Gulf Publishing, 1994.

Blanchard, Kenneth

Originally developed in the 1960s, by Hersey and Blanchard, the situational leadership model identifies employees as followers, who are measured in terms of their readiness to perform a specific job. This is based on their ability and willingness. As can be seen in Figure 5, the relationship between the followers and the leaders is an important one, as leaders are required to adopt a different approach for specific mixes of followers.

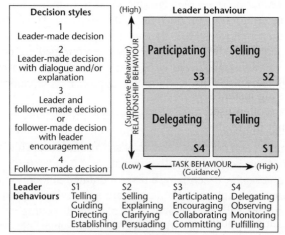

Figure 5   Expanded situational leadership model

Source: Hersey, Blanchard and Johnson, 1996.

Followers in the R4 category need little direct supervision or encouragement and in most cases jobs can be delegated to them (S4). Followers in the R3 category need to be encouraged to participate (S3), whilst those in the R2 category have to be effectively sold the idea by having it clarified or explained to them (S2). The R1 category, given their unwillingness and insecurity, need to be directed and told what it is that is expected of them (S1).

The model itself has been called into question but it is still widely used, particularly in management training programmes, as it is simple to understand and appears to have a degree of validity. Providing the situational leadership model can be dovetailed into a model which looks at goals, then a manager will be able to work using the most effective method of behaviour to deal with a variety of different situations and employees.

Blanchard, Kenneth H. and Hersey, Paul, *Management of Organizational Behavior: Utilizing Human Resources*. Englewood Cliffs, NJ: Prentice-Hall, 1969.

Hersey, Paul, Blanchard, Kenneth H. and Johnson, Dewey, *Management of Organizational Behavior: Utilizing Human Resources*. Englewood Cliffs, NJ: Prentice-Hall, 1996.

Blind ads

Blind advertisements are unusual in the sense that they do not reveal the name of the organization placing the advertisement. Stereotypical blind advertisements are usually related to job advertisements or advertisements offering instant solutions to income generation. Post Office box numbers are often used rather than complete addresses, but it is also possible that the reader is encouraged to call a free phone number or premium rate number for further information.

Bonuses

B

There are a wide variety of different bonus schemes, which are in operation in various businesses. Bonuses usually relate to additional payments made on either a monthly or an annual basis, as a reward for good work, as compensation for dangerous work, or as a share of the profits.

Other businesses will offer bonuses in relation to referrals. This is an integral part of dealing with a human resource department's difficulties in finding new employees for hard-to-fill jobs, specifically those with special skill requirements. Many businesses will offer a referral bonus payment to existing employees for referring qualified candidates who are subsequently employed by the business. Clearly there are strict regulations in respect of the suitability of the candidate and the length of service that the referred candidate actually completes (usually part of the payment is held back until the referred candidate has been working for the business for six months).

There are difficulties in using this system, in particular, as there may be conflicts of interest. Some human resource departments come under intense pressure from existing employees to shortlist candidates that they have referred. In many cases there is also a system set up to ensure that improper promises or assurances of employment to prospective candidates are not made by existing employees.

Keenan, William, *Commissions, Bonuses and Beyond: The Sales and Marketing Management Guide to Sales Compensation Planning.* New York: McGraw-Hill Education, 1994.

Broadbanding

Broadbanding is a policy which describes the restructuring of salaries into consolidated pay grades. Broadbanding usually occurs when a large, formerly **hierarchical organization structure** has removed several layers of management or parts of that management. New, broader salary scales are created, probably eliminating the levels which have been removed in the restructuring exercise. Progress in pay terms within each of the broad bands is encouraged by the acquisition of a wider variety of skills and abilities. In more traditional organizations pay and responsibility is normally linked to a narrow and specialized approach to skills. There are a number of associated problems attached to broadbanding, which include the following issues:

- Under a more traditional system, an employee's salary potential would be capped in line with the ability to acquire the skills for advancement into the next salary scale. Broadbanding, however, has a wider disparity in terms of spread of pay, and therefore there is less salary control in a broadbanded system than in a traditional one.
- **Pay equity** is difficult in many cases as there may be employees who are doing broadly the same work, but of whom one is nearer the bottom of the range whilst the other is nearer the top.
- Broadbanding also requires the opportunity for an employee to advance into a higher salary range, as within each broad band there are fewer salary ranges. The prospect of being able to advance into a new broadband category should encourage **employee retention**.

B

Broadbanding is often seen as a positive move forward and away from a more traditional, structured, rigid and specialization-based hierarchical structure. Most of the broadbanded categories will allow a salary range of around 50 per cent. Within each broad band there are generalized **job descriptions** and advancement rests on the attainment of a broad set of skills which match the **job specifications** in the higher bands.

Institute of Personnel Development, *IPD Guide on Broadbanding*. London: Chartered Institute of Personnel and Development (CIPD), 1996.

Buddy system

Buddy systems, which match an experienced employee to a new employee, are employed by many businesses. In effect the experienced employees operate as guides to the new recruits and show them around the business, introducing them to individuals in various departments and answering many of the questions which the new employee may wish to ask.

Buddy systems can be either formal or informal in their nature. A formalized system will seek to identify the most appropriately experienced employees, who can hope to illustrate to the new employees exactly how their job role and function fits into the overall operations of the business. Many businesses operate a more informal approach where, on an ad hoc basis, an individual within a department to whom the new employee has been assigned is asked to 'buddy' or accompany the new employee and be available to answer any queries or problems which may arise in the first few days of their employment. Buddy systems are often set in place in addition to the more normal **induction** period and any exercises or activities attached to the orientation of the new employee.

Burnout

Burnout is best described as complications arising out of prolonged and substantial stress. It is often exhibited in emotional, mental or physical exhaustion in employees who have been exposed to unreasonable levels of stress which have not been picked up by the management or human resource department.

Burnout has been exacerbated by **downsizing** of businesses and the streamlining of operations in the constant search for ways in which to economize and improve profitability. Whilst these strategies are employed, businesses still seek to be as productive as they had been

B

with larger workforces. Inevitably this places more strain on the remaining employees. The reasons for burnout can thus be described as being a combination of increased work and the fear that the individual may be next on the list of dismissals.

Biggs, Richard K., *Burn Brightly without Burning Out: Balancing the Work You Need with the Life You Lead*. London: Thomas Nelson Publishers. 2003.

Buy back

'Buy back' is a term which is associated with methods used by a business to convince an employee to stay in employment. Buy back involves offering increased wages or salaries in order to dissuade an individual from resigning or to get them to withdraw their letter of resignation.

B

Cafeteria benefit programme

'Cafeteria benefit programme' is the term used to describe a mixture of benefits and services offered by a business to its employees. The employee will be able to choose the exact mix of the benefits and services, which may include variations in **bonuses**, pension rights and working hours.

Career anchors

See **Schein, Edgar H.**

Career break

A career break is a special category of leave usually associated with flexible working arrangements. It is usually granted to those with domestic responsibilities and is often closely associated with the following circumstances:

- after the conclusion of **maternity leave**;
- where a close family member or partner is seriously ill and in need of care;
- where an employee wishes to spend more time caring for pre-school children or children of school age;
- where the employee has an elderly, dependent relative who needs full-time care;
- in the case of other circumstances of a domestic nature which may arise.

Career breaks are common provisions offered by organizations to employees who wish to retain a degree of commitment to the organization and maintain a long-term balance to both their work and domestic responsibilities.

Essentially, most systems consider the career break to be an unpaid leave of absence, yet the individual still remains an employee and therefore there is an expectation that the employee will continue to keep in touch with the organization for the duration of the career break. Usually the employee and the organization determine the proposed length of the career break and a finite number of weeks or months are attached to the break. Career breaks should not be confused with paternity leave, **maternity leave**, **compassionate leave** or **secondment**. Career breaks are often referred to as 'sabbaticals'.

Stevens, Astrid, *Take a Career Break: Bringing up Children without Giving up your Future*. London: Need 2 Know, 1996.
White, Joshua, *Taking a Career Break*. London: Vacation Work Publications, 2001.

Career counselling

Career counselling is a process instituted by a human resource department to assist employees in identifying specific career goals and paths. Career counselling provides help to employees in making informed decisions on their career planning, perhaps identifying training course opportunities and examining different employment options within the business.

Career plateau

A career plateau is simply described as being a temporary halt in the advancement of an individual's career. Career plateauing occurs particularly in the cases of those in the 40–55 age brackets. Often individuals will seek one of the following alternatives as a solution to the problem:

- They will seek a higher position, probably in a business closer to their home.
- They may consider **job sharing** and refocusing their attention on other opportunities which may be afforded to them in the time they have available.
- They may consider a sabbatical or **career break** in order to obtain management or leadership training.
- They may consider moving to a more flexible working pattern and change their role at work.

Bridges, W., *Jobshift: How to Prosper in a Workplace without Jobs*. Reading, MA: Addison-Wesley, 1994.
Saltzman, A., *Downshifting: Reinventing Success on a Slower Track*. New York: HarperCollins, 1991.

Careless worker model

In the history of investigations into health and safety at work, one of the early suggestions was that the majority of accidents occurred as a result of employees' carelessness. The model itself has been largely outdated as a result of more systematic investigations into the nature of the causes of accidents and their associated prevention. It is now widely established that the majority of accidents occurring in the workplace are not as a result of employees' carelessness or negligence, but more to do with long-term or temporary breaches in health and safety procedures and practices.

Casual labour

The employment of casual labour, or casual employees, is seen as a viable alternative by many employers to provide a degree of flexibility, particularly when demand may not be easy to predict. Casual labour is usually taken on a once-off job basis, or the individuals are placed on standby by the employer to come in and occasionally carry out work as and when required.

The term 'casual labour' also implies an employment situation where employees are given low pay, little or no training, no job security, and no sick or holiday pay, and can be discarded as and when the business sees fit. Casual labour has attracted the unfortunate nickname of 'flex-ploitation', which refers to situations where the lowest, minimum wage payments are made, often to individuals who are desperate for work and are prepared to ignore any dangers associated with the work they are asked to undertake.

Philips, Gordon and Whiteside, Noel, *Casual Labour: The Unemployment Question in the Port Transport Industry, 1880–1970*. Oxford: Oxford University Press, 1985.

Chain of command

The chain of command within an organization is typically associated with a business that has a **hierarchical organizational structure**. The chain of command is the formal line of communication, beginning with the board of directors, or managing director, who passes instructions down to departmental managers, section heads, and then to individual employees. The chain of command typifies a pyramid-shaped organization, where increasingly down the pyramid more individuals have to be informed of decisions and instructions. Effectively, the chain of command of the board of directors or the managing director encompasses every individual underneath them in the hierarchical structure. Similarly, the chain of command of a section head is merely the immediate employees who work under that individual's supervision. The term 'chain of command' is closely associated with **span of control**.

Keuning, Doede and Opheij, Wilfred, *De-layering Organizations: How to Beat Bureaucracy and Create a Flexible and Responsive Organization*. London: Pitman, 1994.

Change management

There are many theories regarding change management. Many focus upon the way in which a business thinks about change and the way it drives change. As there are a number of different theories, it is perhaps prudent to focus on just some of the ways in which change management can be achieved. Although change may not necessarily be driven by a human resource department, it is often the role of the department to manage the intricacies and complications arising out of change. There are innumerable theories not only on how to change impacts on individuals and groups within a business, but also on the ideal ways of managing that change.

Doug Stace and Dexter Dunphy took the view that change management could be packaged in terms of its size and complexity and then organized accordingly, as can be seen in Figure 6

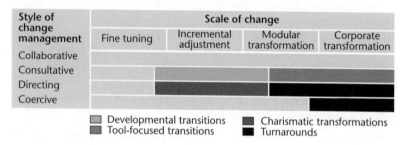

Style of change management	Scale of change			
	Fine tuning	Incremental adjustment	Modular transformation	Corporate transformation
Collaborative				
Consultative				
Directing				
Coercive				

☐ Developmental transitions   ■ Charismatic transformations
☐ Tool-focused transitions   ■ Turnarounds

Figure 6 Stace and Dunphy's view of change

Size of change	Planning and action implications
Developmental	Enables ideas to be generated from and developed by affected employees and involves them in implementation planning.
Transitional	Management needs to be clear about the change and identify similarities and differences between the current and the new procedures. Targets and objectives should be set and progress monitored and reported on. Employees should be acknowledged for their efforts and any successes.
Transformational	The change must be communicated throughout the organization with no possibility of ambiguity or misunderstanding. Employees must be educated as to why the change is occurring, how it will affect them and what the new vision is.

Figure 7 Costello's view of change management

Source: After Costello, 1994.

Costello's approach sought to set the parameters purely by the size and scope of the change being envisioned and then to suggest strategies by which the change could be facilitated (see Figure 7).

Paul Bate, on the other hand, considered the whole process of change to be a cycle which had clearly identifiable phases, as can be seen in Figure 8.

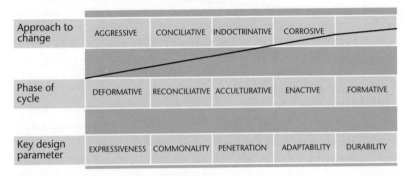

Approach to change	AGGRESSIVE	CONCILIATIVE	INDOCTRINATIVE	CORROSIVE	
Phase of cycle	DEFORMATIVE	RECONCILIATIVE	ACCULTURATIVE	ENACTIVE	FORMATIVE
Key design parameter	EXPRESSIVENESS	COMMONALITY	PENETRATION	ADAPTABILITY	DURABILITY

Figure 8 Bate's view of change management

See also **Hay, Julie; Kotter and Schlesinger** *and* **Lewin, Kurt.**

Bate, Paul, *Strategies for Cultural Change*. Oxford: Butterworth-Heinemann, 1995.
Costello, Sheila, *Managing Change at Work*. New York: Irwin Professional, 1994.
Stace, Doug and Dunphy, Dexter, *Beyond the Boundaries*. New York: McGraw-Hill, 2002.

Chartered Institute of Personnel and Development (CIPD) (UK)

The Chartered Institute of Personnel and Development (CIPD) is the UK's professional body for individuals concerned with the management and development of people.

www.cipd.co.uk/

See also **Society for Human Resource Management.**

C

Civil Rights Act 1991 (US)

This act allows for **compensation** and damages in cases where there has been intentional **discrimination** on the basis of gender, religion or disability. The act prohibits race norming and other discriminatory adjustments of test scores on the basis of race, colour, religion, gender or national origin.

Civil Rights Center (US)

The Civil Rights Center exists to enforce Federal statutes and regulations, essentially in the areas of **discrimination**. It conducts **equal opportunity** compliance reviews and provides compliance assistance and training. The Civil Rights Center's various functions are variously related to issues arising in the Department of Labor (DOL), where it mediates and investigate discrimination complaints filed against the DOL in numerous areas, including disability.

www.dol.gov

Cluster

A cluster is a group of recognized job competences, skills or behaviours which have been identified as being related requirements, in either a **job description** or a **job design**. Human resources departments will seek to identify the inter-connected competences sought in a particular job role, which will help them to categorize the key aspect of that job role and assist in the identification of suitable candidates, or of training, which may be required to periodically update individual employees.

Coaching

Employee 'coaching' is a term closely associated with **mentor programmes**. Coaching is essentially a partnership between a mentor or motivator and another individual within the organization. The purpose of coaching is to help build the individual's confidence, to be clear about their goals, to assist them in dealing with difficult problems and generally to improve their performance. A human resource department may establish a formalized coaching system, having identified and trained key members of staff as mentors or coaches, and assigned them to one or more individuals within the organization. Coaching normally takes place on an informal, but frequent, basis and may also be used in conjunction with an **appraisal** system.

Co-determination

Co-determination as a concept can trace its history back to postwar Germany and is, in effect, a form of worker democracy which gives employees the right to have their representatives present during management decisions, and for them to vote on those decisions. It was initially designed as a means by which potential tension between employers and employees could be balanced. In industries such as coal and steel, five employees would join five shareholders and an eleventh elected member on a supervisory board. The board would then appoint three executive board members (one **trade union** representative and two business-specific specialists) to directly manage the operations of the business. In effect, the system was very similar to the Scandinavian **worker directors**.

More recently in Europe, the **Social Chapter** of the Maastricht Treaty promotes the establishment of **works councils**. There is an inherent problem with co-determination in most countries, certainly from both management and trade union perspectives; it is difficult for both parties to move away from their traditional adversarial positions. Co-determination requires a high degree of compromise, and trade unionists, in particular, are reluctant to be seen as key decision makers which might adversely affect their members.

In practice, many co-determination systems which are in operation in businesses are limited to non-strategic decision making, such as that concerned with **health and safety**. Management is also keen to avoid trade union involvement in a co-determination system dealing with major business decisions, such as acquisitions, closures or restructuring.

From the mid-1990s in the UK there has been a gradual increase in interest and concern with what is known as the 'stakeholder society'. The inference is that employees, as integral stakeholders in any business, should have an involvement in the decision-making process of a business.

Kuhne, Robert E., *Co-Determination in Business: Workers' Representatives in the Boardroom*. New York: Praeger, 1980.

Schneider, Hannes and Kingsman, David J., *German Co-Determination Act*. Frankfurt: F. Knapp, 1977.

Cognitive dissonance

C

'Cognitive dissonance' is a term associated with psychological approaches to changing an individual's attitude or behaviour in the workplace. The term implies that in the cognitive sense, individuals recognise what they have learned and what they understand. Dissonance occurs when there is a lack of harmony. Therefore cognitive dissonance, in the human resource management sense, can mean that employees become confused when new information is given to them which does not correspond, or is at variance with, what they already understand. This means that the individuals feel conflict within themselves. The conflict needs to be resolved and management and human resources can only achieve this by rationalizing the dissonance. Employees are far more likely to accept a rational explanation of why dissonance has occurred, and the fact that it is invariably perfectly normal, providing they are given an explanation by someone they accept as being an expert.

An alternative way of dealing with dissonance, which avoids the requirement to provide rational reasons, is to offer financial inducements. Attitudes and behaviours can be often swept aside providing the financial inducement is strong enough.

Arnold, John, Robertson, Ivan T. and Cooper, Cary L., *Work Psychology: Understanding Human Behaviour in the Workplace*. Harlow, Essex: Financial Times, Prentice-Hall, 1991.

Collective agreement

A collective agreement is essentially a contract negotiated between a **trade union** and an employer, which outlines the terms and conditions of employment. Generally the following rules apply to the way in which collective agreements are arrived at:

- they require everyone to act together;
- they apply to everyone equally, otherwise the agreement is not viable;
- without the inclusion of trade unions in the negotiations, representing the interests of employees, it is difficult to retain either of the above conditions.

Normally collective agreements will deal with all or some of the following issues:

- how pay is determined;
- the length and application of working hours in a week;
- overtime;
- payment for leaves of absence and other leave;
- how pay deductions are calculated;
- pensions.

There are clear benefits in arriving at a collective agreement, as it not only binds all employees to the same sets of rules and conditions, but also ensures that employees themselves are not subject to arbitrary decisions by the employer.

Zack, Arnold M. and Bloch, Richard I., *Labor Agreement in Negotiation and Arbitration*. Washington, DC: BNA Books, 1995.

www.eurofound.eu.int/emire/UNITED%20KINGDOM/COLLECTIVEAGREEMENT-EN.html

Collective bargaining

Collective bargaining seeks to establish, by negotiation and discussion, the means by which disputes and other matters of concern can be resolved. Collective bargaining is, in essence, a joint regulating process which will equally apply to management and employees. There are a number of different ways in which collective bargaining can be achieved, and in this respect there are subdivisions of collective bargaining, which are:

- conjunctive bargaining – which adopts the assumption that an agreement of some sort must be reached in order that operations upon which both the employer and employees are reliant can continue;
- cooperative bargaining – which takes the view that both parties are dependent upon one another and that they can both hope to achieve their objectives more effectively if they win the support of one another.

Normally, collective bargaining is applied to the determination of wages and conditions. Collective bargaining also allows employers and employees to define the rules which will govern their relationship. Usually collective bargaining takes place between an employer and representatives of the employees, which may include **trade unions**. It can take place at various levels, either within a specific business or across a whole sector, which may be regional or national.

Collective bargaining allows employees to exert a collective voice on personnel decisions which may affect them, and may also seek to assist them in gaining rewards for productivity or progress which has been made. As far as employers are concerned, collective bargaining seeks to maintain industrial relations, which may otherwise be interrupted or affected by unrest.

Hilgert, Raymond L. and Dilts, David A., *Cases in Collective Bargaining and Industrial Relations: A Decisional Approach*. New York: McGraw-Hill Education, 2002.
Thompson, Leigh L., *The Mind and Heart of the Negotiator*. Englewood Cliffs: Prentice-Hall, 2000.

www.eurofound.eu.int/emire/UNITED%20KINGDOM/COLLECTIVEBARGAINING-EN.html

Collective redundancy

Collective **redundancy** is a form of **dismissal** that may occur in an organization and notionally is taken to refer to circumstances where the dismissals affect around 10 per cent of employees in a given workplace.

Collective redundancy means that a significant number of the employees will be affected and in most cases employees or the employees' representatives should be contacted 30 days before the first dismissal takes place. During this consultation period both parties will seek to investigate the possibility of avoiding redundancies or reducing the number of employees that are affected. There will also be discussions as to how employees will be chosen for redundancy.

In Europe the Collective Redundancy Directive requires employers to inform and consult workers in the event of collective redundancy.

Combination

'Combination' is a human resource term used to describe a technique used in **job analysis**. Combination involves the concurrent use of at least two different job analysis techniques in order to establish a more reliable picture of the exact nature of a particular job role. Typically, techniques such as **observation** and **interviews** may be deployed.

Commission-based payment

A commission-based pay is an incentive-based pay structure, which is widely believed to produce better results from employees than a traditional pay structure. Typically, sales staff are placed on commission-based pay. Their income is directly related to their performance and in most cases there is no ceiling to the amount of money they can earn. Commission-based structures are seen as a viable means of identifying those who are under-performing and who may require either redeployment or training. One of the many associated problems, however, with commission-based pay structures is that employees tend to focus on the sale of items which provide them with the largest return in relation to their time. Commission-based salaries tend to work when the products or services sold by a business have few variations. This means that employees tend to focus on building relationships with customers in order to provide steady commission payments.

Torkelson, Gwen E., *Contribution Based Pay: Tools to Identify, Measure and Reward Performance.* iUniverse.com, 2001.

Communication standards

This is a formal protocol, often administered by the human resource department, which applies to internal communications within a business. The communication standards set the rules with regard to the elimination of racial, age, gender or other biases in communications within the organization.

Compa-ratio

A compa-ratio (comparative ratio) is used to measure the extent to which average salaries deviate from target salaries. It can also be used to indicate an individual's salary in relation to the mid-point of a relevant pay scale. The ratio is used to identify where limitations in pay may need to be implemented or when a more generous policy may need to be adopted. In order to calculate the compa-ratio, the following formula is used:

Average of all salaries in grade/mid-point of the salary range × 100

This formula can be used to calculate the compa-ratio of a group of employees. A slightly different variation of formula is used to calculate the compa-ratio of an individual employee:

Individual salary/mid-point of salary range × 100

If a compa-ratio of 100 is achieved, then there is an indication that no corrective steps need to be taken. A compa-ratio of 80 would indicate that average salaries are low and possibly there is a need to increase the salaries as they may no longer be competitive within the industry. This lower score could also indicate that there has been a recent influx of new employees into this salary grade. A compa-ratio of 120, however, would indicate that perhaps some staff are being overpaid or that the salary range includes a number of long-serving employees.

Comparative approach

A comparative approach is an extended form of **audit of human resource system** which is carried out by an **audit team** and involves a comparison of the business's human resource practices with those of another business. A comparative approach may involve investigating the relative practices of different parts of a given business, perhaps separate divisions, which have their own human resource departments. Clearly, involving an independent business in a comparative approach audit requires a degree of mutual understanding and trust between the two businesses and may, therefore, only occur when the businesses have a long-standing relationship and are probably not direct competitors. The purpose of the comparative approach is to identify areas of poor performance and if the audit is undertaken as a cooperative exer-

C

cise between two audit teams from different businesses, then the purpose is to reveal information which may be of value to both parties.

Comparative evaluation

Comparative evaluation is a variant form of performance appraisal. It requires the human resource department or managers, supervisors or appraisers to make a direct comparison between an individual employee's performance and that of co-workers. The comparative evaluation relies upon the ability of the individual carrying out the appraisal to compare like with like and, as such, it is common practice to compare those with the same **job description** or function within the business.

Compassionate leave

Although, in the majority of cases, there is no specific entitlement to compassionate leave, many businesses are willing to allow their employees to take leave for a variety of urgent, personal reasons. Compassionate leave may be paid or unpaid, depending upon the business's policy, and would include time off for urgent childcare, care of dependent relatives, or a bereavement. In most cases the granting of compassionate leave will depend upon the urgency of the application and the personal circumstances of the individual. In the case of bereavement, for example, if an individual needs to make funeral and other arrangements, then this will be taken into account. In most cases compassionate leave is dealt with on an as-and-when basis. Although there may be an existing policy within the business to deal with this type of leave, the human resource department, in conjunction with the employee's immediate superior, will agree on the appropriateness of granting the compassionate leave and the probable length of that leave.

Compensation

In terms of human resource management, compensation has two distinctly different meanings. First, 'compensation' can be used to describe the mix of payments and benefits which are exchanged with individual employees for their services. Compensation is usually made on the basis of an individual's education, skills, experience, motivation, the nature of the work, hours worked and a general indication of their commitment to the business or the organization. In this respect compensation often extends far beyond the simple payment of salaries or the availability of **fringe benefits**.

The term 'compensation' can also be applied to situations where it has been proved that an employee has been unfairly treated or penalized by a business. Either the business itself will pay compensation, on the direction of an **industrial tribunal** or, in some cases, a court, or it will be a negotiated package between the employer and the employee.

Compensation audit

A compensation audit, or employee compensation audit, is an investigation and review of salaries, **bonuses**, **incentives** and stock or share options. Many businesses undertake this audit on an annual basis in order to ensure that they are adhering to legal requirements, maintaining their comparative competitiveness in the market, as well as analysing the effectiveness of their systems. Normally the business will examine a number of key areas within the audit, which may include the following:

- Does the compensation plan reflect any changes in business strategy since the last audit? This may include differences in sales strategies which may have underpinned **performance-related pay**.
- Has the business rapidly expanded, either in volume or employment, since the last audit? This requires the business to examine whether the rewards are motivating enough, whether their system is flexible and competitive enough to attract and retain employees, and whether current employees have positive differentials compared with new employees.
- Has there been any problem with recruitment or retention of employees during the period? This could indicate that employee compensation is not adequate.
- Is the compensation linked to individuals, groups, or company performance as a whole? This examines whether it is fair to penalize high performing individuals or teams for failures in other areas of the business, etc.
- Who is setting the performance standards and thus the application of the compensation system? This investigates whether supervisors and managers have been sufficiently trained with regard to **performance appraisal**, and whether performance standards and objectives are consistent throughout the business. This also investigates whether employees feel that their rewards meet, fail or exceed their expectations.
- Is the business satisfied that its current system reflects systems which are in operation in competitors' businesses? There may well be individuals who have recently worked in a competitor's organi-

zation and who could enlighten the audit team as to the effectiveness of alternative systems.

- Does the compensation system comply with current, recent and intended legislation in relation to pay?
- Does the compensation system reflect any changes in the specific duties of employees which have taken place in the past year?

Belcher, John G. Jr., *How to Design and Implement a Results-Orientated Variable Pay System.* New York: Amacom, 1996.

Schuster, Jay R. and Zingheim, Patricia K., *The New Pay: Linking Employee and Organizational Performance.* Indianapolis, IN: Jossey Bass Wiley, 1996.

Competencies

Competencies are taken to mean the skills, knowledge and behaviours which are identified as being crucial to the fulfilling of a particular role by an employee. Ideal competencies form the basis of any **job design** or **job specification** which seeks to identify what will be required of an individual in order to perform a specific series of tasks or fulfil a specific function at a particular level of the business.

Complaints procedure

A complaints procedure may be distinguished from a **grievance procedure** in the sense that it may be a problem encountered by an employee that is not necessarily related to an individual or to a specific practice in the business. A complaint may be an identification of a deficiency in process which has hitherto not been identified as being a specific issue, either by management or by the human resources department. Although there is no clearly defined complaints procedure which can be directly applied to all businesses, many complaints procedures follow a similar format to that of complaints received from external individuals, such as customers. Clearly, any complaint, whether internal or external, which may relate to the way in which the business functions, has to be investigated in order to satisfy the complainant and provide a basis upon which the business can improve its systems and procedures. The chart in Figure 9 provides an indication as to how a complaints procedure could be structured.

Compliance approach

A compliance approach is effectively a review or audit of human resource practices, with the intention of determining whether they

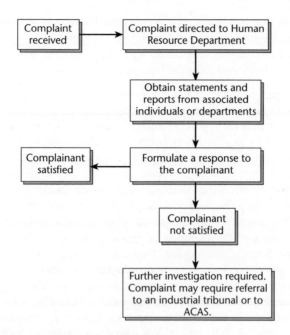

Figure 9   How complaints can be dealt with

conform to the business's stated policies. An integral part of this is also to consider whether human resource practices comply with legal standards. A compliance approach can also encompass an **audit of managerial compliance**.

Compressed working week

The compressed working week is an example of **alternative work arrangements** and is often referred to as a 'compressed time option'. Some businesses will refer to the compressed working week as a 4/10 schedule, which refers to the most common practice of employees working 4 × 10-hour days with the 5th day as leave. Alternatively, the system is referred to as a '9-day fortnight' or '9/80', and in some cases, '9/8 schedule'.

The 9-day fortnight means simply that the employee works for 9 working days in each 2-week block. A 9/80 schedule refers to a system where employees work for 80 hours over 9 days (instead of the normal 10 days). A 9/8 schedule is more complex as employees work for 9 hours on 4 days a week and for 8 hours on the 5th day, or they have a day off.

As far as the US and the UK are concerned, upwards of 25 per cent of private sector employers offer compressed working weeks. There are a number of advantages associated with these more complicated work schedules, which tend to be centred on two key areas:

- Customer satisfaction – a traditional 5-day a week schedule often meant that businesses would be required to take on additional staff to cover periods beyond Monday to Friday. There would be associated breaks in production, coverage, and consistency in relation to dealing with customers. Equally, in times when the business needed extra coverage, there would be a requirement to pay employees overtime. Using a compressed working week, more employees can be deployed at crucial times of the week, with lower staffing levels being maintained when demand is lower. Equally, the timing of the compressed working week can be adjusted to match demand and required turnaround times.
- The other major concern is **employee retention**. It has been a major discovery that a compressed working week actually attracts and adds to the retention strategies of a business. A compressed working week does offer a degree of flexibility. Guaranteed additional time off, sufficient to deal with domestic issues such as childcare, for example, means that a compressed working week is often attractive to employees with young children, or other commitments outside of work.

The compressed working week, however, does have problems associated with it, specifically with reference to issues such as safety and the health of employees. A longer, albeit concentrated, working week does add to the physical strain upon employees, as they will inevitably have shorter breaks between blocks of work within a four-day period. Crucial to the imposition of a compressed working week is the requirement for the business to give employees sufficient time to reschedule their personal lives. Providing the imposition is planned before it is initiated, most employees seem to be receptive to the concept of a compressed working week.

Olmstead, Barney and Smith, Suzanne, *Creating a Flexible Workplace: How to Select and Manage Alternative Work Options*. Indianapolis, IN: Pfeiffer Wiley, 1994.

Compromise agreements

'Compromise agreement' refers to a situation where employment is terminated on mutual terms which have been agreed between the employer and the employee. In all cases, in return for agreeing to the termination of employment, the employee is paid a set sum of money. Enshrined within the agreement is protection for the employer from future claims in relation to the employee's statutory employment rights. Dependent upon the national law relating to employees' rights, usually the following criteria related to a compromise agreement are standard:

- The agreement must be in writing and be signed by both the employer and the employee.
- The employee must have the opportunity to seek advice from an independent legal advisor, whose fees, in most cases, are paid by the employer.
- The advisor must have some form of insurance or indemnity to cover any risks which may be associated with the providing of this advice.
- The advisor is specifically identified in the agreement and may be required to sign the compromise agreement themselves as a witness.

The use of compromise agreements avoids the requirement for the two parties to enter into any form of litigation. Generally, the compromise agreement can ensure the rapid termination of employment in extreme circumstances, usually when **redundancy** may be the only other option.

Computer-assisted interview

Increasingly, computer software is being used by human resource management to assist in the electronic profiling of job candidates and to screen new employees. For several years computer-assisted interviews, or computer-aided interviews, have been used by market research companies to obtain qualitative data as part of a research survey. More recently this application has been transferred into the human resource field, with the establishment of either company-specific computer-assisted interview systems, or, more commonly, the outsourcing of this technique, to internet recruitment specialists.

There has been a considerable increase in the number of **e-recruit-ment** sites, which began by allowing potential job **applicants** the facility to upload their profiles into a searchable database that could then be used by recruiters. This system has now developed to the extent that a randomly generated series of job-specific questions can be posed to the candidates in order to screen and eliminate individuals who do not match specific profiles in terms of skills, comprehension, judgement and other factors.

See also **computer-interactive performance test.**

Computer-based training (CBT)

Computer-based training incorporates both Intranet and internet-based training opportunities. The development of computer-based technologies is now widely applied by many human resource and training departments to internally train and enhance employees. Clearly, the establishment of an Intranet training system incorporates the need to extend the security of the internal system from unauthorized use.

Human resource management is gradually moving towards using computer-based training materials, which may be stored on an Intranet or internet database and, in some cases, on CD-Roms or DVDs. For most businesses the development of computer-based training is not yet cost-effective in areas other than general training, which can be applied to most employees. The costs associated with the creation of CBT often require a business to consider the purchase of general training aids, rather than producing or outsourcing bespoke materials.

One of the major developments has been the creation of an entirely new form of training and learning system. Those professionals who are able to train employees via web-based training programs are often referred to as e-trainers and the CBT as e-learning. It was generally believed, when CBT was first developed, that it would eventually lead to businesses not requiring the services of trainers, as the systems would be smart enough to accommodate the needs of individual learners. Generally this has not proved to be the case and e-trainers are integral parts of e-learning systems. There is still a requirement, no matter how remote each individual learner may be from the e-trainer geographically, that there is a degree of interaction. This need not necessarily be verbal, or, indeed, face-to-face, yet the provision of chat-room and discussion forums has become vital to ensuring understanding, commitment and instruction throughout the programme.

Computer-based training can be seen as the successor to more traditional forms of **distance learning**, which have tended to rely on paper-based materials, supported by occasional seminars or tutorials. Admittedly many distance learning courses did use CD-Roms and websites as backup and as a potential means by which individual learners and deliverers could interact. The implementation of CBT requires human resource management to consider the following issues:

- What are the criteria for success? Does the training have a link to specific business objectives and how will the effectiveness of the training be measured?
- How will the CBT communicate with the trainee, the human resource department and those responsible for overseeing the training on a day-to-day basis?

- How will the CBT be implemented? Where will it appear and how portable will the system be, given the fact that some of the trainees may be in remote locations?
- How will human resource managers ensure that the trainees are committed to the learning?
- What will the system be, to ensure progress and completion?
- How will results be measured? Will the trainees be required to undertake specific examinations, either internal or external, in order to provide proof of their acquired knowledge and skills as a result of the CBT?

Cartwright, Steve R. and Cartwright, G. Phillip, *Designing and Producing Media-based Training*. Burlington, MA: Focal Press, 1999.
Horton, William, *Designing Web-based Training*. Chichester: John Wiley, 2001.
Lockwood, Fred and Gooley, Anne (eds), *Innovation in Open and Distance Learning: Successful Development of Online and Web-based Learning*. London: Kogan Page, 2001.

Computer-interactive performance test

Computer-interactive performance tests can be employed in order to measure skills, comprehension, judgement and spatial visualization in a number of different contexts. The tests can take place during recruitment, in order to screen potential candidates; they can be used during induction in order to identify specific areas of future training for individuals; and they can be used periodically for existing employees in order to test their awareness as a precursor to a **training needs analysis**.

Computerization

Human resource management has not been immune to the gradual switch towards using and depending on technology to store data. In the human resources field there has been an increasing trend to computerize what had hitherto been a traditional data storage system with regard to employee records. Human resource managers have recognized the improvements in efficiency, flexibility and responsiveness as a result of computerizing their data using various types of proprietary software.

Conciliation

Conciliation is the process of involving an independent third party by mutual agreement between an employer and an employee. The third party involved in the conciliation process may be either an organization loosely associated with the government, or an independent private organization with specific conciliation expertise.

See also **Advisory Conciliation and Arbitration Service (ACAS)** and **American Arbitration Association.**

Consolidated Omnibus Budget Reconciliation Act (COBRA) 1993 (US)

COBRA was originally introduced in 1986 and contains provision for certain former employees, retired individuals, spouses and dependent children, giving them the right to have continued health coverage at group rates. COBRA set the minimum standards and benefit eligibility for welfare and medical benefits which were enjoyed through insurance while the individual was in employment.

Constructive dismissal

Constructive dismissal occurs when an employee is forced to leave a job because of the employer's behaviour. In these cases employees feel that they cannot remain in work, and tender their resignation. Typical examples include:

- lack of support;
- **harassment** and humiliation;
- victimization;
- changing job role without **consultation**;
- changing job location at short notice;
- falsely accusing the employee of misconduct;
- excessive demotion or disciplining of employee.

www.eurofound.eu.int/emire/UNITED%20KINGDOM/CONSTRUCTIVEDISMISSAL-EN.html

www.dol.gov/

Consultation

Consultation implies a degree of amicability and discussion between employers and employees. Consultation can occur at various levels of an organization and seeks to involve, and arrive at, a degree of consensus before the implementation of decisions which may affect employees.

Continuous employment

'Continuous employment' refers to a period during which an employee has worked for the same employer without a break. The period includes statutory leave, periods of sick leave, or any other authorized absences. The duration of the period of continuous employment is calculated to determine whether employees qualify for rights accorded to them by virtue of the length of their service. Continuous employment is applicable to a contract with an employer for an indefinite or fixed-term duration. If at any point the continuity of work has been broken, then it is usually taken that the number of weeks worked before the break does not count towards the employee's continuous service calculations. In cases of dispute, **industrial tribunals** will normally determine what was, or what was not, a period of valid continuous employment.

Continuous professional development (CPD)

Continuous professional development is often driven by an individual employee and relies upon the support of human resource management. Continuous professional development is commonly seen as an integral part of the ongoing learning process in which individuals can seek to attain additional skills and competences throughout their working life.

Norton, Bob and Burt, Vikky, *Practical Self-Development: A Step-by-Step Approach to CPD.* London: Institute of Management, 1998.

Contract or contingent workers

Contract or contingent workers are individuals who are hired for a limited period of time, perhaps for as little as a day or even for several years. They can be seen as a necessary adjunct to **core employees** as contingent workers are temporary workers, contractors or other individuals who provide additional labour as and when required by a business. Contingent workers are variously known as 'transients', 'peripheral workers' or 'complementary employees'. They generally fall into one of five categories, as can be seen in Table 5.

George, Helen, *The Professional Contract Workers' Handbook.* New York: McGraw-Hill Education, 1996.
Macdonald, Lynda, *Managing Fixed-term and Part-term Workers: A Practical Guide to Temporary, Seasonal and Contract Employees.* Oxford: Tolley Publishing, 2002.

Contract of employment

The contract of employment, by implication, is a written agreement between an employer and an employee which clearly states the relationship between the two parties. The contract will invariably include

Table 5 Types of contingent workers

Category of worker	Description
Part-timer workers	These are individuals whose working week can generally be adapted to suit the needs of the business. They can also include individuals who are working on a temporary or seasonal basis.
Agency workers	Employees who are, in effect, employed by an agency for which the business pays an additional fee per hour or day worked. The agency is responsible for the wages and tax and other benefits. These individuals can be hired on a daily, weekly, monthly or other basis.
Contract workers	These are usually individuals who provide a form of professional support under contract, for a fixed period of time or a fixed number of hours over a given period of time.
Leased workers	These are either temporary or permanent employees who can be taken on on a long-term basis, usually in the form of a whole group of individuals who perform a specific function.
Direct-hire workers	These are a business's pool of available individuals who can be called in, usually at short notice, to cover unforeseen gaps in the workforce, and may often be retired workers or former employees.

references to the role which the employee adopts and the expectations of that employee in terms of hours worked and other basic information. Normally a contract of employment will have a series of appendices or related documents which will specifically state the exact **job description** and duties to be undertaken by the employee. The contract of employment will also include information regarding pay, benefits and leave entitlement, as well as basic information about employee benefits such as pensions and healthcare. Contracts of employment differ from country to country and in the US they often vary from state to state.

Davies, Paul, Rideout, Roger, and Collins, Hugh (eds), *Legal Regulation of the Employment Relation*. New York: Kluwer Law International, 2001.

Contract Work Hours and Safety Standards Act (1962) (US)

This Act, commonly known as CWHSSA, refers specifically to contractors and subcontractors carrying out federally funded work to the value of over $100,000. The Act requires contractors and subcontractors to pay employees one and a half times the basic rate of pay for all hours worked over 40 hours in a given week, whilst ensuring that the workers operate in sanitary, hazard- and danger-free conditions. The Act specifically refers to construction contracts.

Contributory plans

Contributory plans are systems instituted by an employer which require the employee to make a contribution to benefits which are currently being, or will be enjoyed by the employee, such as pensions and health-care insurance.

Control of Substances Hazardous to Health Regulations (COSHH) 1999 (UK)

These regulations require employers to make regular assessments of the risks from hazardous substances and to ensure that precautions are taken to reduce these risks.

www.hse.gov.uk/hthdir/noframes/coshh

Cooperative methods

Cooperative methods are applicable to **industrial relations** and involve attempts to improve relations between the employer and unions or employee representatives. The techniques employed aim to improve the degree of cooperation and the feeling of mutual direction and benefit between the two groups.

Core competences

Core competences have two specific definitions. The first is identical to that of **competencies**. In other words, the identification of the key skills, knowledge and experience required of an individual to carry out a specific job role.

The other definition refers to the ability of employees or managers to be adaptable in the sense that they could work in an alternate, remote location, particularly abroad. In these cases core competences examine the adaptability and resourcefulness of the managers to operate in what may be an unknown overseas environment.

Stone, Florence M. and Sachs, Randi T., *High-value Manager: Developing the Core Competences for Organizational Demands*. New York: Amacom, 1996.

Core dimensions of diversity

The core dimensions of diversity examine the inherent attributes of an individual and can be defined as either primary or secondary dimensions. It is presumed that the primary dimensions, such as age and gender, exert a powerful influence on all other aspects, values, experiences, assumptions and expectations of an individual. The secondary dimensions, which include education, family status, organizational role and level, are less visible, yet they are significant in respect of the way in which an individual may view certain situations and deal with specific issues. The range of core dimensions is shown in Figure 10.

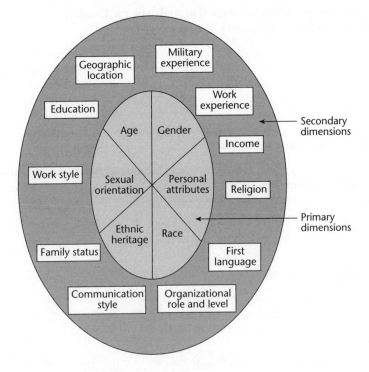

Figure 10 Core dimensions of diversity

Core employees

Core or key employees are individuals who are essential to the running of an organization. Typically, they will be individuals who hold crucial strategic job positions within the organization and have been identified by both the management and human resources department as being vital. These individuals are often provided with additional incentives in order to ensure their retention. Core employees can be distinguished from other employees, and specifically from those considered to be **contract or contingent workers**.

Core skills

See **core competences** *and* **competencies**.

Corrective discipline

Corrective discipline seeks to discourage the breaking of rules, or the continuation of performance and behaviour exhibited by an employee which is considered averse to the effective running of the business. Corrective discipline is usually designed in order to be constructive and to promote employee success. Typically the employee is given specific instruction in order to understand what aspects of his or her work, performance or conduct are unacceptable. The instruction goes on to explain to the employee the implications of continued unacceptable behaviour and what is expected of them in terms of improvement. Inherently the system incorporates the opportunity for the employee to demonstrate this improvement over a given and stated period of time.

Cost leadership strategy

Cost leadership strategy, although it is thought of more as a generic marketing strategy, has considerable implications in terms of human resource management. Cost leadership strategy aims to provide the business with competitive advantage by lowering the costs of its operation. This can inevitably mean that since the drive is towards increased profitability, via the reduction of costs, leading to a reduction in prices, there will be pressure on employees in many different areas of their work. Clearly a policy can be adopted which seeks to reduce the overall demands on the business in terms of pay, which can involve a reduction in the workforce, or it may require each individual to show a higher degree of productivity and contribution towards profit. Another inevitable implication is the use of outsourced labour in order to provide

C

products and services at a lower cost than could be achieved by directly employing a workforce. Businesses will seek to find means by which the human resource department can identify cost savings, either by the reduction of staff numbers, by **job enlargement** or by **multi-skilling**.

Pohlmann, Randolph, Gardiner, Gareth S. and Heffes, Ellen M., *Value-Driven Management: How to Create and Maximize Value over Time for Organizational Success.* New York: Amacom, 2000.

Counselling

At its most basic, counselling involves discussing problems with an employee in order to assist them in dealing with situations they are finding difficult. More broadly, counselling has been identified as an effective means by which emotional and stress-related problems can be addressed in order to offset the high costs of psychological problems encountered by employees, which inevitably lead to their low productivity. Effective counselling requires a careful and staged approach in order to avoid **absenteeism**, stress-related leave, **grievances** and, in extreme cases, violence in the workplace:

- The counselling sessions should be planned in advance, allowing the employee and the counsellor to agree what issues should be discussed.
- The counselling session should encourage openness. The discussions should aim to share responsibility and build a relationship between the counsellor and the employee.

In many cases professional counsellors are not employed by businesses and the function is seen as an additional responsibility of a manager or supervisor.

Craft union

A craft union is a trade union which limits its membership to individuals who share a particular skill or trade. Craft unions are derived from the medieval craft guilds, who were groups of artisans who sought to ensure fair pay for their expertise, specifically during the great building projects of the period. The craft unions, as they are now known, came into existence in the middle of the nineteenth century and were formed to improve wage levels and working conditions.

Kimeldorf, Howard, *Battling for American Labor: Wobblies, Craft Workers and the Making of the Union Movement.* Berkeley, CA: University of California Press, 1999.

www.eurofound.eu.int/emire/UNITED%20KINGDOM/CRAFTUNION-EN.html

Critical incident method

Critical incident method or technique can be defined as a set of procedures which systematically identify behaviours that contribute to success or failure in a particular situation. Human resource departments may choose to use this technique in order to record and analyse the inherent components and processes involved in a particular job role. In this respect, a critical incident can be defined in the following ways:

- an incident which the job holder responds to and which is observable so that its components can be examined;
- an identification of sequences, tools, sub-events, skills and response times associated with the incident;
- an assessment as to the frequency of such events, as this will determine whether it is a critical incident or not.

The critical incident method can be used in order to analyse all sorts of jobs and arrangements at work, as it concentrates on observable incidents as they have happened. Its specific application is in assisting human resource management in selection, as well as **training needs analysis**, development of employees, and even the ergonomic design of work spaces and equipment.

Cross training

Cross training is an essential precursor for a business which desires that its employees are engaged in **multi-skilling**. Cross training, therefore, involves the training of employees to perform tasks and other job functions which are outside the normal parameters of their job role.

Cultural audit

A cultural audit seeks to identify an organization's **culture** and sub-cultures and to discover how they relate to individual members of the organization. The term can also be associated with a retrospective assessment of the range of specific cultures represented in the business by its employees.

Strathern, Marilyn (ed.), *Audit Cultures: Anthropological Studies in Accountability, Ethics and the Academy*. London: Routledge, 2000.

Cultural norms

Cultural norms are the values which may determine the particular behaviour of individuals or groups within an organization. Cultural norms are taken to mean the predominant **culture** which has developed amongst the employees and may well provide an indication as to the way individuals may respond to specific requests or demands from the management or human resources department.

Culture

See **organizational culture.**

C

Dd

Data Protection Act 1998 (UK)

The Data Protection Act 1998 received the Royal Assent in July 1998 and came into force on 1 March 2000. It gives effect in UK law to the 1995 EC Data Protection Directive (95/46/EC). The Act applies to computerized personal data (as did the original 1984 Act), but now also covers personal data held in structured manual files.

The Act applies to the processing of personal data including its collection, use, disclosure, destruction and holding. Organizations (called controllers) which process personal data are required to comply with the data protection principles. These require data to be:

- fairly and lawfully processed;
- processed for limited purposes;
- adequate, relevant and not excessive;
- accurate;
- not kept longer than necessary;
- processed in accordance with individuals' rights;
- kept secure;
- not transferred to non-EEA countries without adequate protection.

www.dataprotection.gov.uk

Deal and Kennedy

See **organizational culture.**

Defined Benefit Plan (DBP)

A Defined Benefit Plan (DBP) is a formula-based plan that provides a lump sum benefit based on an employee's salary, age and years of membership (fees and taxes are included in the formula). Employee (member) and employer contributions are pooled together, invested as a single portfolio, and used, as required, to pay members' benefits.

The purpose of a plan is to reward eligible employees for long and loyal service by providing them with retirement benefits. These benefits must be definitely determinable.

Cotter, Michael L., Remer, Gary M. and Ng, Ho Kuen, *Insider's Guide to IRS Plan Audits: How to Survive an Employee Benefit Plan Audit*. Cincinnati, OH: National Underwriter, 2001

Defined Contribution Plan (DCP)

The Defined Contribution Plan is also known as the Self-Managed Plan. An employee's retirement benefit is based on the amount of money that has been contributed to the plan and the earnings on that money, over time.

Unlike the **Defined Benefit Plan**, there is no guaranteed payout at retirement. The employee decides how to invest his or her contributions and earnings, using one or more of the investment funds the plan offers. If the employees' investments do well, their account grows, but if they make the wrong decisions then the account will diminish. In other words, they bear all the investment risk.

Wrightson, Margaret T., *Private Pensions: Plan Features Provided by Employers that Sponsor Only Defined Contribution Plans*. New York: Diane Publishing, 1997.

Delegation

Delegation is not only an issue for management, but also of considerable importance to human resources, as it involves the active use of the skills and experience of employees in subordinate positions. Delegation usually begins with the identification of an individual suitable to perform a particular task. This person needs to be prepared and, above all, given the authority to carry out the job properly. Delegation does mean that the manager needs to support and monitor progress, and once the task is completed, to acknowledge that the job has been completed successfully. Delegation is a means by which pressured key members of staff can reduce their workload in the certain knowledge that vital tasks will still be performed. It is not always possible to delegate all tasks to other individuals, but delegation can mean greater efficiency, increased **motivation**, skill development and, above all, a more equitable distribution of work throughout a team.

Smart, J. K., *Real Delegation: How to Get People to Do Things for You and Do Them Well*. Englewood Cliffs, NJ: Prentice-Hall, 2002.

Deskilling

Deskilling is the process by which division of labour and technological development may lead to a reduction of the scope of an employee's specialized tasks. Work becomes fragmented and employees lose the integrated skills and knowledge associated with a crafts person. Deskilling has been seen as a negative impact of technology upon a process where a machine can perform a task better than the human hand.

Harry Braverman wrote a Marxist critique of capitalism and in particular of the organization of work under 'antagonistic' social relations. He was concerned with the loss of craft skills in the organization of work. He was one of the first theorists to define the term as 'deskilling', which he described as being the effective separation of mental work and manual work. Deskilling is closely associated with scientific management and is seen as a means by which management can closely control the labour force in the sense that it removes the skills, knowledge and science of the labour process and transfers these to management. An additional concern is that it can mean that manual and mental workers feel diametrically opposed to one another.

Braverman went on to suggest that deskilling leads to decomposition (the dispersal of the labour process across numerous sites and time) and that, as such, deskilling increases the opportunities for management to exploit labour and reduce the capacity of workers to resist their control.

Both **Frederick Taylor** and Henry Ford were deeply involved in early attempts to deskill and initiate decomposition. As scientific management practitioners they attempted to transform the organization of work to improve profitability and to reduce craft skills control of work. The terms **Fordism** and Taylorism are closely associated with the use of the assembly-line. Fordism itself attempts to harmonize the dual desires of mass production and mass consumption.

Deskilling therefore involves the following:

1 the maximum decomposition of the labour process as a series of work tasks across time and space;
2 the separation of direct and indirect labour;
3 the minimization of skill in any work task;
4 the creation of standardized products;
5 the use of specialized machine tools (as opposed to general purpose machine tools);
6 the use of the assembly-line and methods of continuous production (at a pace set by management and not by the workforce).

D

Braverman, Harry, *Labor and Monopoly Capitalism: The Degradation of Work in the Twentieth Century*. New York: Monthly Review Press, 1999
Taylor, Frederick Winslow, *The Principles of Scientific Management*. New York: Dover Publications, 1998.

Differential validity

A visual representation of differential validity or bias can be seen in Figure 11, which illustrates the fact that test results in some cases will show a different set of results for minorities compared with those for the test group as a whole.

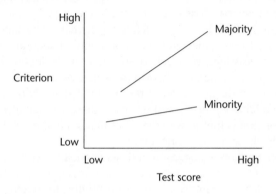

Figure 11 Differential validity

The two lines in the diagram are not parallel, which means that their correlations and thus their validities are different. Under US law, for example, tests which produce results like this cannot be used as a determinant in choosing from job applicants or internal candidates, for three reasons:

1 The tests would need to be differentially weighted by group membership and differential norming (or by weighting by race or gender), but this is forbidden by the Civil Rights Act of 1991.
2 The use of such a test would also represent bias against the minority group because it is less predictive and valid for that group.
3 It is unlikely that such a test would be of value to the business as it would show a low level of predictive efficiency for at least one of the groups.

Linn, R. L., 'Single Group Validity, Differential Validity and Differential Prediction', *Journal of Applied Psychology*, 63 (1978), pp. 507–12.

Direct mail recruiting

Direct mail recruiting techniques can be seen as a complement to traditional methods of recruiting. The process is used to source and select candidates through the coupling of research and targeted direct mail.

One benefit of direct mail is that human resources departments can target searches in specific geographic locations. For example, if there was an opportunity in a well known area, the recruiters could develop a high quality direct mail brochure featuring one or more photographic images promoting the area, text describing the employment opportunity, and a tear-off response card.

Johnson, Paul, 'Interest Group Recruiting', in Allan J. Cigler and Burdett A. Loomis (eds), *American Politics: Classic and Contemporary Readings*. Boston, MA: Houghton Mifflin, 1999.

Disabilities Act 1990 (US)

See **Americans with Disabilities Act 1990**.

Disability Discrimination Act 1995 (US)

The Disability Discrimination Act (DDA) relates to human resources in respect of the clause on employment. Specifically, the Act states that the employment provisions apply to employers with 15 or more employees. Employers are required to consider making changes to the physical features of premises that they occupy (in force since December 1996), in order to accommodate the needs of the disabled. The Act goes on to identify the ways in which an employer might discriminate against a disabled job applicant or employee:

- by treating them less favourably (without justification) than other employees or job applicants because of their disability;
- by not making reasonable adjustments (without justification).

www.legislation.hmso.gov.uk/acts/acts1995/1995050.htm

D

Disabled employees

In the UK, under the Disability Discrimination Act 1995 (DDA), employees, job applicants and customers who are disabled, or who have had a disability, have the right not to be discriminated against because of their disability. It has been estimated that there are some 8.7 million disabled people in the UK and that 18% of the working-age population are disabled. Of this total, 70% of disabled people in employment acquired their disability during their working lives, but fewer than 5% of disabled people are wheelchair users.

According to the DDA, a person has a disability if he or she has a physical or mental impairment which has a substantial, long-term, adverse effect on his or her ability to carry out normal day-to-day activities.

Disability discrimination occurs in one of two ways: either, for a reason which relates to a disabled person's disability, the employer treats that disabled person less favourably than the employer treats or would treat others to whom the reason does not or would not apply, and the employer cannot show that this treatment is justified; or an employer fails to comply with a duty of reasonable adjustment imposed by section 6 of the Act (the duty to make reasonable adjustment) in relation to a disabled person, and cannot show that this failure is justified.

See also **Disability Discrimination Act 1995.**

Disciplinary procedure

When an organization sets down its procedures for handling discipline within the workforce, it is imperative that:

- it is written down;
- all employees have access to the procedure;
- all employees are aware of who operates the disciplinary procedure.

ACAS recommends that the disciplinary procedure should be both fair and impartial and should include the following features in addition to those listed above:

- The employer should clearly state who was involved in any particular disciplinary action.
- The employer should clearly state what kind of disciplinary action would be taken against particular types of infringements of the organization's disciplinary guidelines.
- The employee has the right to have a friend, colleague or **trade union** representative present during all disciplinary interviews.
- In most cases, the employee will not be dismissed for a first offence.
- The employee has the right to appeal against the decision made by the employer.
- All proceedings should be administered in a fair manner.
- The employee should not experience unfair **discrimination**.

Normally an organization's disciplinary procedure would include the following stages of discipline:

1 *Verbal warning* – if the employee's conduct, behaviour or performance does not reach suitable and acceptable standards, then a formal verbal warning will be given. This is the first official stage of

the proceedings. Usually a time limit is set, and provided the employee reaches the acceptable standard within this time then no further action will be taken.

2 *Written warning* – if the employee persists with the same behaviour that resulted in the verbal warning, or if the offence was sufficiently serious, then a written warning will be issued. This is usually issued by the employee's immediate superior.

   The written warning details the complaint and clearly states what must be done by the employee to rectify the situation. The warning will also state how long the employee has, to respond to the warning. If the employee persists, then the next stage of the process will follow. If, however, the employee complies with the requirements then the matter will not be taken any further. There is an opportunity at this stage for the employee to appeal.

3 *Final written warning* – if the employee continues to fail to improve conduct or behaviour, then a formal written warning will be given. In some cases, employees may find themselves at this point in the disciplinary procedure as a result of a serious disciplinary offence. The employee should be aware that **dismissal** is imminent if there is no improvement in behaviour.

4 *Suspension* – as an alternative to, or in addition to, a final written warning, an employer may suspend an individual for up to five working days without pay. This is known as 'disciplinary suspension'.

5 *Dismissal* – the final stage of the disciplinary procedure is dismissal itself. To reach this point, an employee must have failed all the requirements laid down in the early stages of the procedure. The employee's most senior, but related, line manager will take the decision to dismiss the employee, usually in consultation with the human resources department. The employee will be given a written statement which includes the reasons for dismissal and the date of termination of employment. It will also include guidance for the employee in case of appeal.

D

Discipline

See **disciplinary procedure.**

Discrimination

'Discrimination' is a general term which implies differential treatment on the basis of gender, race, colour, nationality, ethnic or national origins, marital status, sexual orientation, pay, or disability. The term also covers the membership or non-membership of a **trade union** or a professional association.

In the UK and US, as well as across much of Europe, there is a raft of legislation, regulations and directives which seek to identify the specific nature of and remedy for, discrimination as and when it occurs.

Monitoring whether discrimination is occurring or may be likely to occur is an integral role of human resource departments. The business, in most cases, cannot argue that it did not intend to discriminate, as the law simply considers the end effect.

Dismissal

If, after having travelled through the stages of an organization's **disciplinary procedure**, employees fail to improve their conduct or behaviour, then they are likely to be dismissed from the job. There are, very basically, four main reasons why dismissal may be the only option open to an employer, in addition to the employee's failure to comply with the disciplinary procedure – these are:

- Capability and qualifications – these reasons relate to an employee's competence to carry out the tasks required of the job role. 'Capability' refers to their skills, health, and physical or mental ability. If an employee shows incompetence or negligence by a series of repeated errors, the employer has grounds for dismissal. 'Qualifications' refers to academic, technical, professional or vocational relevance to the job and could be exampled by an employee's failure to reach a certain standard of qualification within a given time.
- Redundancy.
- Gross misconduct.

An employer must have a valid reason for dismissal and their conduct towards the employee should be seen to be fair and objective. **Discrimination** issues should be uppermost in the mind of the employer at all times. They must be able to prove the employee's guilt, particularly in the following areas of common reasons for dismissal:

- sexual harassment;
- racial harassment;
- wilful destruction of property;
- negligence;
- long-term poor timekeeping;
- sleeping at work;

- gross insubordination;
- inability to do the job the person was employed to do;
- fraud, including the falsification of records;
- abuse of alcohol or illegal drugs whilst at work;
- fighting whilst at work;
- unauthorized access to confidential information.

See also **unfair dismissal, instant dismissal, redundancy** *and* **gross misconduct.**

Dispute resolution

Resolving disputes is one of the key functions of human resource management. The first stage of dispute resolution is trying to avoid disputes. This should be done through consultation with **trade union** representatives or employee associations to form an agreement about **working conditions**. During these negotiations there will be discussions about the formation of a programme or set of procedures which will be followed in the case of a dispute, usually in order to avoid **industrial action**.

Although the procedures put in place will vary from organization to organization, the general content of such an agreement regarding dispute procedures will include the following guidelines:

- The dispute will initially be discussed between the employee and his or her immediate line manager.
- The employee's trade union representative will be called in to meet the line manager, or a member of middle management, should the initial discussion not resolve the issue.
- The trade union representative will meet with senior managers should there still be no resolution.
- If the dispute remains unresolved, senior national representatives of the trade union will meet with senior managers of the organization.

The next stage of the dispute resolution could involve the intervention of an independent arbitrator. It should be noted that the majority of dispute agreements contain a clause specifying that no industrial action will be taken until all the stages of the agreement have been undertaken.

See also **Advisory Conciliation and Arbitration Service (ACAS).**

D

Distance learning

The main advantage of distance learning is that it allows students to study at a time, pace and place convenient to their needs. Learning can therefore be integrated into existing commitments.

Distance learning is an increasingly popular method of course delivery for professionals, with most institutions offering students support through their programme or course of study. This is achieved in a variety of different ways, from face-to-face or telephone tutorials to text-based or electronic study guides. Increasingly, students have the opportunity to network with other learners through a range of media options such as tele-conferencing, video-conferencing and email.

The International Council for Open and Distance Learning (ICDL), operated by the Open University, promotes both open and distance education networks and systems at national, regional and global levels. The ICDL has a database which contains details of over 1,000 institutions worldwide offering distance learning courses.

www.icdl.open.ac.uk/

Downsizing

The term 'downsizing' refers to an organization's need to streamline its activities, perhaps involving the closure of certain operations, along with the associated loss of employees engaged in those areas. Vital in the concept of downsizing is the quality, as opposed to the quantity, of employees.

The downsizing process needs planning by the human resource management as the implications are that some employees will be offered voluntary **redundancy**. Often those who opt to take this method of **dismissal** will be those who are valued by the organization because they have the qualifications, skills and expertise to make them potentially more attractive to competing organizations. In the process of planning for downsizing, the human resource management would have to consider:

- the legal implications with regard to redundancy;
- the implications to the organization of losing key members of staff to competitors;
- how they will communicate their intention to downsize;
- what alternatives are available to them apart from redundancy, e.g. retraining or redeployment of employees.

Fear of downsizing can be stressful for employees and the human resources managers need to ensure that they are communicating with them through appropriate and effective channels. Certainly consultation with **trade union** or employee representatives is essential, as is the provision of an **employee assistance programme (EAP)**.

Downward communication

In several research studies it has been shown that the relationships between employee involvement (EI) and a business's financial performance are very different for large and small businesses. Smaller businesses benefit from the systematic use of one-way downward communication from management to employees. They also benefit from the regular use of direct communication methods such as team briefings, which have the potential for two-way communication between management and employees.

One of the major advantages is that the downward communication system is less costly to maintain. The positive impact of direct communication methods is improved to a large degree by upward problem-solving techniques (e.g. **quality circles**). Whilst one-way downward communication from management to employees improves small business performance, it has a negative effect in combination with upward problem-solving. One-way downward communication of management instructions can bring financial rewards for small businesses, but this rather authoritarian approach conflicts with the need to ensure the smooth operation of upward problem-solving.

Bryson, Alex and Millward, Neil, *The Impact of Employee Involvement on Small Firms' Economic Performance* (paper presented at the 11th International Industrial Relations Association World Congress in Bologna).

Drucker, Peter

Whilst writing in the 1970s Peter Drucker identified, in his 'communication theory', that there were four fundamental aspects of communication:

- perception;
- expectation;
- involvement;
- practical benefits as well as mere information.

Drucker considered that this fitted into **motivation** because it was not simply a case of what was being said, but the fact that something was being said that caused a response from an employee, that was important. In order for employees to understand a particular aspect of the business's activity they needed to realize what they could expect from it, and be involved. It was not enough just to have information; the information had to have a practical basis.

Drucker's research has been considered by many in the development of **performance-related** schemes or **payment by results** and **incen-**

tive schemes. Drucker discovered that employees need to recognize that there is an advantage in including and involving themselves in the system and that the most effective systems have included the employee at the earliest stage possible, ensuring that the employee is understood from the outset. In this way, an employee is much more likely to operate effectively.

Peter Drucker has continued his research and writing on a variety of different aspects of management and leadership.

Drucker, Peter F., *People and Performance*. London: Heinemann, 1977.
Drucker, Peter F., *Management: Tasks, Responsibilities and Practices*. London: Butterworth-Heinemann Management Division, 1988.

Dual-career couple

The term 'dual-career couple' is derived from the phrase 'dual-earner couple'. In the dual-career family or couple, women tend to be more career-oriented rather than simply holding jobs, as in many cases of dual-earner couples. A dual-career couple consists of two spouses who work full-time and possess a high degree of commitment and training in their career area.

Increasingly, university professionals are dual-career couples; the decisions to accept a university position are often made based on the availability of employment for a spouse or partner. Universities, recognizing this fact, make Dual Career Hire funds available for departments to help find employment for talented spouses/partners of candidates being hired for position vacancies. Dual Career Couple Hire funding is often used to support a faculty, academic staff, or classified staff position for the spouse/partner of a new faculty member.

Ferber, Marianne A. and Loeb, Jane W. (eds), *Academic Couples: Problems and Promises*. Champaign, IL: University of Illinois Press, 1997.

D

Economic Dislocation and Worker Adjustment Assistance Act (EDWAA) (US)

The Economic Dislocation and Worker Adjustment Assistance Act (EDWAA) effectively amended Title III of the Job Training Partnership Act (JTPA). It provides funds to States (and local sub-state grantees) to help dislocated workers find and qualify for new jobs.

The EDWAA is part of a broader scheme to aid workers who have lost their jobs (incorporating aspects of the Worker Adjustment and Retraining Notification (WARN) Act and the Trade Adjustment Assistance (TAA) program).

> http://safetynet.doleta.gov/common/edwaa.htm

Educational attainment

The term 'educational attainment' refers to the highest educational level achieved by an individual employee, a group of employees, or the population of the country as a whole.

EEOC regulations (US)

The US **Equal Employment Opportunity Commission** enforces a number of Acts, but publishes an annually updated Title 29 of the Code of Federal Regulations (CFR), which states the other regulations for which they are currently responsible.

Since 2000, they have added the following regulations to their portfolio of responsibilities:

- Final Rule on Application of ADA Standards to the Federal Workforce;
- Final Regulation on 'Tender Back' and Related Issues Concerning ADEA Waivers;
- Amending the Interpretive Guidance on Title I of the Americans with Disabilities Act: Final Rule;
- Sex Discrimination Guidelines and National Origin Discrimination Guidelines: Final Rule;

- 29 CFR Part 1614, Federal Sector Equal Employment Opportunity, incorporating the July 12, 1999 changes;
- Federal Sector Equal Employment Opportunity: Final Rule.

This is in addition to the existing regulations which include:

- 1600 Employee responsibilities and conduct;
- 1601 Procedural regulations;
- 1602 Recordkeeping and reporting requirements under Title VII and the ADA;
- 1603 Procedures for previously exempt State and Local Government employee complaints of employment discrimination under Section 321 of the Government Employee Rights Act of 1991;
- 1604 Guidelines on discrimination because of sex;
- 1605 Guidelines on discrimination because of religion;
- 1606 Guidelines on discrimination because of national origin;
- 1607 Uniform guidelines on employee selection procedures (1978)
- 1608 Affirmative action appropriate under Title VII of the Civil Rights Act of 1964, as amended;
- 1610 Availability of records;
- 1611 Privacy Act regulations;
- 1612 Government in the Sunshine Act regulations;
- 1614 Federal Sector equal employment opportunity;
- 1615 Enforcement of non-discrimination on the basis of handicap in programs or activities conducted by the Equal Employment Opportunity Commission;
- 1620 the Equal Pay Act;
- 1621 Procedures – the Equal Pay Act;
- 1625 Age Discrimination in Employment Act;
- 1626 Procedures – Age Discrimination in Employment Act;
- 1627 Records to be made or kept relating to age: notices to be posted; administrative exemptions;
- 1630 Regulations to implement the equal employment provisions of the Americans with Disabilities Act;
- 1640 Procedures for coordinating the investigation of complaints or charges of employment discrimination based on disability subject to the Americans with Disabilities Act and section 504 of the Rehabilitation Act of 1973;
- 1641 Procedures for complaints/charges of employment discrimination based on disability, filed against employers holding government contracts or subcontracts;
- 1650 Debt collection;

E

- 1690 Procedures on inter-agency coordination of equal employment opportunity issuances;
- 1691 Procedures for complaints of employment discrimination filed against recipients of Federal financial assistance.

www.eeoc.gov/regs

Electricity at Work Regulations 1989 (UK)

These regulations require employers to ensure that all electrical systems are safe and regularly maintained. The Electricity at Work Regulations 1989 is, in practice, an update of the old Factory Act Electricity Regulations of various years, brought together under the Health and Safety at Work Act 1974.

www.hmso.gov.uk/si/si1989/Uksi_19890635_en_1.htm

Employee assistance programme (EAP)

An EAP is a human resource management-driven workplace-based programme which seeks to identify and resolve employee concerns. Essentially, the **counselling** system seeks to be proactive in dealing with both personal and work-related matters which in due course affect performance.

An EAP aims to conform to recognized levels of standards in providing advice, information or counselling as an intervention measure aimed at both individuals and teams of employees. Typical issues related to personal concerns include health matters, family and relationship problems, alcohol and drug abuse issues and anxieties. Directly related to work, an EAP aims to address problems arising out of working relationships (such as **harassment** or bullying) or personal issues (stress and work loads) as well as addressing personal and interpersonal skills and imbalances between work and life outside work.

EAPs can be seen as an integral part of organizational and occupational health in the sense that they seek to address the needs of the individual whilst focusing on the negative impacts of an employee's problems, which may affect the performance of the business. EAPs are seen as recognition of the increasing pressures in business and seek to assist employees in dealing with these pressures.

Typically, an EAP will aim to provide a business and its employees with the following benefits:

- It will give them the ability to deal effectively with either personal or work-related issues that may have an impact upon the performance of individuals or of the business as a unit.

E

- It will address the need to maintain and improve productivity as well as efficiency that may otherwise be affected.
- It will seek to identify and address issues such as **absenteeism**, **labour turnover**, and work-related incidents such as accidents and unnecessary levels of wastage.
- It will foster cooperation and the perception of a caring organization, whilst improving morale and motivation.
- It will recognize and deal with habitual behaviours (such as alcohol abuse) which may affect the performance of the individual and the business.
- It will effectively pre-empt possible causes of grievances arising out of unfair treatment.

Clearly, the effectiveness and impact of an EAP has to be measured in terms of its direct effect on the overall productivity and performance of the business and its employees, against the costs involved in setting up and running the system. EAPs are often made available both to the direct employees of the business and to their close dependants.

www.eapa.org.uk

Employee handbook

An employee handbook is issued to an employee. It explains the key benefits and policies of the organization, as well as giving general information regarding issues such as health and safety or social facilities.

Employee leasing

'Employee leasing' can be defined as being the practice of obtaining specific job functions, such as payroll preparation, from organizations external to the business who specialize in that particular field.

See also **outsourcing**.

Employee log

The completion of an employee log would allow the organization to gather job- and performance-related information from an employee. By requesting that the job holder completes a diary, or other pro-forma document, that summarises their daily tasks, activities and challenges, the organization can glean a better insight into the requirements of the job.

Employee objectives

The term 'employee objectives' refers to goals, targets or deadlines that a human resource department might set an individual employee. The achievement of these objectives set by the organization will not only assist employees in attaining their own personal goals, but will also enhance their contribution to the organization as a whole.

Employee participation

See **participation**.

Employee referrals

Some businesses may positively encourage existing employees to give them assistance in finding new employees for hard-to-fill jobs, specifically those with special skill requirements. Many businesses will offer a referral payment to these employees for referring qualified candidates who are subsequently employed by the business. Clearly there are strict regulations in respect of the suitability of the candidate and the length of service that the referred candidate actually completes (usually part of the payment is held back until the referred candidate has been working for the business for six months).

There are difficulties in using this system in particular, as there may be conflicts of interest. Some human resource departments come under intense pressure from existing employees to shortlist candidates that they have referred. In many cases there is also a system set up to ensure that improper promises or assurances of employment to prospective candidates are not made by existing employees.

Employee retention

Many human resource practitioners have come to realize that the essential relationship between the employer and the employee, in terms of needing one another, has been turned on its head. Increasingly there are far more vacancies available than there are experienced staff. It has therefore become an imperative to ensure that the business retains particularly its most valuable members of staff.

Human resource management adopts several different approaches to transforming business from what had been a culture of high **labour turnover** to one of high retention. Both the **motivation** and retention of employees require close attention and obviously the main responsibilities fall on the shoulders of human resources managers. At its very

E

basic, human resources departments need to create working environments where employees enjoy what they do, feel that they have a purpose, feel that they are adequately compensated and, above all, have a sense of connection with the organization.

The overall approach can be best typified in the acronym PRIDE:

- **p**ositive working environment;
- **r**ecognition, rewards, reinforcement;
- **i**nvolvement;
- **d**evelopment of skills and potential;
- **e**valuation and continuous improvement.

There are, of course, many reasons why employees may add to the retention problems encountered by a business. The most common of these, and their potential remedies, are summarized in Table 6.

Arthur, Diane, *Employee Recruitment and Retention Handbook*. New York: Amacom, 2001.
Wingfield, Barbara and Berry, Janice, *Retaining your Employees: Using Respect, Recognition and Rewards for Positive Benefits*. Los Altos, CA: Crisp Publications, 2001.

Employee Share Schemes Act 2002 (UK)

The Employee Share Schemes Act amended Schedule 8 of the Finance Act 2000, which contained the legislation related to the Share Incentive Plan (SIP), an all-employee share ownership plan.

The ESSA encouraged businesses to involve their employees more closely in the operation of the Share Incentive Plan (by appointing a board of trustees for the Plan which includes professional trustees and employee representatives). The overall intention of the Act was to encourage businesses to acquire substantial shareholdings from owners for transfer under the Plan to the whole workforce.

www.hmso.gov.uk/acts/acts2002/20020034.htm

E

Employee turnover

See labour turnover.

Employers' Liability (Compulsory Insurance) Regulations 1969 (UK)

These regulations require employers to have the necessary insurance in the event of their employees having an accident or suffering from ill health as a result of their work, and for details of this to be on display for staff to see.

Table 6 Employee retention

Reason for leaving	Possible solution
Low pay	Periodic **benchmarking** of pay scales is essential, along with a willingness to make adjustments. The provision of additional benefits, such as **bonuses**, can make the pay package more attractive.
Low involvement	Since many employees believe that decisions are made despite them, possible options include employee **suggestion schemes** and other means by which employees are made to feel that their points of view are taken into consideration.
Inconvenient or too demanding hours of work	Increasingly, businesses are taking a more flexible approach towards working hours. However, this does not necessarily address pressure on employees to remain at work until particular tasks are completed. Steps should be taken to deal with **over-working**.
Working environment	Poor **working conditions** can be easily rectified by the periodic replacement of equipment and furniture and, perhaps, by allocating a budget to each departmental area in order for the employees to personalize their immediate working environment.
Job content	Many of the problems related to job content can be revealed during an **appraisal**. However, regular discussions need to take place regarding current work loads and priorities. **Job enrichment** is a possible solution, as is **delegation**.

Employment Act 1989 (UK)

The Employment Act (1989) included an exemption from the **Sex Discrimination Act** in cases where this occured in relation to employment and vocational training, which had specific statutory provisions relating to the protection of women at work.

The Act further deregulated the labour market by removing protective legislation restricting the employment of women and young persons. At the same time, the Act also relaxed certain employment protection rights, including the restricting of trade union officials' rights to paid time off to carry out their duties, as well as removing the requirement for

E

small businesses to provide employees with details of disciplinary rules and procedures.

See also **Employment Act 2002.**

www.hmso.gov.uk/acts/acts1989/Ukpga_19890038_en_1.htm

Employment Act 2002 (UK)

The Employment Act received Royal Assent on 8 July 2002 and covered a wide range of employment matters including work and parental responsibilities, dispute resolution, improvements to employment tribunal procedures, the introduction of an equal pay questionnaire, provisions to implement the **Fixed Term Work Directive**, a right to time off work for union representatives for learning purposes, work-focused interviews for partners of people receiving working-age benefits, and data sharing provisions.

www.hmso.gov.uk/acts/acts2002/20020022.htm

Employment agencies

Employment agencies are often engaged by businesses or human resource departments in order to seek and provide full-time, part-time, permanent, short-term or long-term employees. Employment agencies may already have an existing bank of potential employees, which can then be matched to the specific requirements of a client, as laid out by the business or the human resource department. Although the final decision as to whether to employ an individual is left to the business itself, much of the time-consuming and tedious work of sifting through **applicants**, as well as placing advertisements, **interviewing** and, perhaps, training individuals to cope with the interviewing, can be avoided.

In the case of employees who are provided on an hourly basis by an employment agency, a premium is paid by the business, which incorporates a commission for the employment agency. The business will pay the agency a gross figure, out of which the employment agency in turn arranges payment for the employee. In these cases the employee remains employed, albeit on a temporary basis, by the employment agency and not the business.

In the case of individuals who are subsequently offered a permanent or fixed-term contract by a business, after having been selected and recommended by an employment agency, the agency levies a charge on the business, which, according to their contractual arrangements, may equate to anything between three months' and one year's equivalent salary for the individual who has been placed in work. Obviously there are parameters and staged payments which take into account the fact that the employee may choose not to remain with the business.

Employment and Training Administration (ETA) (US)

The Employment and Training Administration's main responsibility is to assist in the gradual and continuous improvement of the US workforce through training and more effective matching with available vacancies in organizations. In order to assist them in this task, the O'NET (the Occupational Information Network) has been developed as a comprehensive database of worker attributes and job characteristics. The system, developed for the US Department of Labor, is designed to help direct individuals towards training and placement as well as other employment services.

The database also includes information for employers (in respect of tax issues, incentives, training, grants etc.).

www.doleta.gov

Employment appeal tribunal (EAT) (UK)

An employment appeal tribunal is a body set up to deal with appeals against decisions made by an employment tribunal. EATs can only consider appeals on points of law. In other words, they are able to investigate the incorrect application of law by an employment tribunal. Generally, the appeal must be lodged within 42 days of the receipt of a written confirmation of an employment tribunal's decision.

www.employmentappeals.gov.uk

Employment references

Human resources managers need to consider employment references from a dual point of view, as references are relevant both during recruitment and when existing employees are seeking work elsewhere.

Increasingly there have been problems regarding references and a large minority of employers have chosen to adopt a 'no reference policy', or, at the very least, are restricting the information which they provide. Employers are concerned about possible defamatory statements, or inaccurate references which could give the wrong impression to another prospective employer. Although employers are keen to receive information about prospective employees, all too often they are not willing to give out information about current or former employees.

E

This is coupled with the fact that it is notoriously difficult to check references with any degree of precision. Many employers consider a 'no reference' policy to be a proactive defence: whilst poor employees receive a clean slate because negative information is not passed on, good employees are penalized by the adoption of this policy. In the US, for example, there is also a risk that an employer may make a negligent hiring decision, as there is a duty of reasonable care to protect customers or others with whom the employer is trading. In such cases there is no defence if the employer knew or should have known that the employee would put others at risk. It has, therefore, become essential that US employers in particular diligently check any references, verify education claims and make other background checks.

Reference checking can be **outsourced** but in many cases this is too expensive an option. Testimonials are another useful double-check. One of the most difficult problems is deciding when to check references, as many employees are reluctant to allow their new prospective employer to check their references until a job offer has been made and agreed in principle.

Andler, Edward C., *Complete Reference Checking Handbook: Smart, Fast, Legal Ways to Check Out Job Applicants*. New York: Amacom. 2003.

Employment Relations Act 1999 (UK)

The Employment Relations Act received Royal Assent on 27 July 1999. The following are the main provisions of the Act:

- collective bargaining – recognition of unions' right to take part;
- code of practice on access and method of conducting collective bargaining;
- consultation on training;
- interim relief in cases of unfair dismissal connected with trade union recognition;
- blacklists (giving the Secretary of State powers to introduce regulations to prohibit the compilation, dissemination and use of lists recording individuals' trade union membership and activities);
- ballots and notices;
- leave for family and domestic reasons;
- disciplinary and grievance hearings (right to be accompanied, etc.);
- measures to deal with unfair dismissal of striking workers;
- collective agreements on detriment and dismissal;
- agreement to exclude dismissal rights;
- part-time work (prevention of less favourable treatment);
- national minimum wage;

E

- power to confer rights on individuals;
- Central Arbitration Committee (members and proceedings);
- **ACAS** (general duties);
- partnerships at work (Partnership Fund);
- employment agencies (proper conduct);
- employment rights (employment outside Great Britain);
- unfair dismissal (special and additional awards);
- transfer of undertakings (Transfer of Undertakings (Protection of Employment) Regulations 1981);
- minimum wage.

www.legislation.hmso.gov.uk/acts/acts1999/19990026.htm

Employment Rights Act 1996 (UK)

The Employment Rights Act covers a wide area of employment situations, underpinning many of the basic rights of employees. In this respect, it is one of the key pieces of UK legislation. A summary of the main areas of importance includes:

- The right not to be unfairly dismissed.
- Maternity leave.
- Paid time off for ante-natal care.
- Unpaid time off to care for or to arrange care for dependants.
- The offer of suitable alternative work on not substantially less favourable terms and conditions to pregnant women, and to women who have recently given birth or are breastfeeding.
- Suspension on full pay when a woman is unable to do her usual job on maternity grounds and there is no suitable alternative work.
- The right to receive a statement of employment particulars.
- The right to receive an itemized pay statement.
- The right not to have unauthorized deductions taken from wages.
- A minimum period of notice on termination of employment.
- The right to a redundancy payment.
- The right to a written statement of reasons for dismissal.

www.legislation.hmso.gov.uk/acts/acts1996/1996018.htm

E

Employment Rights (Dispute Resolution) Act 1998 (UK)

The Employment Rights (Dispute Resolution) Act includes an employee's right to be accompanied to a disciplinary or grievance hearing by a trade union official or colleague.

www.legislation.hmso.gov.uk/acts/acts1998/19980008.htm

Employment Standards Administration (ESA) (US)

The purpose of the ESA is to work towards the enhancement of the welfare and rights of American workers. It is, essentially, an enforcement and benefit-delivery agency. The ESA comprises four key programmes:

- **Office of Federal Contract Compliance Programs**
- **Office of Labor-Management Standards**
- **Office of Workers' Compensation Programs**
- **Wage and Hour Division**

www.dol.gov/esa

Employment tests

Employment tests are devices set up by an organization during the recruitment and selection process in order to assess the **applicants'** ability to match the requirements of the job role.

See also **aptitude test; personality test; psychometric test.**

Employment Tribunals Act 1996 (UK)

See **Industrial Tribunals Act.**

Empowerment

The term 'empowerment' applies to individual employees who are allowed to control their contribution within the organization. This means that they are given the authority and responsibility to complete tasks and attain targets without the direct intervention of management. The benefits, to the organization, of empowerment are that it reduces the importance of repetitive administration and the number of managers required at the various levels of the structure. Streamlining management levels often increases the effectiveness of communication. From the employees' point of view, empowerment increases their creativity and initiative, as well as their commitment to the organization, by allowing them to work with **autonomy**.

Entitlements

See **bonuses; fringe benefits; incentives; maternity leave** *and* **parental leave.**

E

Equal Employment Opportunity Commission (EEOC) (US)

The US Equal Employment Opportunity Commission enforces the following acts:

- Title VII of the Civil Rights Act;
- Equal Pay Act of 1963;
- Age Discrimination in Employment Act of 1967 (ADEA);
- Rehabilitation Act of 1973, Sections 501 and 505;
- Titles I and V of the Americans with Disabilities Act of 1990 (ADA);
- Civil Rights Act of 1991.

In addition to this, it publishes the annual Title 29 of the Code of Federal Regulations (CFR), which states the other regulations for which it is currently responsible with regard to enforcement.

See also **EEOC regulations.**

www.eeoc.gov/index.html

Equal opportunities

The importance of complying with equal opportunity legislation has increased dramatically in recent years. Certainly, it is imperative that human resource department employees are fully aware of all UK and European legislation, for which they should receive suitable training and updates. The control of equal opportunity spans from the recruitment stage to the termination of employment, and no decisions can be made that prejudice anyone, based on their race, colour, religion, gender or national origin.

See also **Equal Employment Opportunity Commission (EEOC)** and **Equal Pay Act 1963.**

Equal pay

See **Equal Pay Act 1963 (US) and Equal Pay Act 1970 & 1983 (UK).**

E

Equal Pay Act 1963 (US) and Equal Pay Act 1970 & 1983 (UK)

This US legislation prohibits **discrimination** against individuals on the basis of their gender, with regard to wage payments. The Act clearly states that the payments made to individuals for jobs which require equal skill, effort and responsibilities, in similar working conditions, within the same establishment should be equal.

The Equal Pay Act (1970) aimed to eliminate discrimination in pay between men and women. The Act was amended in 1983 to include work of equal value and most claims of breaches are now in respect of this part of the Act.

The Act itself gives employees the right to claim pay equal to that received by members of the opposite sex provided that it is for work which is rated as equivalent under a **job evaluation** scheme (covering such aspects as effort required, skills and decision making).

www.eoc-law.org.uk/eoceng/dynpages/equal_pay/index.asp

E-recruitment

E-recruitment is the use of an organization's website, or an online recruitment agency, to attract potential employees for current vacancies. It has been estimated that in the UK alone, some 6.3 million individuals use various e-recruitment agencies to seek work. In countries where internet penetration is high, it has been estimated that e-recruitment is growing at a rate of 50 per cent a year. E-recruitment can be both proactive and reactive from the point of view of the potential employee. Many websites now offer the facility to upload CVs or **résumés**, which potential employers can browse to find a close match to their requirements. Alternatively, employers may post their vacancies either on their own company websites or via an e-recruitment agency, in order to attract potential employees and from that point institute a normal recruitment procedure.

Again, in the UK alone, around 1.4 million online job seekers have uploaded their CVs to recruitment sites each year. The efficiency of e-recruitment has become such that many businesses now believe that online recruitment is more effective than placing advertisements in local or national newspapers and trade magazines or using conventional recruitment agencies.

ERG theory

See **Alderfer, Clayton P.**

Ergonomics

The term 'ergonomics' relates to the study of the design of equipment and the working procedures and environment in order to promote employee well-being and organizational efficiency and effectiveness. Ergonomic design can trace its history back to the Second World War, when tank designers acknowledged the fact that a human being should be considered in the design of tanks, guns and planes. Now it is active in the use of computers and their related equipment, such as tables and chairs, and screen design, but ergonomics now also incorporates the human being in much of the commonly found equipment and machinery on the production floor, providing the user with the ability to:

- obtain a stimulus in the use of machinery – by the incorporation of instruments, flashing lights and buzzers so that the tedium is removed to a degree;
- perceive, through touch, smell, sight and sound, whether there is a problem that needs addressing;
- make a decision about what action to take if there is a problem;
- respond, by operating controls on the machinery or by communicating with others.

Ergonomics also takes into account the working environment of the employee and addresses issues such as:

- suitability and level of lighting;
- noise levels;
- suitability of heating and ventilation systems.

Error of central tendency

The term 'error of central tendency' is most closely associated with the **appraisal** of employees. Given that some methods of appraisal involve **job grading** or **job ranking**, one of the major criticisms of the use of these methods is that the manager or appraiser, to avoid the extremes of the grades, i.e. *Poor* or *Exceptional*, sticks to the more central grades of *below average*, *average* and *above average*.

E-trainers

See **computer-based training.**

EU Council Directive 93/104/EC of 23 November 1993

The Working Time Directive (93/104/EC) was implemented in Great Britain by the **Working Time Regulations 1998** (SI 1998/1833).

www.europa.eu.int

EU Council Directive 94/33/EC of 22 June 1994

The Young Workers Directive (94/33/EC), relating to young workers (those between minimum school-leaving age and their eighteenth birthday). The UK opt-out from the restrictions on adolescents' working time and night working within the Young Workers Directive ended on 22 June 2000. The amendment means that adolescents are protected from working more than 8 hours a day or 40 hours a week. Most adolescents will not be able to work between 10 p.m. and 6 a.m. (or 11 p.m. and 7 a.m. where the worker is contracted to work after 10 p.m.).

Those employed in hospitals or similar establishments, agriculture, retail trading, sea-fishing, a hotel or catering business, a bakery, or postal or newspaper deliveries, or in connection with cultural, artistic, sporting or advertising activities, may be able to work between the hours of 10 p.m. and 12 midnight and after 4 a.m. Working between the hours of midnight and 4 a.m. is prohibited except in exceptional circumstances.

www.europa.eu.int

EU Council Directive 94/45/EC of 22 September 1994

The establishment of a European Works Council or undertakings for the purposes of informing and consulting employees. The main provisions of the Directive were to establish a European Works Council or a procedure for informing and consulting employees in every Community-scale undertaking and every Community-scale group of undertakings, following agreement between the central management and a special negotiating body.

www.europa.eu.int

EU Council Directive 97/74/EC of 15 December 1997

Directive 97/74/EC extends the scope of **EU Council Directive 94/45/EC** to the United Kingdom.

www.europa.eu.int

EU Council Directive 97/81/EC of 15 December 1997

Council Directive 97/81/EC of 15 December 1997 concerned the framework agreement on part-time work. The bill closely follows the wording of the original European social partner agreement in establishing a right for part-time workers not to be treated less favourably than 'comparable' full-time workers, unless different treatment can be justified 'on objective grounds'.

The Directive allows Member States the scope to define what these 'objective grounds' are.

www.europa.eu.int

EU Council Directive 98/23/EC of 7 April 1998

Directive 98/23/EC extends Directive 97/81/EC to the United Kingdom. The purpose of the agreement is to eliminate discrimination against part-time workers and to improve the quality of part-time work. It also aims to facilitate the development of part-time work on a voluntary basis and to contribute to the flexible organization of working time in a manner which takes into account the needs of employers and workers.

www.europa.eu.int

EU Council Directive 98/59/EC of 20 July 1998

The Council Directive 98/59/EC (known as the Collective Redundancies Directive 98/59/EC) of 20 July 1998, on the approximation of the laws of the Member States related to collective redundancies.

www.europa.eu.int

EU Council Directive of 20 October 1980

Council Directive 80/987/EEC of 20 October 1980 (known as the Insolvent Employers 80/987/EEC), on the approximation of the laws of the Member States relating to the protection of employees in the event of the insolvency of their employer.

www.europa.eu.int

E

EU Council Directive of 25 June 1991

The Council Directive of 25 June 1991 supplements the measures to encourage improvements in the safety and health at work of workers with a fixed-duration employment relationship or a temporary employment relationship (91/383/EEC).

www.europa.eu.int

EU Council Directive of 14 October 1991

The Council Directive 91/533/EEC of 14 October 1991 (known as the Written Particulars Directive 91/533/EEC), which states an employer's obligation to inform employees of the conditions applicable to the contract or employment relationship.

www.europa.eu.int

EU Council Directive 1999/63/EC of 21 June 1999

Council Directive 1999/63/EC refers to the organization of seafarers' working times. The objective of this Directive is to protect the health and safety of seafarers by laying down minimum requirements with regard to working time.

www.europa.eu.int

EU Council Directive 1999/70/EC of 28 June 1999

This EU Directive, adopted on 28 June 1999, put into effect the framework agreement on fixed-term work concluded earlier that year (by the European Trade Union Confederation, the Union of Industrial and Employers' Confederations of Europe and the European Centre of Enterprises with Public Participation and of Enterprises of General Economic Interest). The Directive's primary purpose was to:

- prevent fixed-term employees from being less favourably treated than similar permanent employees;
- prevent abuses arising from the use of successive fixed-term contracts; and improve access to training for fixed-term employees;
- ensure that fixed-term employees are informed about available permanent jobs.

www.europa.eu.int

E

EU Council Directive 2000/34/EC of the European Parliament and the Council of 22 June 2000

Directive 2000/34/EC of the European Parliament and of the Council, of 22 June 2000, amends Council Directive 93/104/EC concerning certain aspects of the organization of working time to cover sectors and activities excluded from that Directive.

www.europe.osha.eu.int/legislation/directives

EU Council Directive 2001/86/EC of 8 October 2001

This Regulation and the **EU Council Regulation (EC) No. 2157/2001** on the Statute for a European Company (SE) supplement the Statute for a European Company with regard to the involvement of employees. It comes into force in 2004. It states:

> The rules relating to employee involvement in an SE (Societas Europaea) are laid down in Directive 2001/86/EC, the provisions of which are designed to guarantee that the creation of an SE does not entail the disappearance or erosion of systems of employee involvement that exist within the companies participating in the establishment of an SE. Given the diversity of rules and practices in the Member States as regards the manner in which employees' representatives are involved in decision-making within companies, the Directive is not intended to establish a single European model. Nevertheless, it lays down that SEs must have procedures for informing and consulting their workforce on a supranational level. When rights of worker participation exist within one or more of the companies forming an SE, those rights will be preserved through their transfer to the SE on its establishment, unless the parties involved, acting through the special negotiating body representing the employees of all the companies involved in the SE, decide otherwise.

www.europa.eu.int

EU Council Directives of 14 February 1977, 98/50/EC of 29 June 1998 and 2001/23/EC of 12 March 2001

The Council Directive of 14 February 1977 on the approximation of the laws of the Member States relating to the safeguarding of employees' rights in the event of transfers of undertakings, businesses or parts of businesses (77/187/EEC). The Directive has been consolidated with Directives 98/50/EC and 2001/23/EC.

www.europa.eu.int

E

EU Council Recommendation of 27 July 1992

This was the Council Recommendation of 27 July 1992 which concerned the convergence of social protection objectives and policies (92/442/EEC). In presenting the recommendation, the Commission emphasized the essential link between convergence of economic policies and that of social protection policies. This means, in particular, that convergence of economic policies can make a useful contribution to developing an advanced social protection system.

www.europa.eu.int

EU Council Regulation (EC) No. 2157/2001 of 8 October 2001

This is the Council Regulation 2157/2001 on the Statute for a European Company (SE). After some 30 years of stalling, the EU adopted the European Company Statute (ECS), establishing the first pan-European company, the Societas Europaea (SE). Legislation implementing the ECS comes into force in Member States of the EU on 8 October 2004.

The SE will enable pan-European businesses to have one corporate vehicle with a common management and reporting structure, operating under one set of legal rules, without the need for a network of branches and subsidiaries. Other advantages include the ability to move the SE's registered and head office between member states without having to re-register or wind up its operations.

The key aspect of the SE in relation to human resources is employee involvement, recognizing the differences between countries with a tradition of worker participation in management (e.g. Germany) and those where mandatory worker participation in management is rare (e.g. the UK). A compromise was adopted which requires negotiations between management and employee representatives on employee participation before a European company is created. Assuming these are unsuccessful, a standard set of principles will apply, dependent on the incorporation method chosen and the level of participation previously enjoyed by the employees.

www.europa.eu.int

EU Directive 96/71/EC of the European Parliament and of the Council of 16 December 1996

The Directive 96/71/EC of the European Parliament and of the Council, of 16 December 1996, concerned the posting of workers in the framework of the provision of services. The Posted Workers Directive's intention was to ease the interchange of services between countries and secure the rights of employees, thus preventing 'social dumping'.

This Directive applies to undertakings established in a Member State which, in the framework of the trans-national provision of services, post workers to the territory of a Member State. The term 'posted worker' means a worker who, for a limited period, carries out his work in the territory of a Member State other than the State in which he normally works.

Member States must ensure that workers posted to their territory are guaranteed the same treatment as their own workers. Exceptions to this are provided when the period of posting does not exceed one month.

www.europa.eu.int

EU Directive 2002/14/EC of the European Parliament and of the Council of 11 March 2002

March 2005 sees the deadline for implementation of the Information and Consultation Directive (2002/14/EC), which will require the creation of National Works Councils for employers with 150 or more employees.

This historic Directive should ensure that employees are consulted prior to decisions that seriously affect them. The Directive will require employers to facilitate wide-ranging disclosure of information, and consultation with employee representatives, with a 'view to reaching agreement' on changes in terms and conditions of employment and work organization.

www.europa.eu.int

EU Directive 2002/74/EC of the European Parliament and of the Council of 23 September 2002

Directive 2002/74/EC of the European Parliament and of the Council, of 23 September 2002, amending Council Directive 80/987/EEC on the approximation of the laws of the Member States relating to the protection of employees in the event of the insolvency of their employer.

www.europa.eu.int

E

European Employment Strategy

The Luxembourg Jobs Summit (November 1997) launched the European Employment Strategy (EES), based on the new provisions in the Employment Title of the Amsterdam Treaty. The intention was to achieve considerable progress within five years. By 2002, it had been established that there were still major challenges and issues for EES and there was also a requirement to more closely align policies with the Lisbon goal of sustained economic growth, together with more and better jobs and greater social cohesion by 2010.

At the Lisbon European Council (March 2000), the European Union set itself a new strategic goal for the next ten years. The desire was to become the most competitive and dynamic knowledge-based economy, which could sustain economic growth whilst ensuring more and better jobs together with closer social cohesion. The ultimate goal was full employment by 2010 (actually measured at 70% of males and 60% of females).

The Stockholm European Council (March 2001) had added two intermediate targets and one additional target:

- employment rate to be raised to 67% by 2005;
- employment rate to be raised to 57% for women by 2005;
- employment rate to be raised to 50% for older workers by 2010.

The Barcelona Council (March 2002) confirmed that full employment was a primary goal of the EU, calling for an Employment Strategy to underpin the Lisbon strategy (given that the EU would be greatly enlarged by 2010).

In 1997, the Luxembourg European Council initiated the European Employment Strategy (EES), also known as 'the Luxembourg process'. A framework for coordination of national employment policies was therefore built around the following areas:

- Employment Guidelines, which set out the common priorities for Member States' employment policies.
- National Action Plans to be drawn up each year by every Member State showing how the Employment Guidelines would be put into practice on a national basis.
- A Joint Employment Report, which would be a summation of all of the National Action Plans as a Joint Employment Report.
- Recommendations from the Council to issue Member State-specific Recommendations after a proposal by the Commission.

In this way, the Luxembourg process aimed to deliver a rolling programme of yearly planning, monitoring, examination and readjustment as and when required.

Following the 2002 evaluation, the Barcelona Council concluded that the European Employment Strategy (EES) had made considerable progress but that a reinforced strategy was required to streamline the policies and the coordination issues. On 14 January 2003, the Commission presented an outline for the revised strategy with associated objectives and targets. There are three main objectives for the next five years, which are:

- full employment;

- quality and productivity at work;
- cohesion and an inclusive labour market.

The Commission also stressed the importance of a tighter control and delivery of the EES. After April 2003, the Commission would submit its proposals in this respect.

www.europa.eu.int

European works councils (EWCs)

The function of European works councils is to provide information and consultation between employers and employees, primarily in international businesses, which operate in Europe. EWCs are also known as European Committees or Forums. EWCs aim to:

- increase trust between managers and employees;
- encourage greater employee involvement in business;
- assist employees in understanding why management decisions are made;
- assist in the creation of a positive corporate culture;
- assist businesses in demonstrating their concern for their employees.

The Directive which established the role of EWCs (the European Works Council Directive) was derived from the Social Chapter and came into law in the UK on 15 January 2000. It provides for businesses under specific circumstances to be able to set up **works councils**. Normally this refers to businesses with at least 1,000 employees in Europe, of whom there are at least 150 employees in two different Member States.

www.eurofound.eu.int

Evaluation interview

E

An evaluation interview seeks to collect specific information on a review or perception basis. The interviews could take place both prior to and after a selection process or training period, to illicit information regarding changes in perception or pre-conceived ideas as part of an assessment of how this has affected the participant.

Evaluation interviews are also, of course, an integral part of **job evaluation**.

Fear, Richard A. and Chiron, Robert J., *The Evaluation Interview*. New York: McGraw-Hill, 1990.

Exit interview

Increasingly, exit interviews are being seen as a means by which issues surrounding staff retention can be investigated. Given the fact that many businesses are spending an increasing amount of money in recruiting suitable staff each time an employee chooses to leave, this is now seen as an opportunity to reduce the **attrition**.

Exit interviews throw light on why individuals are choosing to leave employment. They may reveal a trend, rather than a specific single employee-orientated reason for leaving. Pay and conditions are not the sole reasons why individuals choose to leave employment (see Figure 12), and an exit interview aims to identify the following:

- the precise reason why the employee is leaving;
- an indication of the measures which could have made them choose otherwise;
- the necessary background data to provide a process by which **labour turnover** can be reduced.

Clearly there are occasions when individuals feel that they are being discriminated against for some reason, which may be the root cause of their decision to leave the business, and there are also incidences when **core employees** choose to tender their resignation on account of the fact that they have been offered a more desirable package with a competitor.

Effective exit interviews can also convince employees who are retiring to continue their association with the employer, perhaps on a part-time or a temporary basis.

Exit interviews do not always provide as much information as an employer would wish, particularly if some employees are reluctant to give their exact reasons for choosing to leave. This could be because they think this may affect the business's decision to provide them with an adequate **reference** for future employment.

Drake, John D., *The Exit Interview*. New York: DBM Publications, 1998.

E

Expectancy theory

See **Vroom, Victor.**

Experiential learning model

Experiential learning is a form of educational training based on the idea that rather than studying a particular concept or set of circumstances, the individual has an encounter with that concept. In doing so, the individual undergoes a learning process.

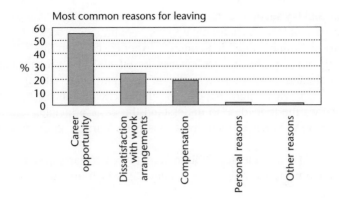

Figure 12   Reasons for leaving employment

There have been a number of different views and theories expounded regarding experiential learning, many of which were initially related to traditional classroom experiences. Experiential learning, however, can be typified as existing primarily in post-school educational situations, which provide an opportunity for personal growth and self-awareness.

One of the key theories on experiential learning was put forward by David A. Kolb and Roger Fry. They created a model (see Figure 13) based on work carried out by **Kurt Lewin**.

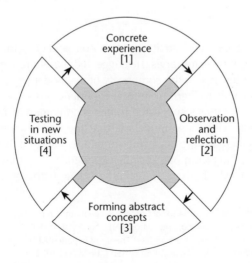

E

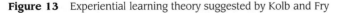

Figure 13   Experiential learning theory suggested by Kolb and Fry

Kolb and Fry suggested that the learning cycle can begin at any one of four points and that the learning cycle is a continuous process. Typically the process will begin with a concrete experience, when the individual carrying out a particular action sees its effects. The second step is to understand how these effects, in this particular situation, can help predict what might happen in similar circumstances. The third step allows the individual to understand the basic principles and then to move on to consider using what has been learned, in other sets of situations.

Kolb and Fry also identified four different types of learning styles using the stages in the learning cycle (Figure 13), which are summarized in Table 7.

Table 7   Learning styles

Learning style	Learning characteristic	Description
Converger	3 and 4	Good at practical application of ideas.
Diverger	1 and 2	Good imagination and idea generation.
Assimilator	2 and 3	Strong ability to create theoretical models.
Accommodator	1 and 4	Practical, willing to take risks.

A more complex view, albeit based on Kolb and Fry's model, was the approach set out by Peter Jarvis. He suggested that there were a number of different routes, hence the complexity of his model (Figure 14), which allowed individuals to learn from their experiences.

A summary of Jarvis's suggested routes is contained in Table 8.

The problem with these models is that they do not recognize that many of the processes are occurring simultaneously and that while individuals are learning from one specific experience, they may be encountering another which they are still wrestling with, or indeed have rejected.

Jarvis, P., *Adult Learning in the Social Context*. Beckenham: Croom Helm, 1987.

Kolb, D., *Experiential Learning*. Englewood Cliffs, NJ: Prentice-Hall, 1984.

Kolb, D. and Fry, R., 'Toward an Applied Theory of Experiential Learning', in C. Cooper (ed.), *Theories of Group Process*. Chichester: John Wiley, 1975.

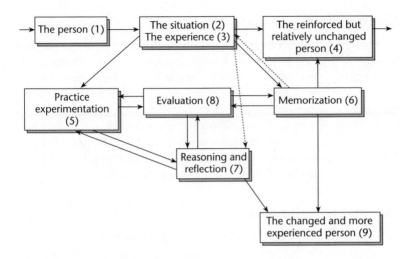

Figure 14 The Jarvis model

Table 8 Routes to learning using Jarvis's model

Type of learning	Route	Description
Presumption	1–4	Interaction through patterned behaviour.
Non-consideration	1–4	No response to a learning situation.
Rejection	1–3, 7	Sees no value in the experience.
Pre-conscious	1–3–6 then either 4 or 9	No real thought of what is happening.
Practice	1–5–8–6 then either 4 or 9	Repetition and gradual building of skills.
Memorization	1–3–6 then 8–6 then either 4 or 9	More concern with remembering what has occurred than learning from what has occurred.
Contemplation	1–3–7–8–6–9	Situation is seriously considered and then an intellectual decision is made.
Reflective	1–3–5–7–5 or 6–9	Serious consideration to all aspects of what has been learned.
Experiential	1–3–7–5–8–6–9	A pragmatic approach.

E

External equity

External equity relates to an employee's perception of current pay and benefits in relation to pay and benefits received by others outside the organization. Perception of relative rewards may be derived from a number of different sources, including job advertisements and conversations with employees from other organizations in the course of normal business interactions. Although the overarching perception may be that the pay is not on an equitable basis, the external equity concept does not take into account other factors which may make the jobs being compared somewhat different in a number of respects.

External recruitment

External recruitment can be differentiated from internal recruitment in the sense that the business seeks to attract candidates for job vacancies from outside the organization. There are a number of different methods which can be employed by a business wishing to recruit externally, which normally depend upon the type of vacancy that is available. Recruitment agencies, which specialize in finding specific types of worker tend to be used to identify skilled or professional employees. For senior management positions a business may employ **head hunting** services. Local or national newspapers are usually appropriate for semi-skilled workers, whilst clerical, administrative and unskilled workers are usually recruited through government or private **employment agencies**.

Another form of external recruitment involves setting up an arrangement with a university, or a number of universities. Recommended students, who match the criteria required, are then introduced to the business by the university staff or the university's own job-finding services.

One of the major problems associated with external recruitment is the cost, as in most cases external agencies will require some form of payment for their services. Normally the procedures involved in external recruitment include the following:

- applications are received, usually by means of an application form, a letter of application and/or a CV;
- the human resources department then sorts through the applications and creates a short list of candidates who will be invited to **interview**;
- a panel is then formed, consisting of a representative from human resources, a manager from the area or department to which the **applicant** is applying, and an independent panel member;

E

- in most cases the choice of candidate is made by the panel, but there may be a **personality test** or an **aptitude test** in order to further sort the candidates;
- once candidates have been selected they will formally start their job and go through an **induction** in order to familiarize themselves with their new place of employment.

The main advantages of external recruitment can be seen as:

- the introduction of new blood, with new ideas;
- the opportunity to see a wider range of candidates, giving the business more choice;
- the opportunity to take advantage of training either already personally undertaken or having been paid for by another business, which not only increases the overall skills available, but also reduces the potential training costs.

Extrinsic rewards

Extrinsic rewards are additional forms of reward which are outside the control of the employee. Pay can be seen as an **intrinsic reward**, but most other benefits associated with employment can be considered as an extrinsic reward. In other words, extrinsic rewards are very similar to **Hertzberg**'s hygiene factors, and therefore include **incentives**, **share options**, **pension schemes**, insurance and crèches. As Hertzberg pointed out, lack of attention to these details can lead to dissatisfaction and de-motivation. It is not uncommon for management to ignore these factors, considering that they provide sufficient pay, and pay alone, to compensate the employee for any shortcomings, which may be apparent to the employee but not valued by the management itself.

E

Ff

Fair Labor Standards Act (FLSA) 1996 (US)

The FLSA sets the Federal minimum wages ($4.75 per hour 1996, and $5.15 per hour 1997). Exemptions include employees less than 20 years of age ($4.25 per hour during their first 90 consecutive calendar days of employment with an employer) and specifically identified groups of full-time students, student learners, apprentices, and workers with disabilities, provided the employer is in receipt of a special certificate issued by the Department of Labor.

www.dol.gov/dol/compliance/comp-flsa.htm

Family and Medical Leave Act (FMLA) 1993 (US)

FMLA provides an entitlement to eligible employees to take up to 12 weeks of unpaid, job-protected leave in a twelve-month period for specified family and medical reasons.

www.dol.gov/dol/compliance/comp-fmla.htm

Fayol, Henri

In 1916 Henri Fayol, a French industrialist, wrote his views and theories about the problems commonly encountered by organizations. His view was that many of the root causes of industrial failure were down to management and personnel. Fayol was a 'top–down' theorist who believed that change must begin with the board of directors or the managing director (see Figure 15).

Fayol began by identifying the three main aspects of management, which are:

- the activities of the organization;
- the elements of management;
- the principles of management.

Fayol identified the six main categories of activities of an organization as being:

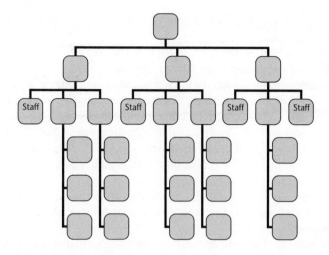

Figure 15 Fayol's management structure

- technical activities – which include production, manufacture and adaptation;
- commercial activities – which include buying, selling and exchanging;
- financial activities – which include the seeking of finance and deciding the best use of that finance;
- security services – which include the protection of the organization, its employees and its property;
- accounting services – which include the production of balance sheets, costings, statistical data and stock inventories;
- managerial activities – which includes forecasting and planning, organization, giving instruction, coordinating and controlling employee activity.

Fayol then identified 14 elements and principles of management which were key qualities and functions:

- division of work – ensuring that all employees know what their duties are;
- authority – the ability to give clear, complete and unambiguous instruction;
- discipline – to be rigid and firm when appropriate but always to ensure understanding;
- unity of command – to ensure that all aspects of management within the organization are uniform;

F

- unity of direction – to ensure that the business has a clear corporate strategy;
- subordination – the ability to put the organization first and personal needs and commitments second;
- remuneration – the need for a fair wage for a fair day's work;
- centralization – to ensure that tasks are concentrated and not duplicated, in order to maintain cost effectiveness;
- clear scalar chain – to ensure that all individuals within the organization know their position (Fayol suggested that this could be achieved through the production of an organization chart);
- internal order – to strive to avoid internal conflict;
- equality – to ensure equal opportunity within the organization and avoid discrimination by age, sex, sexual orientation, disability or religion;
- stability of tenure – to ensure that employees feel their job is secure, so that they need not be concerned with their own security;
- initiative – to encourage idea creation and to accept ideas from employees without, necessarily, enforcing senior management input;
- esprit de corps – to encourage a company spirit where individuals are proud to support the objectives of the business.

Fayol also identified some rules which he considered management should follow. He wrote that an individual who specializes would become more skilled, efficient and effective, but also considered that the manager should have the ultimate accountability for the employees.

Boje, David and Dennehy, Robert, *Managing in the Postmodern World*, 3rd edn, September 2000, at http://cbae.nmsu.edu/~dboje/mpw.html

Summary of Fayol's work at www.comp.glam.ac.uk/teaching/ismanagement/manstyles1f.htm

F

Feedback

The word 'feedback' relates to any information that helps to evaluate the success or failure of an action that has taken place.

Field review method

'Field review method' refers to a form of **performance appraisal**. The usual situation involves the head of department or the employee's immediate line manager carrying out the appraisal interview. In the field review method, however, representatives of the human resources department contact the employee's head of department or line manager and gather information from them about the employee's performance or qualities. The human resources department representative then produces the appraisal report.

Fire Precautions Act 1971; Fire Precautions (Factories, Offices, Shops and Railway Premises) Order 1989; Fire Precautions (Workplace) Regulations 1997; Fire Precautions (Workplace) (Amendment) Regulations 1999 (UK)

This series of Acts and subsequent amendments and additions require employers to have a valid fire certificate, specifically in the case of hotels and boarding houses, and factories, offices, shops or railway premises. In the second case a certificate is needed if more than 20 employees are working in the building or more than 10 employees are working on a floor other than the ground floor.

www.hmso.gov.uk/si/si1989/Uksi_19890079_en_1.htm

http://194.128.65.3/si/si1997/97184001.htm

www.hmso.gov.uk/si/si1999/19991877.htm

Fixed-term contracts

A fixed-term contract is a **contract of employment** for a definite period, set in advance. Employment ends when the contract expires and no notice need be given by the employer. Fixed-term contracts sometimes provide the organization or the **temporary contract** worker with the option that they can be ended, by notice on either side, before the expiry date of the contract. Termination by one side alone where there is no provision for early termination may leave the other open to liability for the remainder of the contract. Contracts may also be agreed which end on the completion of a particular task rather than on a specific date.

From 1 October 2002, employees on fixed-term contracts have the right to be paid the same rate as similar permanent employees working for the same employer, and in general terms should not be treated less favourably than permanent employees. This means that employees on fixed-term contracts will have broadly the same rights to statutory **redundancy** payments, written reasons for **dismissal** and the right not to suffer **unfair dismissal** as permanent employees. Any redundancy

F

waiver included in a fixed-term contract which is agreed, extended or renewed after 1 October 2002 will be deemed invalid.

See also **Fixed-term Employees (Prevention of Less Favourable Treatment) Regulations 2002.**

Fixed-term Employees (Prevention of Less Favourable Treatment) Regulations 2002 (UK)

Under the terms of this Act, a fixed-term contract is defined as being:

- a contract that lasts for a specified period of time; or
- a contract which will end when a specified task has been completed; or
- a contract which will end when a specified event does or does not happen.

(Note that the Act defines the second and third descriptions as 'task contracts').

Prime examples of fixed-term contracts include those for employees who are covering for long-term sickness or maternity leave, seasonal workers, casual workers and those employed for a definite period to cover increased demand. The Act came into force on 1 October 2002 and guaranteed fixed-term contract employees the following rights:

1 Not to be treated less favourably than comparable permanent employees.
2 To receive a written statement from their employer setting out the reasons for any less favourable treatment.
3 To treat their contract as a permanent contract if it is successively renewed for more than four years.
4 To qualify for statutory redundancy payment if they have been employed for the necessary 2-year period.
5 To receive information on permanent vacancies within the organization.
6 For employees on 'task contracts' as well as specified-period contracts to claim unfair dismissal at the end of the fixed-term contract if it is not renewed, and to receive a written statement from the employer giving reasons for the dismissal.
7 For employees on fixed-term contracts of 3 months or less to have a right to Statutory Sick Pay and to Payments on Medical Suspension, and guaranteed payments (once they have been employed for 1 month).
8 For employees on fixed-term contracts of 3 months or less to have a right to receive 1 week's notice after they have served 1 month's

F

continuous service if the employer wishes to bring the contract to an end before it is due to expire. They must also give 1 week's notice to the employer if they wish to terminate the contract themselves before the expiry date.

9 To have access to the employer's occupational pension schemes.

(Note that the rights under 1, 3 and 9 can be denied by the employer if this can be justified on objective grounds.)

www.hmso.gov.uk/si/si2002/20022034.htm

Fixed Term Work Directive (EU)

See **EU Council Directive 1999/70/EC of 28 June 1999.**

Flat organization structure

A flat organization structure is a **hierarchical structure** in the sense that it is in the shape of a pyramid, but has fewer layers. Often a hierarchical structure can be de-layered in order to create a flat structure. This de-layering process often allows decisions to be made more quickly and efficiently because the layers are able to communicate more easily with one another. This enables the organization to become less bureaucratic and is a simpler structure often used by organizations operating from a single site. The directors and other major decision makers are more available for consultation with employees, who often find that they feel more a part of the process. This encourages motivation, particularly amongst junior managers, who are likely to be given more responsibility through delegation from the senior management level of the structure.

Flexibility agreement

A flexibility agreement is a **collective agreement** made between employer and employees. The flexibility agreement would concern the agreement of employees to carry out any tasks within their own capabilities and expertise, in exchange for a promise from employers that **trade union** representatives would be involved in any decision-making negotiations to implement a structure for the application of the flexible practices involved.

Flexible staffing

Flexible staffing aims to provide the business with a responsive approach to the deployment of its employees. Flexible staffing means

F

that the business will have a small number of **core employees** supported by a number of either **part-time** workers or **contract** workers available when needed. Part-time workers' hours can be changed or amended in order to fit with additional pressures of work or demand, whilst contract workers can be brought in or outsourced from **employment agencies**. **Temporary contracts** can be offered to individuals for fixed periods of time and, once the immediate problem period has passed, staffing levels can then return to their normal pattern.

Flexiplace

The term 'flexiplace' refers to the location of the employees while they are carrying out the duties of their job role on behalf of the organization. Often this can be at their home or in another remote location, linked to the organization by means of computer networks and telecommunication systems. There are control problems associated with the widespread use of home working as a primary method of carrying out core activities, since there will be a reliance on the various outworkers completing the series of tasks at precisely the right point. At the same time, the organizational structure has to be capable of accommodating the requirement of continuous communication and supervision of remote workers.

An employee could also be required to show flexibility by being geographically mobile. Individuals, particularly those who are involved in maintenance, carry out their duties in a variety of locations, very often in other countries. The flexibility requires the willingness of the employee to travel, and some form of reward from the organization to compensate the employee for the inevitable disruption to domestic life.

Flexitime

F

Flexitime allows employees to choose, within set limits, when they wish to begin and end work. They are required to work during core times and must work an agreed number of hours during a given period (usually four weeks). Outside the core times there are flexible bands of time during which employees may choose whether to be at work. The total period for which the workplace is open is known as the 'bandwidth'. The starting and finishing times of lunch breaks and the maximum and minimum lunch period entitlements also have to be calculated. The employee's hours of attendance are recorded and added up at the end of each period and, within expressed and agreed limits, employees can carry over any excess or deficit in the number of hours they are required to work. Some schemes allow employees to take excess hours as additional leave, known as 'flexi-leave'.

Flexitime is typically used for office-based staff below managerial level in both the public sector and private sector service organizations. Manufacturing organizations are less likely to operate a flexitime system.

Those carrying out **shift work** are usually excluded from flexitime schemes, as are senior managers or key personnel. Other groups of workers for whom flexitime systems are rarely an option include those who serve the public during specific organizational opening times.

For employers, flexitime can aid the recruitment and retention of staff. It can also help provide staff cover outside normal working hours and reduce the need for overtime. Additionally, flexitime can improve the provision of equal opportunities to staff unable to work standard hours.

Flexitime can give employees greater freedom to organize their working lives to suit domestic commitments, and travelling can be cheaper and easier if it is out of peak time. However, the use of a flexitime system can result in increased administration costs, including the costs of keeping records, and of extra heating and lighting, as well as of providing adequate supervision throughout the bandwidth.

An effective flexitime system can be developed, provided the organization is willing to do the following:

- involve managers and **trade union** or employee representatives at an early stage, possibly by means of a working group, to plan, implement and monitor the scheme;
- ensure supervisors and line managers are kept fully informed on the development of the scheme;
- pilot the scheme for a trial period and receive feedback on opinions;
- identify individuals who will participate in the scheme – often it is more appropriate to ask for volunteers rather than impose compulsion;
- ensure there are procedures in place for dealing with medical appointments, absence, etc.;
- set up a system by which employees and line managers can easily record time worked.

F

Fordism

The term 'Fordism' takes its name from Henry Ford (1863–1947), who, although not inventing the assembly line system, brought this means of production into the public eye. Ford broke down the production process into hundreds of individualized, highly specialized parts. This, in effect, created a complex division of labour in which individual workers could specialize in being able to complete a specified task, or series of related tasks, in a much shorter period than had been the case before the production line system was introduced. In effect Ford rationalized the production system, whilst simultaneously **deskilling** his workforce.

Alongside the division of tasks and deskilling, Ford introduced higher wages than the industry norm to encourage the employees and partially compensate them for the fact that they would now be working as part of a three-shift system, allowing the plant to run 24 hours a day. It was a measure of the effectiveness of this introduction that the price of a model T Ford fell from $950 in 1908 to $290 in 1927, yet the turnover of the business increased significantly over the same period.

Ford, however, did not wish to proceed beyond the process of deskilling to introduce full automation of his factory. He still believed that employees were essential in being able to create quality products. Fordism remains at the heart of much of the mass production standards of products to this day.

Matthews, Richard A., *Fordism, Flexibility and Regional Productivity Growth*. New York: Garland Publications, 1997.

Freedom of Information Act 2000 (UK)

The Freedom of Information Act 2000 received Royal Assent on 30 November 2000 and provides clear statutory rights for those requesting information. Under the terms of the Act, anyone can apply for access to information held by bodies across the public sector.

The main features of the Act are:

- Right of access to information held by public authorities in the course of carrying out their public functions, subject to certain conditions and exemptions.
- Where information is exempted from disclosure there is a duty on public authorities to disclose where, in the view of the public authority, the public interest in disclosure outweighs the public interest in maintaining the exemption in question.
- The establishment of an Information Commissioner and a new Information Tribunal, with wide powers to enforce the rights.
- Public authorities must be prepared to adopt a scheme for the publication of information. The schemes, which must be approved by the Commissioner, will specify the classes of information the authority intends to publish, the manner of publication and whether the information is available to the public free of charge or on payment of a fee.

www.legislation.hmso.gov.uk/acts/acts2000/20000036.htm

Fringe benefits

The term 'fringe benefit' refers to any reward given to employees in addition to their wage or salary. Fringe benefits can include:

- a company pension scheme;
- employee sick pay scheme;
- subsidized meals;
- company products or services at a discounted price;
- company cars;
- private medical health insurance;
- counselling or mentoring services;
- occupational health screening;
- social and recreational facilities;
- legal and financial service support.

Fringe benefits are not necessarily related to merit, but often increase with employee status and length of service. They do not necessarily benefit all employees but are established and monitored after an initial analysis process. Once established, however, it is difficult for an organization to remove them as this could affect **employee retention**. Fringe benefits are considered important because they improve **job satisfaction** provided they are consistently and fairly administered.

Frustration of contract

Frustration of contract occurs when one or both parties, i.e. employer and employee, can no longer give or receive what had originally been agreed in a **contract of employment**. A prime example of this would be a situation where an employee suffered from ill health to such an extent as to be unable to work for a considerable period of time, or, perhaps, never able to work again. In these cases there comes a point when it is no longer feasible to allow the contract of employment to continue. The employer has to make a judgement as to whether it has reached a point where it is no longer reasonable to keep the post open for the absent employee.

   In the UK, for example, on the basis of various case laws, frustration of contract cannot occur until the period of legal right to sick pay has elapsed. Frustration cannot be claimed until the sick pay period has reached the point expressly stated in the individual's employment contract. The **Employment Appeal Tribunal** states that the following matters should be taken into account:

- the length of the previous employment;

F

- how long it would have been expected that the employment would continue under normal circumstances;
- the nature of the job;
- the nature, length and effect of the illness suffered;
- the need for the employer to have the work done and the need for a replacement to be found to do that work;
- the potential obligations, as far as the employer is concerned, in respect of **redundancy** payment or **compensation** for **unfair dismissal** if the employee is replaced;
- whether the wages or salary of the employee have continued to be paid;
- how the employer has behaved in relation to the employment;
- whether a reasonable employer could be expected to wait any longer.

Functional structures

A functionally based organizational structure is designed around specific sections of the organization, usually those that produce, market and sell the organization's product or service. Functional structures can be a sub-structure of **hierarchical** or **flat organization structures** and similarly will be controlled by a managing director, supported by relevant senior function or departmental managers. The creation of positions and departments around a specialized function is an integral

Table 9 An evaluation of functional structure

Advantages	Possible disadvantages
Promotes skills specialization and reduces duplication of resources.	It tends to limit the organization to having a relatively short-term horizon.
There is a clearer career progression route.	Managers of each department could become parochial, thus limiting career advancement.
There are clearer lines of communication, which could lead to higher productivity and performance within the department.	There is a chance of restricted communication between departments.
	If one department does not reach expectations, this has a knock-on effect to other departments.

F

part of the functional structure. There will be common themes, in terms of function or process within each department, enabling the management to concentrate on specific issues within their own technical area of expertise. This form of organizational structure has a number of advantages and disadvantages over other types of structure, as shown in Table 9.

Sutherland, Jon and Canwell, Diane, *Organization Structures and Processes*. London: Pitman Publishing, 1997.

F

Garden leave

'Garden leave' is a term used to describe the period after an employee has been made redundant or has resigned. If an organization or employer no longer requires employees to turn up for work once the redundancy has been announced, or resignation accepted, then the employees are placed on leave, with immediate effect. Although they will continue to draw a salary from the organization for the duration of the notice period, they are not required to report for work. Contractually the redundant individuals are not permitted to take up additional employment during this time. The main organizational motive behind offering garden leave is to inhibit aggrieved employees from sabotaging organizational activities or working for the competition. However, some organizations prefer to make a lump-sum payment to the employee, thus freeing them from their contractual obligations

Gilbreth, Frank and Lillian

Frank and Lillian Gilbreth were pioneers in time and motion studies. They developed a view of management contemporary with, but independent of, that of **F. W. Taylor**. They analysed the performance of a specific job, breaking down each activity into component parts. They then judged the most efficient means of carrying out each of those components, added the ideal times assigned to each of them, and arrived at an aggregate time for the whole activity.

Glass ceiling

The term 'glass ceiling' refers to what has been described as an invisible, but real, obstruction which inhibits the career advancement of women and minority groups. The glass ceiling is renowned for causing frustration amongst those affected by the barrier to progression, often resulting in a lack of **job satisfaction** and increased **labour turnover**.

See also **Glass Ceiling Act (1991) (US)**.

Glass Ceiling Act (1991) (US)

The Glass Ceiling Act established the Glass Ceiling Commission, which is empowered to investigate and make recommendations aimed at eliminating artificial barriers to promotional opportunities in the case of women and minorities. The commission itself is also empowered with fostering improvements in opportunities and development for women and minorities in management and, as such, administers a national award for 'Diversity and Excellence in American Executive Management'.

Godfather system

The godfather system is widely used in Japanese industry. The system encourages a more senior member of the organization to act in a pastoral role to a new employee. The new employees are guided through a system that enables them to glean information from all aspects of the organization, by ensuring that they rotate their duties through all functional sections and activities.

See also **buddy system** and **job rotation**.

Grade drift

Grade drift is a phenomenon which occurs particularly in organizations that base their remuneration systems on **job evaluations**. There is a tendency, both in the regular process of job evaluation instituted by human resources departments, and from the point of view of the individual post-holders, that during the job evaluation process the job is re-graded. Inevitably there are instances where the **job specification** has changed and the employee subsequently requests a re-grading. The reclassification of the job upwards to take into account additional duties and responsibilities provides the employee with a means of obtaining increased earnings without a separate conversation regarding an increase in pay rates. Grade drift is also known as 'grade creep'.

Grapevine communication

Grapevine communication is an informal method which often allows the passing on of messages to be one of the speediest forms of communication. Often considered to be gossip and rumour, grapevine communication can be extremely unreliable. Snippets of information get passed from one individual, or group of individuals, to another and the message can become extremely distorted. Grapevine communication is not a method to be encouraged by managers, who should attempt to convey information to employees in a more formal way, stating facts rather than part-truths. A high degree of grapevine communication within an organization, if it is not adequately dealt with by management, can lead to low morale. Although this method of communication is quite natural and prevalent in all organizations, it should be tackled in an appropriate manner so that employees hear a message from the appropriate level and through the appropriate channels.

Graphic response test

A graphic response test is carried out by an organization during the recruitment and selection process. This type of test would be undertaken in order to ascertain the level of the **applicant**'s honesty, by the use of computer software that measures the individual's body responses to particular questions.

Graphology

Graphology is the study and analysis of handwriting and is used by an increasing number of organizations, particularly within Europe, in the selection and recruitment process. Much can be gleaned from an individual's handwriting, particularly if graphology has been studied in depth.

Grievance audit

Periodic grievance audits are carried out by human resources departments in order to discover the source and nature of grievances which have been expressed by employees. The purpose of the audit is to discover whether there are underlying trends or patterns in the types of grievances and whether remedial action needs to be taken in order to combat these.

Grievance procedure

Frustration and change can often result in a grievance from an employee against the organization. Often this can be as a result of a misunderstanding or lack of appropriate communication. Simple day-to-day grievances are usually dealt with by supervisors and line managers, but on occasion they require further intervention.

A well constructed and well laid out grievance procedure will enable the human resource management to resolve grievances quickly, without the need for further intervention or **industrial action**. A formal grievance procedure is a set of agreed rules that have been drawn up to provide strict guidelines as to how grievances are dealt with. Organizations have found that it is in their own interests to have formal grievance procedures established, particularly in cases where legal intervention has been necessary, primarily due to the fact that an employer has to be seen to be attempting fairness. A formal grievance procedure would:

- attempt to ensure that both parties involved in the issue are impartial and behave responsibly;
- ensure that both parties understand the process and progress of the procedure;
- use written procedures to allow the necessary consistency to be applied even when **trade union** or employee representatives, or senior managers from within the organization, have been replaced by new individuals;
- ensure that authority for decision making is clarified;
- ensure that the timescale for registering a grievance is clear;
- ensure that the opportunity and deadline involved for lodging an appeal is clear;
- institute a formal procedure that allows the content of the hearing to be minuted, thus allowing for comparison in future disputes;
- increase employee security and peace of mind.

Gross misconduct

Acts of gross misconduct within the workplace are one of the reasons for **dismissal**. The term 'gross misconduct' can cover quite a wide area, but it does include the following:

- **absenteeism**;
- lateness for work on a regular basis;
- insubordination, when an employee refuses to take instruction from a superior;
- incompetence, when an employee shows a continuous inability to complete vital tasks within the job;
- immorality, in the form of unacceptable behaviour while at work;
- endangering the lives of others by unsafe working behaviour;
- theft of the organization's property, or sometimes the property of colleagues.

G

Essentially the gross misconduct category of dismissal falls into two main sections:

- Statutory contraventions – where an employee breaks a legal requirement, e.g. being under the influence of alcohol while driving a vehicle during the carrying out of the job role.
- Other contraventions – which would include any of those listed above, but often refers to the employee's inability to do the job, or signs of gradual deterioration in performance.

In all cases of dismissal through gross misconduct, the employer must be able to prove that they have acted reasonably throughout, and be able to specify where and when the misconduct took place, how it affected the employee's job and/or colleagues and how the organization was, or was likely to be, harmed by the actions. The organization further has to ensure that any extenuating circumstances, together with the employee's previous work, were taken into account prior to the dismissal and that the dismissed employee has not been selected unfairly from others who were equally guilty. They have to be sure that dismissal was the only option, that warning had previously been issued and that the correct procedures were followed throughout the process.

Group think

The term 'group think' was coined by Irving Janis, who related the term to a phenomenon within **groups**. Janis considered that group think occurs when a group of individuals are so determined to make a decision that they ignore all major considerations and alternatives, as well as any disagreements within the group, in order to achieve this. Groups suffering from group think are often thought to be over-cautious and to lack necessary creativeness. They bond with each other, and the individuals see themselves as secure because they belong to the group. The group members have little doubt about the effectiveness or vulnerability of the group and consider the views of anyone not involved within the group to be those of insignificant outsiders. According to Janis, the symptoms of group think are:

- a feeling of invulnerability in that the members consider they cannot be touched;
- inappropriate rationale in that they consider things are unlikely to happen to them;
- a sense of morality, in that they think they know what is best;
- stereotyping other groups by considering them all to be less effective than they are;

G

- pressurising other groups;
- exerting an element of self-censorship by not communicating all, but selecting what they consider to be appropriate, information to other groups or relevant individuals;
- unanimity, by assuming a consensus when some of the individuals do not speak;
- mind-guards – referring to the fact that they do not allow any other thoughts to contradict what they have already decided.

Suffering from group think can make groups ineffective. Janis considered that management would have to encourage the individuals within the group to:

- consider and examine all alternatives;
- feel able to express their own doubts within the group;
- listen to criticisms from outside the group;
- challenge those who have firmly held beliefs;
- actively seek feedback, advice and information from outside the group;
- create subdivisions within the group;
- avoid **grapevine communication**.

Group think can lead to ineffective decision-making through insufficient attention to alternatives and risks.

Groups

The definition of a group, within human resource management, is two or more individuals who come into contact with one another in a work situation on a regular and continued basis. Within most organizations there are a number of groups who come together for a particular reason. Groups can be either formal in nature, or informal. The informal type of group often come together to support activities, both within and outside the organization, and cooperate and collaborate with one another in order to carry out certain tasks and fulfil individual job roles.

A formal group is often formed in order to pass on and share some form of information. Very often groups assist in the decision-making process and are seen as an official function within the organization. Formal groups include **quality circles**, which invariably will exist for a longer period of time than some of the other formal groups. Most formal groups consist of a variable number of representatives from different areas of the organization's activities. They are often given responsibility and authority to implement ideas and amend working practices, giving input into the possible impact of expected change.

G

Halo effect

The term 'halo effect' has a number of different definitions, depending on the functional area of the business activity. In human resource management terms, 'halo effect' refers to the selection and recruitment process. It is the situation that can arise when an **applicant** has one of the characteristics required for the position, and, because of this, the interviewer or interviewing panel wrongly infer that he or she has the other characteristics or attributes required as well.

Handy, Charles

Charles Handy's main areas of research have been centred around organizations and how they are structured, particularly with regard to their cultures and progression, together with the progression of individuals within the organization.

In 1985 Charles Handy was concerned with career development from the point of view of both the organization and the individual's ability to plan the right moves for success. He described the process of planning for career development as a 'human hurdle race', often with too many hurdles to make it achievable, even for highly motivated employees. The added complication, according to Handy, is that if the attempt at one of the hurdles, during the early stages of development, is considered a failure, then the individual has little chance of re-attempting it. Added to this is the speed of the expectation of success and the fact that often individuals are so focused on the next hurdle that they become blinkered in their outlook and disregard anything that is not appropriate to the achievement of the next stage of development.

Handy identified the relevance of the **organizational culture** and structure as being a determining factor in an individual's ability to gain promotion or see any success in the development of a career. The result, from an organizational point of view, of the lack of appropriate planning for career development could be high levels of **labour turnover**. From the individuals' point of view, being employed by an organization that fails to plan for career development and promotion could restrict their progression.

See also **organizational culture**.

Handy, C. B., *Understanding Organizations*. Harmondsworth: Penguin, 1985.

Harassment

In human resource terms, harassment is usually taken to mean an institutional or management victimization of an employee. In the US, for example, there are increasing numbers of harassment suits against employers who, employees claim, have created a 'hostile environment' to the degree that it is 'severe and pervasive'. This seems to be the **benchmark** in the levelling of harassment charges against employers and it is the human resource department that needs to ensure not only that harassment is eliminated, but in cases where harassment occurs, that the process of investigating it is transparent. Providing an employer can prove that reasonable efforts have been made to either prevent or correct harassment, such as by instituting a **complaints procedure**, most courts will consider that the employer has done as much as could be reasonably done. The prevention of harassment requires organization-wide exposure and, perhaps, training, to instil policies regarding harassment and a clear knowledge of the obligations of all employees, particularly management.

Hard management

The fundamentals of hard management can be closely associated with a quote from **Peter Drucker**: 'Doing the right things is more important than doing things right.' This seems to be the fundamental ethos behind hard management, in as much as the primary role of all private businesses is to be competitive and to produce a profit. All other considerations, as far as hard management is concerned, are subservient to this.

Hard management would, therefore, transcend all areas of the business, including human resources, and rather than focusing on employee **job satisfaction**, **motivation** or even **employee retention** the drive is to achieve a competitive advantage, make the best return on investment and meet or exceed the organization's objectives. Proponents of hard management believe that if this holistic approach is adopted, then management will do the right thing, which may mean that particularly valued employees are not only well rewarded but also well treated. Hard management is to be distinguished from **soft management** by virtue of the fact that the latter focuses on human resource factors as much as on the other objectives and strategies of the business.

H

Harrison, Roger

See **organizational culture.**

Hawthorne effect

See **Mayo, Elton.**

Hay, Julie

Julie Hay's approach used transactional analysis to understand how change could be managed by considering three sets of seven interrelated aspects. Her three areas of concern were:

- individuals' responses to change;
- the needs of an individual going through change;
- the seven acts of management to meet the seven stages of change and the needs of employees.

Her theory, often referred to as the 'seven, seven and seven approach', is summarized in Table 10.

Hay, Julie, *Working it Out at Work: Understanding Attitudes and Building Relationships.* Watford: Sherwood Publishing, 1993.

Hay, Julie, *Transactional Analysis for Trainers.* Watford: Sherwood Publishing, 1996.

Head hunting

The term 'head hunting', sometimes also known as 'executive search', describes a form of recruitment process, carried out either by the organization itself or by use of an outside organization, known as a head hunter. Assuming that a head hunter is used, they will undertake to find a suitable candidate to fill a managerial or senior managerial post that has arisen within the organization. It is not always the case that suitable candidates apply for the jobs advertised, probably because they are not actively seeking alternative employment at the time. Suitable candidates will therefore be searched for by the head hunter, using organizational literature, trade and magazine reports and by networking among competing organizations. The individual concerned is then approached and invited to attend the organization to discuss the option of joining the business.

Health and safety

Health and safety is primarily concerned with the well-being of employees. In most large organizations all health and safety issues are coordi-

Table 10 Julie Hay's approach to the management of change

Criteria	Responses	Needs	Management
Immobilization	Shock. Individual does nothing.	Seeks reassurance.	Make information available and give employees time and space.
Denial	Acting as if nothing is happening.	Needs the organization to show patience.	Listen, and recognize that this is the most difficult stage.
Frustration	Blaming others for changes. Internal fighting between colleagues.	Needs the organization to recognize that this is normal, and needs space and time.	It is normal that anger is directed towards management.
Acceptance	Realizing that the past is gone, and positively considering the future.	Needs help to redefine their new position.	Offer advice and be employee-focused.
Development	Gradual acquisition of new knowledge and skills.	Requires training and coaching and possibly a role model.	Offer more advice and provide training and coaching when needed.
Application	Realization of where the individual fits in.	Needs positive encouragement and a means of monitoring progress.	Encourage.
Completion	Now settled and competent, without considering the past.	Contentment and a strong advocate of the change.	Continue to encourage and help develop.

H

nated by a particular individual who is concerned with the maintenance of a safe working environment and safe working practices. Businesses are required by law to ensure that their employees' health does not suffer as the result of their work. Various statistics are collected, primarily fatal injuries, major injuries and other injuries. There is a continued concern that accidents at work are under-reported by employers.

The Health and Safety Commission estimates that there are at least 80,000 new cases of work-related disease occurring each year and that half a million people suffer from continuing damage to health at work. The principal legislation in Britain is the **Health and Safety at Work Act 1974**, requiring, as far as is practicable, that employers ensure the health, safety and welfare of those who work for them. Britain's national legislation has been modified in recent years to incorporate European Directives on health and safety. The initial framework directive led to the Management of Health and Safety at Work Regulations (1992) which detailed more specific duties for employers, requiring them to carry out risk-assessment, appoint competent individuals to develop preventative measures and to ensure that employees and others have sufficient information.

The Health and Safety Executive is a public agency responsible for the inspection and the enforcement of health and safety legislation. Its powers include the issuing of improvement notices and prohibition notices. The inspectors may initiate criminal proceedings if the regulations are continually flouted.

Health and Safety at Work Act 1974 (UK) (HASAWA)

The HASAWA places a duty on employers to ensure the health, safety and welfare at work of all their employees (as far as is practicable). The Health and Safety Executive and local authorities enforce HASAWA and there are criminal sanctions for breaches or failure to comply.

In addition to this legal responsibility, employers also have an implied responsibility to take reasonable steps, as far as they are able, to ensure that the health and safety of their employees is not put at risk. Employers are required to assess the levels of risk against the costs associated with the elimination of those risks in order to make a judgement as to whether they have taken all reasonable steps. Usually the employer's responsibility is only to his or her own employees and premises; however, the responsibility can be extended in some circumstances.

www.hse.gov.uk

Health and Safety (Display Screen Equipment) Regulations 1992 (UK)

These regulations are specifically related to work with visual display units (VDUs) or computer screens. The specific obligations with regard to employers can be summarized as in the Table 11.

H

Table 11   Regulations concerning VDUs

Obligation	Towards own employee who is a user	Towards other employee (e.g. working for Temp agency) who is a user	Towards self-employed person who is an operator
Assess risks at workstation	YES	YES	YES
Inform staff about rights and what has been done	YES	YES	YES
Plan work and provide breaks	YES	YES	NO (individual responsibility)
Offer eye-tests and special glasses if necessary	YES	NO (main employer is responsible)	NO (individual responsibility)
Provide training in safe use	YES	NO (main employer is responsible)	NO (individual responsibility)

www.hmso.gov.uk/si/si1992/Uksi_19922792_en_1.htm

Health and Safety (First Aid) Regulations 1981 (UK)

These regulations address the requirement of an employer to provide first-aid cover and trained personnel.

www.hse.gov.uk

Health and Safety Information for Employees Regulations 1989 (UK)

These regulations require employers to display a poster informing their employees of what they should know about health and safety.

www.hmso.gov.uk/si/si1989/Uksi_19890682_en_1.htm

H

Health and Safety (Safety Signs and Signals) Regulations 1996 (UK)

These regulations came into effect following a European Union Directive. They require employers to provide safety signs where there is a risk which has not been avoided or controlled by other means. The safety signs are aimed at reducing the risks. They cover matters such as the regulation of traffic, and the marking of dangerous substances or areas, and incorporate fire safety signs, including directions to exits.

www.hmso.gov.uk/si/si1996/Uksi_19960341_en_1.htm

Health Insurance Portability and Accountability Act (HIPAA) 1996 (US)

The Health Insurance Portability and Accountability Act (HIPAA) ensures fundamental rights and protections for participants and beneficiaries in group health plans.

HIPAA includes protection under group health plans, prohibits discrimination against employees and dependants based on their health status, and allows employees the opportunity to enrol on a new plan in certain circumstances. HIPAA also gives employees the right to buy individual coverage if they are no longer covered under Continuation of Health Coverage (COBRA).

www.dol.gov/dol/topic/health-plans/portability.htm

Hertzberg, Frederick

Frederick Hertzberg developed his two-factor theory, which included his hygiene factor and his motivator factor, during his investigation of accountants and engineers in the USA. This brought about his angle on the theory of leadership, motivation and management. According to Hertzberg, the five major motivating factors are:

- Achievement – employees need to feel that something has been accomplished by their labours.
- Recognition – employees need to feel that management and others realize that the role they are playing within the organization is an important and appreciated one.
- The work itself – the employees should feel that their job role meets or reaches their own potential.
- Advancement – employees need to feel that they have a chance of promotion and that their skills and performance warrant such a promotion.

H

- Responsibility – employees need to feel they have enough freedom to make their own decisions.

The hygiene factors that Hertzberg identified are features of the workplace, or the organization itself, that help to make the employees feel good about themselves, and include:

- wage or salary paid;
- bonuses/commissions paid;
- working conditions;
- quality of supervision;
- the working environment;
- job security.

The hygiene factors do not motivate employees, and they can never reach a stage of either complete satisfaction or of complete dissatisfaction, but remain in a neutral zone.

Hertzberg's motivators are concerned with the work that the employees undertake and their performance within each task (see Figure 16). An employee cannot be motivated if the organization is not offering them any of the following, and they will remain in the neutral zone:

- attainment;
- advancement;
- responsibility.

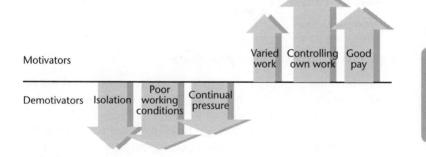

Figure 16   Hertzberg's motivational hygiene model

Hertzberg, F., *Work and the Nature of Man*. London: HarperCollins, 1966.
Hertzberg, F., *Motivation to Work*. Somerset, NJ: Transaction Publishers, 1993.

Hierarchical organization structure

A hierarchical organization structure is best imagined by using an image of a pyramid. At the top are the major decision makers, who are few in number, and further down the pyramid the shape of the organization broadens as more employees become involved at the lower levels. At the base of the pyramid are the majority of the workers.

Power, responsibility and authority are concentrated at the top of the pyramid and decisions flow from up to down. An organization would choose this form of structure when decisions needed to be made by those who had expertise and experience, together with the authority to ensure that decisions were implemented.

The most common version of this form of structure is the steep pyramid where there are many different layers of management, possibly within an organization that operates in several different locations, needing to fulfil different administrative functions. Equally, organizations of a complex nature may choose this structure.

There are some disadvantages to those lower down the hierarchical structure in that if the pyramid is too multi-layered and complex, they often find difficulty in understanding how and why decisions are made. The organization may also find itself too bureaucratic in nature and the result could be that the decision-making process becomes too complicated and time consuming because there are too many layers involved.

See also **chain of command.**

Hierarchy of needs

See **Maslow, Abraham.**

High involvement work practices

Pil and MacDuffie studied motor vehicle assembly plants to test a series of factors which affect what they termed 'high involvement work practices' (HIWPs). The practices include job rotation, the use of teams and suggestion schemes. They considered that HIWP was more difficult to change than normal human resource policies because the work practices are more integral to the core business processes and coordination requirements of the organization.

Pil and MacDuffie discovered the following:

- Plants are more likely to increase their use of high involvement work practices when they already have implemented complementary human resource management practices.
- Higher levels of managerial tenure have a positive association with

greater increase in the use of HIWPs, suggesting that longer-term relationships provide a possible basis for greater trust.

- Actions which reduce employee trust, such as management layoffs, production-worker layoffs and early retirement programmes have no statistically significant association with the introduction of HIWPs.

Pil and MacDuffie found that businesses in developing countries use HIWPs and not automation. They tend to use training, performance-based pay, and selective recruitment and hiring more than an investment in automated processes.

Pil, F. K. and MacDuffie, J. P., 'Organizational and Environmental Factors Influencing the Use and Diffusion of High Involvement Work Practices', in P. Cappelli, *Employment Practices and Business Strategy*. Oxford: Oxford University Press, 1999, pp. 81–106.

Holland, John

John Holland identified six personality types and six different working environments. Holland suggested that employees prefer to work in environments which are similar to their personality types. His theory can be summarized as in Table 12.

Table 12 Personality types and corresponding work environments

Personality type	Description	Compatible work environments
Realistic	Practical, mechanical and avoids social activities.	Realistic, investigative and conventional.
Investigative	Systematic and a good problem solver, avoids leadership and selling.	Investigative, realistic and artistic.
Artistic	Avoids repetitive activities as creation is important.	Artistic, investigative and social.
Social	Values helping people, friendly and trustworthy.	Social, artistic and enterprising.
Enterprising	Strong on leadership and persuasion, energetic and ambitious.	Enterprising, social and conventional.
Conventional	Number-based, orderly, values success and working to a set plan.	Conventional, enterprising and realistic.

H

Holland, John H., *Emergence: From Chaos to Order*. Oxford: Oxford University Press, 2000.

Horizontal communication

Horizontal communication involves the often informal communication between peers or colleagues on the same level of the organizational structure.

Human resource accounting

The term 'human resource accounting' refers to the systematic recording, measurement and analysis of all the costs involved in a department's activities. In addition to identifying the costs, the financial benefits to the organization will also be calculated. The costs and financial benefits will include:

- the recruitment and utilization of human resources;
- an estimation of training costs;
- an assessment of the effects of training programmes;
- an assessment of the effects of staff development programmes;
- an investigation into the consequences of wage and salary increases;
- an investigation into the consequences of the introduction of **incentive** schemes;
- any other financial implications connected to the continued utilization of human resources.

Human resource audit

A human resource audit examines and reviews an organization's policies, procedures and practices across the human resource function. Typically, elements included in a human resource audit are:

- personnel policies;
- review of personnel files;
- performance **appraisal**;
- evaluation processes;
- termination processes, including **exit interviews**;
- compliance with employment law;
- recruitment procedures;
- review of benefits and compensations;
- review of employee status and classifications;
- review of **job descriptions** and **job specifications**.

H

Human resource information system (HRIS)

Human resource information systems, or HRIS, are gradually beginning to replace manual or partially computerized and partly manual systems used by human resource departments. Despite the availability of complex, integrated HRI systems, many businesses still retain a form of paper records, but are gradually moving across to scanned documents which are stored electronically, rather than retaining the originals.

One of the biggest advantages in using an HRIS is that the system can be used with an integrated payroll. In this way common data needs only to be entered once and can be maintained by either human resources managers or those in charge of the payroll. Other businesses opt for stand-alone HRIS, which does mean that it is sometimes difficult to coordinate with the payroll.

Clearly, a decision whether to purchase an HRIS very much depends on the nature of the business and its present capacity to deal with human resource issues, and, indeed, whether it wishes to integrate this into a payroll system. Generally, basic systems can be purchased for a little in excess of $300, whilst a larger organization, with several thousand employees, may find that the cost is closer to $1 million.

One of the inherent problems with any proprietary HRIS software is that it does not necessarily reflect a business's needs and therefore needs to be configured or customized specifically for the task which the business has in mind. Most software vendors will offer support but, in the longer term, businesses realize that in-house support is essential to maintain the system.

HRIS can handle pay, benefits, **applicant tracking**, **recruitment**, time and attendance, skills inventories, health and safety, **compensation** and **retirement** plans.

Pinto, Jeffrey and Millet, Ido, *Successful Information System Implementation: The Human Side*. New York: Project Management Institute, 1999.

H

Human resource plan

The human resource plan is the department's attempt to forecast the number and type of employee needed for future requirements, and their anticipation of how likely this need is to be realized. The current human resources will be compared with future likely needs, and programmes will be set up for recruitment drives, training, the possible redeployment of current employees, or the **redundancy** of others. This planning process can assist human resource management in:

- recruitment;
- the avoidance of redundancy, or plans for redeployment;
- training;
- professional development needs;
- the costs involved in supplying the required number of employees;
- ensuring that productivity targets are met;
- ensuring that other resources, such as accommodation, are available when needed.

Clearly, a human resource plan will have to be continuously monitored and readjusted as the company objectives change or are affected by unforeseen internal and external considerations. Most organizations would produce both a short-term (usually up to 1 year ahead) and a longer-term (usually 5 years ahead) plan, which would include the following considerations:

- organizational objectives;
- human resource objectives;
- current utilization of human resources;
- internal organizational environment;
- external environment;
- the potential supply of labour.

Planning for resource implications gives an organization the ability to cope with the human resource consequences of any changes in circumstances that may arise. It could also assist in developing new and improved methods of managing employees in order to avoid labour shortfalls or surpluses in the future. The duplication of effort amongst the different sections of the organization can also be avoided, provided the planning has improved the coordination and integration of employees.

Human Rights Act 1998 (UK)

The Human Rights Act incorporates into UK law some of the specific rights and freedoms contained within the European Convention on Human Rights. It came into force on 2 October 2000.

The major implications with regard to human resource management are the adoption of Articles 8, 11 and 14, which cover the following aspects:

- Article 8 addresses situations where employers interfere with communications by employees; this includes intercepting telephone calls or emails. The article also addresses the disclosure of information about an employee to a third party without the employee's consent.

- Article 11 addresses the right to freedom of association, which by inference includes the membership of a **trade union**. It also may subsequently cover an employee's entitlement to request time off for religious holidays or recognized days of rest.
- Article 14 addresses the rights of employees to be protected against **discrimination** on the grounds of gender, race, colour, language, political opinion, national or social origin, birth, status, disability or sexual orientation.

There are other articles within the European Convention which may, in time, depending upon interpretation by the European Court of Human Rights, have an impact on human resources management, including Articles 9 and 10.

Wadham, John and Mountfield, Helen, *Blackstone's Guide to the Human Rights Act 1998.* London: Blackstone Press, 2000.

Huselid, Mark

Huselid was one of the first human resource specialists to look at the connection between human resource practice and a business's performance outcomes. Specifically, he investigated **selection process** and **recruitment**, **training**, **job design**, employee involvement and participation, information sharing, **compensation**, **motivation** and **performance appraisals**. Huselid discovered that there was a close relationship between human resource practices, **labour turnover** and productivity. He also noted that the more sophisticated the human resource function is within a business, the greater the value per employee in terms of productivity and profit. He noted that, initially, human resources management can have an immediate impact, but that its effectiveness plateaus and only when the function becomes more focused can it deliver a longer-term value to the business.

Huselid, Mark, Becker, Brian and Ulrich, Dave, *HR Scorecard: Linking People, Strategy and Performance.* Cambridge, MA: Harvard Business School Press, 2001.

H

Implementation of the Non-discrimination and Equal Opportunity Provisions of the Workforce Investment Act (WIA)

This refers to the Implementation of the Non-discrimination and Equal Opportunity Provisions of the Workforce Investment Act of 1998; Final Rule (11/12/1999)].

See **Workforce Investment Act 1998.**

www.access.gpo.gov/nara/cfr/cfrhtml_00/Title_29/29cfr37_00.html

Incentives

See **fringe benefits** *and* **inducement.**

Indexation

Indexation is a method by which an organization, or human resources department, can attempt to estimate their future employment needs by matching employment growth with a specific index. Typically, figures such as the ratio between employees involved in production, or administration, would be compared with actual sales. In this way a business may be able to predict whether the number of employees engaged in a particular operation is disproportionate to (lower or higher than) what may reasonably be required on the basis of forecasted figures.

Inducement

The term 'inducement' covers pay, benefits and other intangible **incentives** which are part of an overall package offered by an organization in order to attract potential employees. The inducements represent the total benefits or compensations which the employee would expect to receive as a result of accepting a job offer from a particular organization.

Induction

Induction training is a vital function carried out by human resources departments as it provides new employees with their first impressions of the organization. Induction should be seen as part of a continuing process and a vital addition to the overall **recruitment** process. An induction programme helps new employees to understand their new role and to adapt to the **organizational culture**.

The induction process provides an ideal opportunity to effectively indoctrinate new employees with a basic understanding of how their behaviour and attitudes may need modification in order to fit into the organization's expectations of their role. Whilst induction is, in essence, an orientation process, it gradually transforms new employees into individuals who are able to settle into their jobs far more quickly and effectively than those simply thrown in at the deep end and expected to manage without any direction or assistance.

An induction programme does not simply begin when the employee walks through the door on their first day of work. Orientation can begin with what is known as the pre-arrival stage, when information can be relayed to the new employee prior to them officially entering employment. This ongoing dialogue continues through the induction process itself, which is often referred to as the 'encounter' stage. Once the majority of the orientation has taken place the employee then enters the 'metamorphosis', which refers to the stage when they have made the necessary adjustments to the values and norms prevalent in the business.

Fowler, Alan, *A Good Start: Effective Employee Induction*. New York: Hyperion Books, 1990.

Industrial action

Industrial action is often the result of lack of agreement in **dispute resolution**. Industrial action can take a number of different forms, all of which will have been the centre of discussions between **trade union** members, their representatives and the management of the organization. If, after a series of negotiation discussions, there is no resolution to the issue, then trade union representatives have the following options to present to their members:

- To withdraw cooperation with management by ending negotiation and assistance in future dispute resolution, and the compilation of agreements, until the industrial action issue has been resolved.
- To insist on formal rights – this means that the trade union repre-

sentative would bring to the attention of management every issue that arises, however trivial. Normally such trivial incidences would have been dealt with in a less formal manner.

- To withdraw willingness to work **overtime** – this means that employees would not be prepared to work additional hours to those stipulated as their normal working hours. This form of industrial action can have serious implications for an organization that relies on employee cooperation to meet production output targets.
- To work a 'go-slow' – this means that employees will continue to adhere to the requirements of their **contract of employment**, but will not carry out any additional duties, nor respond to urgent requirements or rush jobs as they may emerge.
- Withdrawal of labour – in effect this is strike action, when either a trade union calls for an *unofficial strike*, which could be for short periods of time until the dispute is finally resolved, or in some cases an *official strike* is called, usually when the dispute has remained unresolved for a length of time or a **collective agreement** is thought to have been broken by the employer.

Industrial relations

The term 'industrial relations' has largely negative connotations since it is often preceded by the words 'poor' or 'bad'. As a general term, 'industrial relations' refers to the ongoing dialogue or relationship between employers and employees, which may, or may not, involve aspects of **collective bargaining**, discussions regarding **working conditions**, rewards, job structures and a variety of other human resource topics. Industrial relations also implies an underlying conflict between those who own and control industry and those who provide the labour in order to fuel it. In most countries industrial relations have had periods during which the relationship between employers and employees (largely represented by **trade unions**) has been extremely poor, confrontational and irreconcilable, on the basis that their objectives are mutually exclusive.

The term 'industrial relations' is also interchangeable in many respects with the term 'labour relations', which again refers to the ongoing attitudes of employers and employees towards one another, and their ability or willingness to cooperate on various matters. There is an underlying suspicion for both parties that decisions and stances are taken without regard to the other's desires.

Industrial tribunals

The exact nature and makeup of an industrial tribunal is very dependent upon the individual country involved. For the most part, however, industrial tribunals are concerned with matters such as **unfair dismissal**, **discrimination**, or other alleged breaches of employment law which have resulted in the termination of employment or other disciplinary measures taken against an employee. Increasingly, in most countries, as the result of more stringent legislation, industrial tribunals are becoming more legalistic and formal and have begun to adopt an adversarial nature, rather than being more inquisitorial, as in the past. Industrial tribunals require both parties to present relevant evidence, including documentation and witnesses, in order to pass a judgement based on that country's employment law. For the most part, in Europe, employment law has become standardized as the result of a number of European Directives which, in England, for example, have led to the establishment of **employment appeal tribunals**. The normal composition of an industrial tribunal is a fully qualified, legal representative, who chairs the tribunal, supported by two lay members, normally nominated, one each from an employer organization and an employee organization. The industrial tribunal will hear the case, leaving open the option for either party to make an appeal, first through an employment appeals tribunal and then, perhaps, through a higher court, depending on the complexity of the case.

Industrial Tribunals Act 1996 (UK)

Confusingly, this legislation is known as either the Employment Tribunals Act 1996 or the Industrial Tribunals Act 1996. This Act consolidates information relating to industrial tribunals and the **employment appeal tribunal**.

www.legislation.hmso.gov.uk/acts/acts1996/1996017.htm

Industrial union

An industrial union is a **trade union** which only recruits members from one industry. Notably, however, an industrial union is a vertical union in the sense that it recruits members from all grades, either manual or non-manual, within that industry. There are very few industrial unions left in existence as over the past quarter of a century many unions which had formerly been industrial unions have merged or amalgamated with one another in order to improve their bargaining strength and ensure their continued existence. Membership of industrial unions became extremely fragmented during this period and many of the unions opted for horizontal recruitment, thus making them general unions.

In-house complaints procedure

In-house complaints procedures can be both formal and informal in nature. Clearly, most of the stages, particularly in the case of a formal procedure, have been laid down by policies derived from human resources. These in-house complaints procedures provide employees with an opportunity to begin by making direct contact with their supervisor or manager with a specific complaint. If they are dissatisfied, then they complain to the next tier of management. The procedure continues, rising up the levels of management until a resolution has been achieved.

For the most part, however, in-house complaints procedures tend to be somewhat informal in their nature and are typified by organizations which have an **open door policy**. This allows an employee to speak directly with the person with whom conflict or a problem has occurred. However, it also allows employees the opportunity to refer the matter to someone higher in the **chain of command**, should they feel that it is inappropriate to discuss the matter with their immediate manager or supervisor.

Other organizations choose to use an external service provider in the case of internal complaints. These individuals, although funded by the organization, are deemed to take an objective view of the situation and have been given the responsibility and the authority to investigate matters of complaint. They will seek a resolution within guidelines agreed with the organization.

In-house training

In-house training is seen as a possible alternative to sending individuals out to external training providers or inviting external training providers into the organization itself. The implication of in-house training is that the training itself is delivered by existing employees. Normally, in-house training will be hosted, partially delivered, and organized by human resources departments, who will then identify suitably experienced members of staff who can deliver information or training programmes to other employees. Clearly there are financial benefits in not employing external trainers to carry out this work. However, there may be a limited supply of sufficiently experienced individuals who are prepared to deliver the training within the organization.

The major advantage of in-house training is that organization-specific information can be delivered by practitioners, which is clearly of direct relevance to those assigned to the training programme.

Instant dismissal

Instant dismissal occurs when cases of **gross misconduct**, gross **negligence** or incompetence have taken place. This is the most extreme form of **dismissal** and to be able to justify instant or summary dismissal, an employee's action must have serious repercussions. Generally, theft, assault, drunkenness, drug taking and extreme rudeness to either colleagues or customers are taken to be acceptable examples of cases where instant dismissal is allowable.

Clearly, employees can challenge whether an employer took the right decision in instantly dismissing them. The onus is then on the employer to prove that the employee broke their **contract of employment** by the act. Tribunals or courts will then judge whether the employer's response was justified.

Integrity test

An integrity test usually occurs during the recruitment procedure and is a form of **personality test** which seeks to establish the applicant's trustworthiness and honesty.

Internal equity

Internal equity as a concept is not unlike **external equity**. It differs in the sense that employees feel that an organization's pay structure is fair and transparent. Internal equity suggests that the organization will have made the positive decision to provide similar rewards (although, perhaps, not identical) to those in similar jobs throughout the organization. In other words, those individuals who have broadly the same duties and responsibilities are rewarded financially in exactly the same manner.

Internal recruitment

Internal recruitment involves the matching of an individual who already works for the organization to a vacancy. In the majority of cases an organization would routinely offer vacancies or forthcoming vacancies to their existing employees prior to, or simultaneously with, an **external**

recruitment drive. Internal recruitment has a number of advantages, which are:

- The applicant will already know the organization and the way in which work is carried out, and will therefore be more likely to settle in quickly.
- Recruitment costs are significantly reduced, although an interviewing process may be necessary if there are multiple internal applications. Human resources managers would still have to match the candidate's skills and expertise against the vacancy, but most of the normal recruitment procedure is unnecessary.
- Internal recruitment, and particularly the opportunity to gain promotion, is a strong motivator for existing employees.

There are, however, a number of disadvantages, which are:

- The range of applicants will be limited.
- The applicants may not be able to offer anything particularly new, which might have been the case had an external applicant been considered.
- The need to externally recruit will still be there because when the internal applicant has been assigned to the current vacancy, a new vacancy will arise when they leave the previous job.

Internet recruiting

See **e-recruiting.**

Interviewee error

The interviewee is the person being interviewed. The term 'interviewee error' relates to mistakes that may have been made by this individual during the interview process. Typically, errors such as lack of preparation, lack of concentration or not listening sufficiently to questions posed are common, as are the interviewee's tendency to boast about their accomplishments. Such errors tend to reduce the usefulness and validity of the interview and do little to assist the **applicant** or the interviewer.

Interviewer error

The interviewer is the person conducting the interview. The term 'interviewer error' relates to mistakes that an interviewer can make during the interview process that may affect the interviewee's performance or interest in joining an organization. Typical examples of interviewer error include showing a strong bias about an aspect of the questioning, or portraying a dominant attitude towards the interviewee.

Interviews/interviewing

An interview is a face-to-face meeting, often held between employees and managers of the same organization, but often involving an individual who is external to the business. Very often interviews will be a regular part of the function of human resource departments in order to discuss the effectiveness, or otherwise, of programmes, systems and activities in place within the organization. In addition, human resource department personnel could be involved in interview situations for any of the following reasons:

- A selection interview – which involves the meeting with an **applicant** for a position within the organization. The selection interview would aim to give a greater insight into the candidate's ability to do the job. It also allows the human resources personnel to judge the candidate's motives, personality and behaviour, evaluate the relevance of their qualifications and experience and provide the candidate with further information about the organization and the job role involved. Often the selection interview is carried out on a one-to-one basis, but it is not uncommon for an organization to be represented by more than one current employee. These *multiple interviews* can take the form of what are known as *panel interviews* or *board interviews*. In these cases a cross-section of the senior management of the organization will interview the potential new employee.
- A **counselling** interview – which is used in order to discuss problems and provide advice and information to an individual employee. Counselling interviews tend to be informal in nature and to always be held in private, uninterrupted conditions.
- A **discipline** interview – which seeks to reprimand an employee as a result of a complaint made regarding their conduct or behaviour while at work. The employee has the right to have a **trade union** representative present at such an interview and in cases of a serious discipline problem; a written confirmation of what has been discussed will be required.

Intrinsic reward

Intrinsic rewards are intangible rewards which are largely personal in nature. Intrinsic rewards include feelings of satisfaction and accomplishment at having completed a particular task. Intrinsic rewards are not usually derived from mundane or routine duties or tasks, but rather they are related to challenging situations which require a degree of application in order to complete. Within any **job design** there should be an inherent opportunity for the worker to feel an intrinsic reward for having completed certain aspects of that job.

Investors in People (IIP) (UK)

'Investors in People' as a standard of good practice in the training and development of employees was developed during 1990 by the National Training Task Force (in partnership organizations such as the Confederation of British Industry (CBI), the Trades Union Congress (TUC) and the Institute of Personnel and Development (IPD) as well as the Employment Department).

The standard aims to provide a national framework for the improvement of business performance and competitiveness by developing people to achieve these objectives. The IIP standards are based on four key issues or principles:

- Commitment to invest in people to achieve business goals.
- Planning how skills, individuals and teams are to be developed to achieve these goals.
- Taking action to develop and use necessary skills in a well-defined and continuing programme directly tied to business objectives.
- Evaluating outcomes of training and development for individuals' progress towards goals, the value achieved and future needs.

www.iipuk.co.uk

Janis, Irving

See **group think.**

Jarvis, Peter

See **experiential learning.**

Job analysis

Job analysis is a process which seeks to identify the component parts or elements of a particular job role. There are several different areas which provide sources of information regarding the exact nature of the job which are integral to analysing a job successfully (see Table 13).

The process of analysing a job usually follows a fixed set of procedures, also known as a **job analysis schedule**.

Prannick, Michael T. and Levine, Edward L., *Job Analysis: Methods, Research and Applications for Human Resource Management in the New Millennium*. Thousand Oaks, CA: Corwin Press, 2002.

Job analysis schedule

A job analysis schedule is a multi-stepped process which aims to analyse the exact nature of a specific job. The chart in Figure 17 describes one such way in which this may be achieved.

The steps are more clearly described in the following manner:

- Identify jobs and review existing documentation – typical documentation would include **job descriptions**, organization charts, previous **job analysis** information. In identifying the job itself, analysis can take the form of analysing an individual job or specific **job roles** within a division or the whole organization.
- Explain the process to managers and employees – it is imperative that both managers and employees receive an explanation as to why the job analysis is under way, what steps will be involved and, if possible, the timescale. This will enable the analyst to encourage these individuals to participate and identify who should be contacted when issues arise.

Table 13 Sources of information for job analysis

Information source	Description
Work activities	What is actually done? What are the tasks which make up the job and what is their relative timing and importance? Are the tasks complex or simple?
Job context	Where is the job physically located? What are the working conditions? Is supervision necessary?
Work aids	What equipment, machinery or tools are immediately required to carry out the work?
How job is performed	What are the precise operations involved? How are they measured and what standards do they need to conform to?
Personnel requirements	What experience, training, education, physical abilities, dexterity, aptitudes or social skills are required of the individual doing the job?
Job relations	How reliant is the job on cooperation? Is immediate supervision required? What advancement opportunities are there and what are the usual patterns of promotion?
Job tangibles and intangibles	In terms of tangibles, what resources are consumed or required by the job? With regard to intangibles, what services are required in order to facilitate the job?

- Conduct the job analysis – typically interviews may be conducted, observations made or questionnaires used to collect the specific information.
- Prepare job descriptions and specifications – on the basis of the information collected, new job descriptions and job specifications can now be drafted. It is vital that existing employees and their managers are encouraged to participate and amend as necessary.
- Maintain and update job descriptions and specifications – rather than having to periodically repeat the entire process, job analysts should routinely review and update job descriptions and specifications, should circumstances and the nature of the job visibly change.

Mathis, Robert L. and Jackson, John Harold (eds), *Human Resource Management: Essential Perspectives*. Mason, OH: South-Western College Publications, 2001.

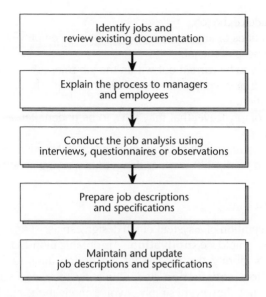

Figure 17   Example of a job analysis schedule

Source: Adapted from Mathis and Jackson, *Human Resource Management: Essential Perspectives*.

Job code

Job codes are often employed by human resources managers in order to facilitate the rapid identification of a particular job and its content. Job codes consist of a series of letters or numbers, and in some cases both, which summarize the description of a job and its immediate associations.

Job description

The main purpose of a job description is to define the job role and the intended tasks to be carried out within that role. It is vital to the success of the selection process of recruitment that the job description is exact in its nature, both for the benefit of the organization and for the new employee. Typically, a job description would include the following:

- The title of the job.
- The location at which the work is to be carried out. This might be a branch of the organization or the department or section within which the new employee will be based.
- The title of the new employee's immediate line manager.

- The grade of the job.
- The job titles of any subordinates of the new employee.
- The purpose of the job.
- The tasks to be carried out within the job role.
- Details of any equipment, machinery or other job- or skill-specific information.
- Details of any travel that may have to be undertaken as part of the job role.
- Details of any additional work requirements, such as overtime, weekend work, shift work or dangerous working conditions.

Job design

The implementation of a system of job design can assist an organization in increasing employee **motivation**. An organization that carries out **job analysis** during the process of job design aims to improve its employees' **job satisfaction** and ultimately their performance. Job design does not, however, simply involve motivation, but has added determining factors which may restrict or limit the job. These are:

- technology;
- the cost of providing essential equipment or materials;
- resistance from current employees or their representatives;
- the organizational structure of the business.

If a job has significantly changed, then an organization might choose to amend the job by using **job enrichment**, **job enlargement**, **job rotation** and accordingly amend the employees' **job descriptions**, rather than go through the costly and time-consuming process of a new job design.

Wall, Toby and Parker, Sharon, *Job and Work Design: Organizing Work to Promote Well-Being and Effectiveness*. London: Sage Publications, 1998.

Job enlargement

As an alternative to designing a new job, an organization might decide to redesign the parameters of an existing job to incorporate additional required tasks. Job enlargement involves an employee having to expand his or her job role to carry out additional, but similar, activities. Although it is often hoped that this enlargement of tasks will lead to a higher level of **job satisfaction** and **motivation**, it has to be remembered that once the enlarged job has been orientated, then there is a risk that this job, too, will become boring. An organization would need to ensure that this job enlargement process does not simply incorporate into a tedious job yet another set of equally tedious tasks. However, it has been concluded that the job enlargement process does give employees a greater degree of job satisfaction and that their performance is improved as a result of the process as compared with those who remain in restricted job roles. From an organizational point of view, however, the job enlargement process can be a costly exercise, with few guaranteed benefits.

Job enrichment

Job enrichment is, effectively, another form of **job enlargement**, but one in which the employee often finds a higher degree of **job satisfaction** and **motivation**. The closest type of job enrichment to job enlargement is known as 'horizontal job enrichment', which involves the incorporation of similar tasks into the job for the employee. This often proves not to be as satisfactory as the more successful form of job enrichment, known as 'vertical job enrichment'.

Vertical job enrichment involves an individual employee being given the opportunity to see the task in hand through to its completion. This allows the employee to become involved in related but not necessarily similar tasks, allowing a higher degree of motivation. Research has identified that this type of job enrichment has both short- and longer-term effects. After approximately three months the employees' performance levels have been shown to decrease, possibly as a result of the difficulties faced in taking on board the added considerations of their enriched role. However, after approximately six months these employees show an improvement in their original performance levels, possibly because they have had the time to develop confidence in what they are doing.

Peters, Tom, *Projects 50: Or, 50 Ways to Transform Every Task into a Project that Matters.* New York: Alfred A. Knopf, 1999.

Savall, Henri, *Work and People: An Economic Evaluation of Job-enrichment.* Oxford: Oxford University Press, 1981.

Job evaluation

An organization can undertake a process of job evaluation in a number of different ways, the three most common being:

- by placing the different jobs in ranking order so that the value of each job can be identified;
- by grading the job from the **job specification** point of view;
- by giving each job a points rating, again from the job specification point of view.

The considerations of each of these job evaluation methods are given in Table 14.

The job evaluation process is carried out by the human resource department, in collaboration with functional managers, in order to ensure that the pay structure matches the demands and conditions of jobs. The process looks in detail at:

- the tasks involved in each job;
- the responsibilities and obligations of each of the post holders;
- the skills used in each job;

Table 14   Job evaluation methods

Job evaluation method	Considerations
Ranking	A committee will often be established to rank different jobs according to their worth to the organization. This is an inexpensive and speedy process for smaller organizations to use, provided they have a sensible pay structure in place. Larger organizations may have difficulties using this method as experience has proved that issues regarding pay inequality have been the outcome.
Grading	Normally this process is taken from the job descriptions, with the job requiring the lowest degree of skills or the highest level of supervision being the starting point. Jobs are then graded from this starting point according to the skills, knowledge and responsibility involved. This is a straightforward way of carrying out the job evaluation process, although there are significant numbers of routine jobs that are difficult to categorize in this way, particularly again in larger organizations.
Points rating	This is possibly the most popular way of carrying out job evaluation. Several factors contribute to the measurement of the job, including the skills and degree of effort required, the responsibilities undertaken and the working conditions within which the job is undertaken. These basic starting points are often expanded by creating subdivisions within each factor with a number of points being allocated for each. Where one particular skill or level of expertise is imperative to a job, then this score is then doubled, trebled or quadrupled to reflect its importance.

- the knowledge required for each job;
- the initiative required by each of the post holders;
- the ability of each individual post holder to cope with stress;
- the organization's requirements to plan for the future;
- the organization's need to control employees;
- the overall coordination of the organization's environment.

Having established a need for the job evaluation process and categorized each job using the most suitable method, the organization would place a monetary value on each of the jobs. They would do this to ensure that:

- the pay administration process is as uncomplicated as possible;
- internal rates of pay can be harmonized;
- each of the jobs receives a reasonable rate of pay;
- each of the post holders can see the possibility of promotion to a higher job grade.

Quaid, Maeve, *Job Evaluation: The Myth of Equitable Assessment*. Toronto: University of Toronto Press, 1996.

Job families

Job families can be typified as attempts to group jobs which are closely related. Each job within the job family will share a common set of responsibilities, duties or skills. The identification of job families can assist human resources managers in the processes of defining **cross-training** opportunities, **multi-skilling**, and potential transfer of individuals from a current role to another job-related role. Job families can also help define the fundamentals of a salary structure, identifying the scale of related and interconnected jobs within the organization, through which an individual may be able to logically progress.

Typically job families will encompass broad ranges of jobs, including finance, general administration, information technology, technical or sales departments and customer relations, etc.

Job grading

Job grading is an appraisal method that gives each individual employee an allocation in a set of predetermined categories, based on their overall performance in the job role. The grades are:

Poor   Below average   Average   Above average   Exceptional.

Job grading is used to assess the likely future uses of the employee and to determine pay scales for each job. The appraiser has to know the individual employee quite well for this process to be undertaken and often there is criticism in the form of an **error of central tendency**.

Job identity

In many respects job identity is rather similar to a **job code** in as much as it is an identification of the key aspects of the **job description**, job title, grade or rank (in terms of its status), and of where, physically, an individual holding this job would be based (geographic location or department). Job identities are used by human resources management as a short-cut means of identifying specific jobs, which may aid them in **job grading** and the grouping of jobs into **job families**. They can also form the basis of early assessments, such as **job evaluation** and **job design**.

Job performance standards

See **performance standards**.

Job progression ladder

A job progression ladder is the formal identification of a specific career path within an organization. Typically, job progression ladders will be constructed as part of the identification of **job families**. The progression or possible career path of the jobs within the ladder identify the prerequisites in terms of skills, training, education or experience which may be required as an individual gradually moves up the ladder in the organization.

Job ranking

Job ranking follows similar lines to job grading in that it requires managers to rank employees on their merit and capabilities of carrying out the set of activities involved in their job role. This form of performance appraisal does not identify any training or retraining and development needs, but simply establishes the merit of the employee, often for purposes of pay increases or the future use of the employee within the organization.

Job redesign

See **job analysis**; **job analysis schedule**; **job enlargement**; **job enrichment**; **job evaluation**; and **job rotation**.

Job rotation

Job rotation is a way of extending or enlarging the tasks carried out by employees. It involves the training, or retraining, of employees so that they are capable of exchanging jobs with one another, often on a regular and pre-determined basis. Job rotation can often lead to increased **job satisfaction** because employees feel that they have a fuller picture of the related jobs and feel more involved in the organization as a whole. The employees also feel more versatile and consider that the scheme gives them a wider variety of tasks, as well as eliminating the need for them to carry out difficult or disliked tasks regularly, as they only have to confront these tasks on an infrequent basis.

The main benefits to an organization of introducing a job rotation system are that they have constant cover for periods of holiday or sickness. Individual employees can, however, feel that they are constantly on the move and not given sufficient time for the development of specific skills, particularly if the process is carried out during times of high demand, when they often consider they have left a job with too many loose ends still not dealt with. Additionally, levels of competence also have to be reasonably parallel, otherwise some employees could find themselves completing the bulk of the tasks involved in the job whilst the next employee finds little to do.

The question of **motivation** through job rotation is a questionable one as often employees are motivated at the introduction of the system, but once they have grasped the aspects of the new tasks involved, they find little reason to continue to strive. The job rotation scheme is an ideal system to be put in place by an organization employing large numbers of unskilled or semi-skilled workers.

Job satisfaction

The term 'job satisfaction' refers to the attitude employees have to the work they carry out. Clearly a positive attitude is more favourable for all concerned than a negative one. Sometimes the degree of job satisfaction that an individual employee has depends on the degree of involvement they have in the organization as a whole. Researchers have found that employees tend to have a higher degree of job satisfaction if they:

- are in a job which suits their personality and expertise;
- carry out a balanced number of mentally challenging tasks;
- feel they are being justly rewarded by receiving a fair day's work for a fair day's pay;

- have the appropriate resources available to them within a good working environment;
- have supportive managers and colleagues.

Research has also discovered, however, that job satisfaction does not necessarily lead to increased productivity, particularly for unskilled and semi-skilled workers.

Robbins, Stephen, *Organizational Behaviour*. Englewood Cliffs, NJ: Prentice-Hall, 1991.

Job sharing

Job share is one of the ways an organization can arrange **alternative work arrangements**. This working arrangement has become more popular in recent years as managers have discovered that job sharing can be beneficial to the organization and that employees often find it more convenient. Job sharers find that they can approach the job in a fresher and more positive manner because they are only working for a part of the week, as opposed to a complete week. Commonly employees embarking on a job share scheme are able to choose the hours that they work and this is often arranged via negotiation with their partner job sharer. This gives each of the job sharers time to deal with domestic issues whilst maintaining a percentage of their income from the organization. There can be drawbacks for an employee, however, particularly if one of the job sharers is more organized than the other, or if one of the days worked is the busiest time of the week for the organization. Like all part-time workers, job sharers have the same employment rights as full-timers

From an organizational point of view, employers often benefit from the fact that there are two individuals, each with different ideas, available to input into the activities of the business. Job sharing can increase flexibility when used to meet peak demand, for instance by both sharers being present when workloads are heavy. There is greater continuity because one sharer can carry on with at least half the work if the other partner is absent through sickness, holiday or **maternity leave**.

Disadvantages can include the extra costs of induction, training and administration. There may also be problems if the individuals sharing a job perform differently and thus produce an inconsistent output or level of productivity. Job sharers may also find it difficult to communicate with each other as they are not usually at work at the same time. If one job sharer leaves, it may be difficult to find someone to complement the hours worked by the remaining sharer. If the job share involves the managing or supervising of staff, this may create difficulties for the employees involved as they may find the two sharers have differing styles of management.

Job specification

A job specification would be drawn up by an organization in order to identify a number of key issues related to a post. Initially a **job analysis** would be completed and from this research into the nature of the job, the job specification would define:

- the qualifications required;
- the experience, knowledge and skills required;
- the personal qualities required;
- any other special demands the job might have.

The purpose of the production of a job specification is to enhance the **interview** stage of the recruitment process and to enable the interviewer to ask appropriate and enlightening questions of the potential new employee. It is vital that the level of qualification required is precise in the job specification and that the requirements are not pitched at either too high or too low a level. There are two recognized ways of analysing the information on a job specification, the seven-point plan and the five-point plan.

The seven-point plan was developed by Alec Rodger and covers:

- physical make-up required – this looks at health, physique, appearance, bearing and speech issues;
- attainments – this is where the education, qualifications and experience required will be stipulated;
- general intelligence – this is the intellectual level required;
- special aptitudes – this is where considerations such as manual dexterity, communication or number skills or those in the use of particular equipment or machinery will be included;
- interests – this section would identify whether the individual needs to be physically fit, practical, artistic etc.;
- disposition – this section would identify whether the individual has to be of a certain nature, for example, steady, reliable, self-reliant, able to influence others;
- circumstances – this would relate to the individual's domestic circumstances and the occupations of their family.

Munro Fraser designed the five-point, or five-fold, grading system, which is often considered to be simpler and concentrates more on the previous career of the **applicant**. The five-fold system looks at:

J

- Impact on others – this looks at issues such as the potential employee's physical make-up, appearance, communication skills and general manner.
- Acquired qualifications – education, training, qualifications and, where appropriate, work experience carried out.
- Innate abilities – this aspect considers the potential employee's aptitude for learning, and quickness of comprehension.
- Motivation – this aspect considers whether the potential employee has set personal goals, aims, targets or objectives and whether or not they have achieved them.
- Adjustment – this considers issues such as emotional stability, ability to deal with stressful situations, and the individual's nature with regard to getting along with others.

Prannick, Michael T. and Levine, Edward L., *Job Analysis: Methods, Research and Applications for Human Resource Management in the New Millennium*. Thousand Oaks, CA: Corwin Press, 2002.

J

Kanter, Rosabeth Moss

Rosabeth Moss Kanter has written a wide variety of different books, primarily on management and management techniques. One of her main concepts brought together **empowerment**, organizational **change management** and bureaucracy. Kanter is a strong supporter of participative management and claims that management should use employees in order to achieve synergy within the organization. She also is a strong supporter of **flat organization structures**, with less **hierarchical** control over the organization, which she feels would stifle empowerment and entrepreneurial opportunities.

Kanter, Rosabeth Moss, *Rosabeth Moss Kanter on the Frontiers of Management*. Cambridge, MA: Harvard Business School Press, 1997.

Kennedy and Deal

See **organizational culture.**

Knowledge management

Knowledge management can be seen as one of the key factors of organizational development. Knowledge management recognizes that information and ability are among the most valuable assets an organization possesses. In the past, organizations have not been able to quantify or recognize this aspect as being one of their prime assets, as it is intangible. Knowledge is not just information or data, it needs to have a meaning and a purpose, and in human resources this means the ability to apply and use information. In other words, knowledge management is all about people and the ability to use information. There is no compelling definition of the term 'knowledge management' and it has been variously described as intellectual capital or property, amongst a variety of other different attempts to explain its purpose and worth.

The key concern for human resources is the retaining of individuals who are able to impart knowledge as an essential function of their relationship with the business. This knowledge management is a complex process, but includes questions as to how to share knowledge, how to find it, how to use it and how to convert it or transfer it from one individual to another.

Davenport, Thomas H. and Prusak, Laurence, *Working Knowledge: How Organizations Manage What They Know*. Cambridge, MA: Harvard Business School Press, 2000.
von Krogh, Georg, Ichijo, Kazua and Nonaka, Ikujiro, *Enabling Knowledge Creation*. Oxford: Oxford University Press, 2000.

Knowledge test

A knowledge test is essentially an examination which seeks to quantify an employee's knowledge or understanding of information.

Knowledge workers

A knowledge worker is typified as being an employee who may have a job title such as business analyst, researcher or practice consultant. In essence, a knowledge worker is an individual who generates, processes and analyses ideas on behalf of the organization. These are the individuals who are the primary subject of **knowledge management** as it is their ability to manipulate information and data, and process it in such a way as to be of value to the business, which can give the organization a competitive edge and the ability to understand the environment in which it operates. Knowledge workers will usually apply information and data to theoretical models or ideas, test them and assess their value in terms of their applicability to the organization.

Cortada, James (ed.), *Rise of the Knowledge Worker*. Oxford: Butterworth-Heinemann Management Division, 1998.
Feldman, Susan F., *Surviving the Information Age: Online Users' Guide for Today's Knowledge Worker*. Independent Publishing Group, 1997.

K

Kolb, David

See **experiential learning**.

Kotter and Schlesinger

Kotter and Schlesinger recognized that many employees are inherently resistant to change. There are enormous implications arising out of change, which could affect an individual's opportunities of promotion, pay, or the fact that they may need to travel to an alternative location. The theorists attempted to classify why employees may be resistant to change and suggested four broad categories, as described in Table 15.

Table 15 Why employees resist change

Reason for resisting change	Description
Parochial self-interest	This category suggests that individuals are more concerned with the impact of change on themselves and how it might affect their future, rather than considering the continued success of the business. Change for these individuals means losing something which they value and, as such, they will resist the change. There is a danger that if enough individuals feel this way, then they will collaborate to block the change.
Misunderstanding	Essentially this is a communication problem. Inadequate information has been passed to the employees by the management and, as a result, much of what the employees know and understand has been derived from **grapevine communication**. At the root of this, the employees do not trust the management and will seek to find alternative explanations as to why the management are instituting the changes.
Different assessment of the situation	Not all employees will see that there are good enough reasons for instituting the changes. Each will seek to find reasons why the changes are being proposed and they will come to their own conclusions, which may inevitably lead to resistance. It should not be assumed that even with the most complete and open consultation process, all individuals will reach the same conclusions.
Low tolerance to change	These individuals value their security and stability in work. The introduction of new systems or processes will tend to undermine their self-belief. The management will need to recognize that there is fear, and reassure the employees, otherwise they may resist the change.

K

Kotter and Schlesinger suggested a number of ways in which management could seek to minimize resistance to change:

- through education and communication;
- through participation and involvement;

- through facilitation and support;
- through negotiation and agreement;
- through manipulation and co-opting;
- through explicit and implicit coercion.

Kotter, J. P. and Schlesinger, L. A., 'Choosing Strategies for Change', *Harvard Business Review*, 57 (1979), pp. 106–14.

K

L

Labor-Management Reporting and Disclosure Act (LMRDA) 1959 (US)

The Labor-Management Reporting and Disclosure Act, also known as the Landrum–Griffin Act, resulted from the perception of improper activities in the fields of labour and management (collusion between dishonest employers and union officials, the use of violence and the diversion and misuse of labour union funds).

The Act regulated internal union affairs, and banned former Communist Party members or former convicts from holding office for at least five years from the time of their resignation from the Party or release from prison. The Act supports a union member's right to freedom of speech and secret elections. Secondary boycotting and picketing are restricted by the Act.

www.dol.gov/esa/regs/statutes/olms/lmrda.htm

www.dol.gov/dol/compliance/comp-lmrda.htm

Laboratory training

Laboratory training is a specific form of group training which is primarily used to improve the participants' interpersonal skills. Typically, laboratory training will be directed at existing teams; they are given a series of scenarios in which they will be required to cooperate and interact, using their collective skills and experience, in order to successfully achieve pre-determined goals.

Labour flexibility

Labour flexibility is a measure of a business's ability to change the jobs or the nature of the jobs carried out by its employees. Labour flexibility depends on employee attitudes, specifically their resistance to change. It may also be restricted by a **trade union** or an employee's representative's view of how their members should be employed. One of the other key factors is the ability of the workers to engage in **multi-skilling**.

Labour intensive

'Labour intensive' describes workplace situations where the processes involved in either producing or managing the production of a particular product require a higher than usual level of staffing.

Labour market analysis

The term 'labour market analysis' has two distinct meanings. The more generalized definition involves a government or industry's attempts to identify and quantify trends across a local, regional, national or international labour market. Typically they will attempt to identify shifts or possible shifts in the makeup of the overall labour market in order to predict the possible impact of an increase or decrease in demand for employees in specific areas of industry. In analysing the market, governments, or agencies working on behalf of governments, can seek to predict where labour shortages may occur, or where there may be instances of over-supply of particular employees.

The term is also applicable to a specific business, although the basis of much of the research may be centred around information which has been gathered by governments or agencies. In relation to a business's current trends in terms of sales and potential demand, it too will forecast, or try to predict, its presumed employee requirements into the future. The business will need to ascertain what the manpower requirements may be and how fluctuations in the labour market may affect its ability to attract sufficient employees at some possible point in the future. This labour market analysis will enable human resources managers to take immediate steps to search for suitable employees and, perhaps, review the overall payment and benefits packages in order to attract employees in cases where certain skills are likely to be in short supply.

L

Labour mobility

'Labour mobility' refers to the willingness of potential employees to seek work in a broader, or different, geographical location. It is distinct from occupational mobility, as this is a measure of an individual's propensity to move between jobs. Occupational mobility can often become a key factor in a human resources department's function in attracting ideal candidates to fill specific job roles, despite the fact that they may live a considerable distance from where the job is physically located.

Labour stability

Labour stability examines a business's ability to sustain or retain as many of its employees as possible. Typically, the level of labour stability is measured on a year-by-year basis, comparing the proportion of individuals who started in employment with the business at a certain point with those who still remain one year after that date. In effect, it is an alternative measure of **labour turnover**.

Labour turnover

Labour turnover, or employee turnover, is a measure of the rate at which employees are leaving a business. There are two effective measures in calculating labour turnover, these are:

Number of employees who left the organization/the total (average) number of employees in the organization × 100

This provides a percentage figure. Alternatively, turnover rate can be calculated as:

Number of employees who left the organization/total number of employees in the organization.

Turnover rates can differ widely from business to business and, indeed, from industry to industry. It is more common for younger and newer employees to leave a business than for older or more established members of staff.

Having identified the labour turnover rate, a business now needs to address why the turnover rate is at the level it is. There are obvious circumstances in which management has no control over the turnover rate, these typically include factors such as illness, pregnancy, marriage, or the relocation of a partner or spouse. Most other reasons can actually be avoided by effective human resource policies and procedures and, in many cases, a considerable change in outlook by the management itself. In order, therefore, to work out the underlying trend of labour turnover, it is imperative that a further calculation is made using the following formula, which counts only those who have left for unavoidable reasons. The formula is:

Total number of employees leaving for unavoidable reasons/total number of employees

This figure provides the business with the underlying trend. The loss of employees or a business's inability to retain its staff or deal with **attri-**

L

tion represents a considerable expense, as not only are there interruptions in productivity, as it is often the employees who have learned to do the job efficiently who have chosen to leave, but there is also the additional expense of having to launch a recruitment drive to replace them. Typically, reasons for high turnover may relate to comparatively low pay, low morale, ineffective or authoritarian leadership, or more attractive job opportunities elsewhere.

Learning and Skills Act 2000 (UK)

The Learning and Skills Act 2000 established the Learning and Skills Council (LSC), with 47 local arms, to be responsible for the planning, funding and quality assurance of all post-16 learning and skills delivery in England. The Act also provided for:

- Comprehensive and rigorous independent arrangements for the inspection of post-16 learning in England (Ofsted and the Adult Learning Inspectorate).
- Establishment of the Connexions Service to provide integrated support services for all 13- to 19-year-olds, including information, advice and guidance services.
- The setting up of individual learning accounts offering discounts on learning, and incentives for employers who contribute to their employees' learning.
- The creation of City Academies to replace seriously failing secondary schools in urban areas.

www.legislation.hmso.gov.uk/acts/acts2000/20000021.htm

Learning curve

A learning curve shows the relationship between an individual's performance and the amount of time he or she spends learning, but can also be interpreted as an individual's level of ability or motivation. Very often the individual will reach a stage known as the *learning plateau*, where little progress is seen to be made. However, this tends to be a temporary stage, sometimes due to lack of motivation, but also likely to be as a result of the need to refresh or revise what has been learned to date before further progress can be achieved.

The rate of learning very much depends on the difficulty of the task involved and often the learning plateau is reached on more than one occasion (see Figure 18).

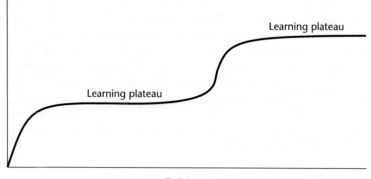

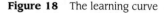

Figure 18   The learning curve

Learning organization

An exact definition of the term 'learning organization' is somewhat problematic since there are a number of different categories of learning organization. The essential encompassing concept is that organizations learn from external stimuli and, as a result, alter or amend their internal framework to match those opportunities. This requires a re-evaluation of goals and, in extreme circumstances, a change in **organizational culture**, organizational structure, and patterns of work, in order to take advantage of the new opportunities.

The main recognized categories of learning organizations are:

- the knowing organizations – which tend to be businesses in static or mature markets;
- the understanding and thinking organizations – which are prepared to adapt their culture and structure within certain parameters;
- the learning organizations – which accept change as being both necessary and desirable, and are ultimately the businesses which drive their competitors to mimic them.

Clearly a human resources department which operates in a learning organization, of whatever type, has to be far more adaptable and flexible, as well as effective and efficient, in driving changes within the organization. It has been recognized that there are two stages of evolution in a learning organization, of which human resources are an integral part. The first is known as a single-loop or adaptive learning organization, where new techniques and ideas are assimilated. The second type

L

of learning organization is known as a double-loop or generative learning organization. In this case the business continually evaluates its goals and objectives, as well as its organizational culture, to suit any emerging external opportunities. Both forms of learning organization offer considerable challenges to human resources departments, who have to quickly learn that they are in an ever-shifting and adaptive organization.

Chawla, Sarita, *Learning Organizations: Developing Cultures for Tomorrow's Workplace*. New York: Productivity Press, 1995.

Kline, Peter and Saunders, Bernhard, *Ten Steps to a Learning Organization*. Arlington, VA: Great Ocean Publishers, 1998.

Leniency bias

This is a tendency to rate employees higher than their performance justifies. The term is most usually associated with performance appraisals. Leniency bias may exist because supervisors are concerned about damaging a good working relationship by giving an unfavourable rating or they may wish to avoid giving negative feedback. Both objective and subjective assessments can give rise to biases. Objective assessments cause too much effort to be diverted towards the easily measurable tasks. Subjective assessment gives rise to 'leniency bias', where supervisors are reluctant to give bad ratings to workers, and/or 'centrality bias', where ratings are overly compressed.

Mathis, R. L. and Jackson, J. H., *Human Resource Management*. St Paul, MA: West Publishing, 1994.

Lewin, Kurt

Kurt Lewin, in the 1950s, identified three stages which individuals, groups or organizations pass through when dealing with change (see Table 16).

Lewin, Kurt, *Field Theory in Social Science: Selected Theoretical Papers*. London: Tavistock Publications, 1967.

Lewin, Kurt, *Resolving Social Conflicts and Field Theory in Social Science*. Washington, DC: American Psychological Association, 1997.

Likert, Rensis (1903–81)

Likert was a management theorist concerned with human behaviour within organizations. He examined different types of organization and styles of leadership. At the heart of his theories he believed that an organization needed to make optimum use of its human assets in order to

Table 16 Stages in coping with change

Stage	Description
Unfreezing	This stage calls on the management and human resources personnel to make it clear to employees that there is a requirement to make a change in the business. Employees are consulted, changes are planned, and organized, and schedules and appropriate training is arranged.
Changing	This is the actual implementation of the changes, which rests upon the flexibility of the planning process and the steps which have been taken during the unfreezing stage.
Refreezing	Now that the change has been implemented, an assessment needs to be made of how effective and satisfactory the change has been. Whatever the new systems or procedures which have now been put in place, these are effectively the new ways of doing things and should now be fully accepted by the employees and the organization as a whole.

achieve maximum profitability, via good labour relations and high productivity. Likert believed that the workforce should be organized into work groups supported by other similarly effective groups. Likert identified four different types of management style:

- *Exploitative/authoritative* – where decisions are made by the management alone and motivation is ensured by threats. Higher-level management has the bulk of the responsibilities whilst lower-level management has little responsibility other than day-to-day operations. The system is characterized by having poor upward and downward communication, as well as the absence of teamwork.
- *Benevolent/authoritative* – this is essentially a master and servant relationship between the management and employees. It is on this basis that trust is maintained, and motivation is assured through rewards. Management is made to feel responsible for the employees, but there is little communication up and down the organization, neither is there any developed form of teamwork.
- *Consultative* – this system shows that managers have a degree of trust in their employees, but not a total belief in their abilities or ideas. Motivation is achieved through reward and the opportunity to be involved, at least partially, in the decision making. Higher management are primarily responsible for achieving organizational

goals. Horizontal communication and vertical communication, as well as teamwork, are used moderately.

- *Participative group system* – this illustrates circumstances where the management has confidence in its subordinates. Motivation is based on economic rewards, firmly based on goals which have been set in participation. All personnel have a responsibility to achieve the organizational goals. As a consequence, all forms of communication work well and cooperative teamwork is encouraged. This is the system which Likert believed is the ideal in order to ensure both profit and concern for employees.

Achieving the participative group system may take an organization a considerable period of time. Likert recognized that there were four primary factors which would need to be put into practice in order to achieve the ideal:

- Old systems of rewards and threats needed to be swept away and replaced with more modern principles.
- Management would need to recognize that employees had their own needs, values and desires and that employees' self-worth needed to be fostered.
- In order to achieve the objectives of the organization, employees needed to be organized into close and effective workgroups.
- Within these workgroups not only mutual respect was required, but also internal and external supportive relationships.

In creating these workgroups, at the centre of a participative group system, the groups themselves should have the following features:

- Membership roles should be clear and there should be skilled leadership within each group.
- After a period of existence, each workgroup would be able to work with relaxed relationships.
- Group loyalty and mutual trust would aid the effectiveness of each group.
- The values and goals of the group should be an expression of the needs and values of its membership.
- Each group should recognize the goals of other workgroups in order to foster harmony across the organization.

Likert, Rensis, *Human Organization: Its Management and Value*. New York: McGraw-Hill, 1967.

Line authority

The term 'line authority' is applied to individuals who have a direct management responsibility for a number of subordinates. The concept of line authority is integral to the **chain of command**, in which successive levels of management have line authority (responsibility) for all those individuals who are technically, in the hierarchy, lower than them in the organization. Line authority is distinguished from staff authority in the sense that the latter refers to management or supervisors, who have a specific responsibility for an aspect of an employee's work. Examples of staff authority would include human resources personnel, who, technically, have authority in certain respects towards all employees, regardless of grade or position in the hierarchy. Line managers, however, have line authority and can, on a daily basis, exert decisions upon those over whom they have responsibility.

Locus of control

Julian Rotter developed his theory of locus of control in order to determine what happens to people as a direct result of past experiences. His research concluded that there were two types, or extremes, of individuals, the internalizer and the externalizer. Rotter's conclusions about internalizers and externalizers are given in Table 17. Further research into this concept was carried out by Blau, Storms and Spencer, **Rosabeth Moss Kanter** and Paul E. Spector during the 1980s. Their conclusions have also been included in the table.

Spector's conclusions included the fact that many of the newer leadership and management styles are more suited to internalizers than to externalizers, who often prefer what are now considered old-fashioned or traditional management styles.

Kanter, Rosabeth Moss, *The Change Masters*. London: Allen & Unwin, 1985.

L

Luthans, Fred

Although Fred Luthans has systematically amended his views on a number of management and organization issues over the years, the central core of his theories revolves around what he referred to as a contingency approach. The contingency approach suggests that there should not be a rigid authoritarian leadership which tightly controls all aspects of a business's operations, and specifically all employees. The theory also suggests that the type of management applicable to certain individuals should differ according to the employee's role and purpose

Table 17   Internalizers and Externalizers

Internalizer characteristics	Externalizer characteristics
Believe they control their own fate.	Believe their fate is out of their own control.
Understood from an early age why they were punished for bad behaviour and rewarded for good.	As children they never understood how punishment and reward related to their own behaviour.
Tend to become entrepreneurs and are more likely to leave a job.	Tend to talk about leaving a job but never get around to doing anything about it.
Do not often become frustrated or aggressive at work.	Are more likely to show frustration and aggression at work.
More safety conscious.	Not so safety conscious.
Not likely to remain in employment that is not satisfying them.	More likely to remain in a job that is not satisfying them.
Responsive to financial reward.	Not so responsive to financial reward.
Do not need a high degree of supervision.	Respond better with closer control.
Like and welcome change.	Not so capable of dealing with change.

within the organization. Some may need tight authoritarian control, whilst others may require a more hands-off approach by their managers.

See also **organizational culture**.

Luthans, Fred, *Organizational Behavior*. New York: McGraw-Hill, 2001.

L

Management by objectives (MBO)

The concept of management by objectives was developed by **Peter Drucker** in the 1950s. This management concept relies on the defining of objectives for each employee and then comparing their performance, and directing that performance, against the objectives which have already been set. MBO requires that clear objectives are set, and that every employee is perfectly well aware of what is expected of them, a factor which often means that the employees themselves have a considerable input into the setting of the objectives. Also at MBO's heart is **delegation**, as it requires employees to take a responsibility for the achievement of objectives. It is recognized that employees are much more able and willing to seek to achieve their objectives if they have some degree of independence in how those objectives are achieved, rather than being led or directed overtly by management.

MBO has at least one fatal flaw, in as much as the objectives of individuals within different departments can be different. When they are required to act together collaboratively, the objectives of one of the individuals may override those of another individual who has a different set of priorities and a different set of objectives. Inevitably, conflict or inertia may occur, which will clearly have an impact on productivity. Provided the business has thought the whole process through, objectives need not be mutually exclusive, but can be compatible – a compatibility which would seek to impel all collaborative projects forward and facilitate inter-disciplinary cooperation.

Management by walking about (MBWA)

The driving force behind this approach to management was the belief that senior managers, in particular, were perceived by employees as being elitist and unwilling to expose themselves to the realities of day-to-day business operations. In effect, the managers sought to isolate themselves in their offices and dispense orders from a distance, without any real conception as to the realities of shop floor life. The concept probably derives from Japan and was originally applied primarily to manufacturing industries. As the term suggests, managers are encouraged to visit the shop floor and see what is happening, solve problems on the spot and interact with normal employees. In Japan, management by walking about is actually termed *Gemci Genbutsu*, which literally means 'go and see'.

There are a number of human resource management implications arising out of the adoption of a management by walking about system. The fact that senior managers are out and about in the factory or offices of an organization means that they may inevitably interfere with normal lines of communication, authority and supervisory management decisions. Clearly the imbalance that might result from a senior manager becoming involved in what would normally be a situation that could be handled using day-to-day management and procedures could cause unnecessary friction within the organization. Human resource management would, therefore, need to ensure that a clear notion of cooperation, communication and demarcation is established.

Management of Health and Safety at Work Regulations 1999 (UK)

These regulations require employers to carry out risk assessments and to make arrangements to implement any necessary measures. Competent individuals should also be identified to pass information on to other employees and to carry out the necessary training.

These Regulations set out broad general duties, which apply to almost all work activities, aimed mainly at improving health and safety management and can be seen as a way of making more explicit what is required of employers under the Health and Safety at Work Act. They also introduce requirements contained in the European Health and Safety Framework Directive, into British law.

www.hmso.gov.uk/si/si1999/19993242.htm

M

Managing diversity

Managing diversity is the process of being able to successfully control and direct employees with radically different sets of cultural values. It has long been recognized that not all employees respond to the same type of management approach as each other. For a manager, dealing with radically different viewpoints and stances, on not only work, but also views of the world, is becoming an increasingly complex task. It is a measure of the importance of the management of diversity that increasing numbers of training programmes revolve around the recognition and respecting of diversity within groups.

Manual Handling Operations Regulations 1992 (UK)

These regulations cover the movement of objects in the workplace, either by hand or by force.

The regulations do not set legal limits for weights that can be lifted; neither do they explicitly require training to be given in manual handling techniques. The Regulations do require, where reasonably practicable, that manual handling is eliminated. In cases where this is not possible, then a risk assessment must be carried out where there is a risk of injury due to the manual handling operation.

www.hmso.gov.uk/si/si1992/Uksi_19922793_en_1.htm

Markov analysis

In the human resources sense, Markov analysis is used to attempt to predict or forecast the possible employee availability in the future. The analysis involves the use of a matrix which examines historical or expected changes or movements of employees, and tries to match instances of change which are predictable in some sense in order to ascertain what may occur in the future.

Maslow, Abraham

Maslow initially started his theory of the hierarchy of needs with seven basic needs that individuals have. This was ultimately reduced to the five needs shown in the well-known pyramid associated with Maslow's theory (see Figure 19).

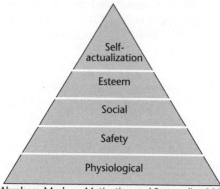

M

(Abraham Maslow, *Motivation and Personality*, 1954)

Figure 19   Maslow's theory of the hierarchy of needs

Fundamental to Maslow's theory is that employees start at the bottom of the pyramid and only when they have satisfied their basic needs do they begin to move up the pyramid. According to Maslow, once a need has been fulfilled it is no longer a **motivation** and it is possible that employees get a desire to progress to the next level of the pyramid before their base-level needs have been fulfilled. The levels of Maslow's pyramid are described in Table 18.

Table 18 Maslow's hierarchy of needs

Pyramid level	Description
Physiological	This basic needs level is seen as the lowest and includes the need for food, water, a roof over our heads, and sex.
Safety	According to Maslow the second level only becomes important when the physiological needs have been met. Employees look for a safe and secure working environment from their organization or employer.
Social	Once the physiological and safety needs have been met, employees then turn their attention to their social needs. This is the time that employees feel the need to make friends and to feel loved, and want to be accepted by those they work with.
Esteem	This level concerns self-respect. According to Maslow, once employees have fulfilled the first three basic needs, they then have a desire for success. They want to be praised and regarded as being good at what they do.
Self-actualization	The top level of the pyramid can only be reached once all the other needs have been fulfilled. This level concerns the employees' need to realize their full potential and develop their innovative and creative side.

Maslow's theory is popular with management and trainers and it is considered to be an essential learning tool in most programmes of study about motivation. However, it was not initially intended by Maslow as a management tool but is more about how individuals progress through their personal lives. Certainly it is quite possible that an individual could progress quite satisfactorily through the first two levels of the pyramid without the need to work.

Baker, Betsy and Sandore, Beth, 'Motivation in Turbulent Times: in Search of the Epicurean Work Ethic', *Journal of Library Administration*, 14(4) (1991), pp. 37–50.

Evans, G. Edward, 'Motivation', in *Management Techniques for Librarians*, 2nd edn. New York: Academic Press, 1983, pp. 174–98.

Nadler, David A. and Lawler, David E., 'Motivation: a Diagnostic Approach', in *The Management Process: A Selection of Readings for Librarians*, ed. Ruth Person. Chicago, IL: ALA, 1983, pp. 315–26.

Maternity and Parental Leave Regulations 1999 (UK)

The right to parental leave is contained in the Maternity and Parental Leave Regulations 1999. These regulations were made under the Employment Rights Act 1996 (as amended by the Employment Relations Act 1999). The Regulations came into force in December 1999.

www.legislation.hmso.gov.uk/si/si1999/19993312.htm

Maternity benefit

Rules and conditions related to maternity benefits and leave differ from country to country, but a generally accepted set of conditions includes the right of the woman to attend clinics and other related medical appointments prior to the birth. She is also entitled to have an 18-week break from work directly following the birth and the further right to attend ante-natal care.

In the UK, maternity leave is available to women, regardless of how long they have worked for an employer. During the first 18 weeks, statutory maternity pay is available to women who have worked continuously for 26 weeks prior to the birth of their child (this is counted from 15 weeks before the baby was due).

In most countries women are entitled to a fixed number of weeks fully paid, after which an additional number of weeks can be taken unpaid. During this time their job is still protected. From 1 April 2003 the maternity leave period was increased from 18 to 26 weeks, with the further provision of another 26 weeks unpaid.

See also **Maternity and Parental Leave Regulations 1999 (UK).**

M

Maternity leave

See **maternity benefit.**

Matrix structure

The use of a matrix organizational structure allows the opportunity for **teamwork and team building** to be developed in order that particular tasks can be undertaken. Matrix structures often develop in stages, with the first being the establishment of temporary teams, who, having studied a particular problem and suggested recommendations, might be considered significant enough to be retained on a more permanent basis. These teams will consist of a number of different individuals from the different functions of the organization (see Figure 20).

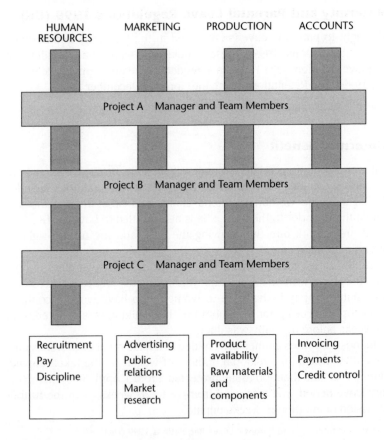

Figure 20   Example of a matrix structure

As can be seen in Table 19, a matrix structure has some advantages and disadvantages.

Sutherland, Jon and Canwell, Diane, *Organization Structures and Processes*. London: Pitman Publishing, 1997.

Weiss, Joseph, *Organizational Structure and Processes*. Cheltenham: Nelson-Thornes, 1999.

Table 19   Pros and cons of a matrix structure

Advantages	Disadvantages
Good use can be made of specialist and functional knowledge from within the organization.	Because there is not a clear line of command and authority, this may affect a manager's ability to understand requirements and make changes.
Enhanced communication can be facilitated between departments, providing a greater level of consistency and efficiency of policies.	There is often a higher level of stress and a feeling of constant competition with added responsibility.
The availability of multiple sources of power allows the establishment of recognized mechanisms to deal with different forms of culture.	Demand on individuals and departments may be inconsistent, resulting in a high demand in some areas and only a limited demand in others.
The structure enables the organization to adapt to environmental changes by moving the main emphasis from a functional one to a project-based one.	There may also be inconsistency between individuals with the ability to flourish and those who are more technically minded. This could cause exclusion for some employees by those who are competitive enough to wish to manage the project teams.

Maturity curve

Maturity curves are a statistical-based calculation used by human resources management to calculate pay and benefits for employees. Maturity curves rely on the examination of an employee's seniority and performance as key indices of where their remuneration should fall within a specific range. Typically, maturity curves are used to calculate the remuneration packages for employees in either technical or professional fields.

Mayo, Elton

Elton Mayo was employed by the Hawthorne Works during the 1920s and 1930s to attempt to improve the electrical company's productivity. As a result of this work he developed a theory which has since become known as the Hawthorne Effect.

Initially Mayo adopted the scientific management theory of **F. W. Taylor** in his attempt to discover what environmental features of the workplace were affecting productivity. He made amendments to the lighting, the heating and the availability of refreshments then went on to make changes to the length of the work day and week. Each time he made a change the rate of productivity increased. Puzzled by his findings, Mayo reversed his actions by removing tea-breaks and reducing the level of lighting, but productivity continued to increase. Mayo's conclusion was that the changes had been made in consultation with the employees and that this factor had been the determining influence on productivity, together with the fact that the employees had a good working relationship with their supervisors. This research became known as Mayo's Hawthorne experiments.

Further research was then undertaken in another department of the organization. Two different groups of employees were working on complex equipment; one group considered that their status was high because of the complexity of the **job role**. The second group considered themselves to be lower in status and this resulted in a degree of competition between the two groups. Both groups had established their own sets of rules and code of behaviour and each had established the pace of work and degree of output. Individuals within the group who did not comply with these standards were put under pressure from the other members of the group.

Each group was given a target output for the day by the management of the organization. On some days these targets were exceeded but the groups simply reported that they had reached the target figures and included the excess in the target figure for the following day. Mayo's conclusions from this were:

- The groups had been given a **benchmark**. Their benchmark had been the employer's output targets and they had been able to compare this with their own output totals.
- They had established for themselves a concept of a fair day's output and did not feel they needed to exceed these targets.

Mayo felt that lessons could be learned from this research in that a group's needs have to be in accord with organizational rules. Consultation was the key to achieving this, together with close monitoring of day-to-day organizational activities.

Mayo made three interesting discoveries from his research, which form the basis of this 'solidarity theory':

- Output and motivation improved when employees were being observed.

- Peer pressure contributed to the level of support from the individuals within the group.
- The group had strong feelings about what was possible and reasonable. This was as important to the group as their reaction to the demands of their managers.

Bratton, John and Gold, Jeffrey, *Human Resource Management: Theory and Practice.* Basingstoke: Palgrave Macmillan, 2003.

Mayo, Elton, *Social Problems of an Industrial Civilization.* London: Routledge, 1998.

McClelland, David C. (1917–98)

As a behavioural scientist, McClelland studied the human need for achievement for over 20 years at Harvard. McClelland is best known for his research on achievement **motivation**, distinguishing between three types of motivation:

- a need for achievement (nACH), where individuals seek personal responsibility, attainable but challenging goals, and feedback on performance;
- a need for affiliation (nAFFIL), where individuals have a desire for friendly relationships, sensitivity to the feelings of others, and a preference for roles with human interaction;
- a need for power (nPOW) where individuals have a desire to make an impact, to be influential and effective.

Power Needs (nPOW) show a high need for power, expressed as 'personalized power' or 'socialized power'. The key characteristics are:

- high personalized power with little inhibition or self-control, and the impulsive exercise of power; there are tendencies for these individuals to be rude, use alcohol, sexually harass, and collect symbols of power (e.g., big offices, desks, fancy cars, etc.);
- when they give advice or support, it is with the intent to bolster their own status;
- they demand loyalty to themselves rather than to the organization;
- when the leader leaves the organization, disorder is likely and a breakdown of team morale and direction.

Achievement Need (nACH) is reflected as attaining challenging goals, setting new records, successful completion of difficult tasks, and doing something not done before. Key characteristics are:

- a preference for a job in which success depends on effort and ability rather than on chance and factors beyond their control (**locus of control**);

- a preference for tasks that enable them to exercise their skills and initiative in problem solving;
- frequent and specific feedback about performance so they can enjoy the experience of making progress toward objectives;
- for managers in large organizations, moderate to high achievement is secondary to higher power needs; if achievement is dominant, the manager may try to achieve objectives alone rather than through team development;
- typical jobs include sales representatives, real-estate agents and owner-managers of small businesses.

Affiliation Need (nAFFIL) revolves around establishing or restoring close and friendly relationships, joining groups, participating in social activities, and enjoying shared activities. Key characteristics are:

- cooperative, supportive, and friendly behaviour;
- the valuing of belonging and conformity to a group;
- satisfaction from being liked and accepted by others;
- a preference for work with others, with group harmony and cohesion;
- a person low in affiliation tends to be a loner, who may lack motivation or energy to maintain high social contacts in networking, group presentations and building close personal relations with peers and subordinates;
- a person with high affiliation tends to be reluctant to let work interfere with harmonious relationships;
- moderate affiliation is related to effective management, since strong needs often lead to avoidance of unpopular decisions, permitting exceptions to rules, and showing favouritism to friends. However, this can lead to subordinates feeling confused about rules and playing to the manager's preferences.

M

McClelland argues that, on the basis of his research, nAFFIL (a desire to be liked) handicaps managers, who are led to make exceptions when they should not. He describes the nPOW manager as being dedicated to the organization, committed to the work ethic with energy and devotion. The best leader, he argues, is the nACH individual. The ideal combinations of these three needs are shown in Figure 21.

McClelland, D. C., *Power: The Inner Experience*. New York: Irvington, 1975.

Large organizations	Entrepreneurial small organizations or autonomous subsidiaries of large organizations
nPOW (high)	nPOW (high)
nACH (moderate)	nACH (moderate)
nAFFIL (moderate)	nAFFIL (low)

Figure 21   Best combinations of three types of motivation

McGrath, M. R.

See **organizational culture.**

McGregor, Douglas (1906–64)

McGregor was a management consultant theorist and a social psychologist. In 1954 he became Professor of Management at the Massachusetts Institute of Technology and he later taught at Harvard where he helped establish the Industrial Relations section. Douglas McGregor's book *The Human Side of Enterprise* was published in 1960, examining the behaviour of individuals at work. He formulated two models, which he called Theory X and Theory Y.

Theory X assumes that the average human has an inherent dislike of work and will do all that is necessary to avoid it. This assumes the following:

- because people dislike work they have to be controlled by management and often threatened in order to work hard;
- most people avoid responsibility, need to be directed by management but seek security within work as a primary concern;
- managers who adhere to the Theory X approach rarely give their subordinates any opportunity to show traits other than those associated with Theory X.

Theory X has given rise to what is often known as tough or **hard management**, typified by tight control and punishment. **Soft management** adopts the alternate view, which aims to create a degree of harmony in the workplace.

M

Theory Y, on the other hand, assumes the following:

- Most people expend the same amount of energy or effort at work as in other spheres of their lives.
- Providing individuals are committed, or made to be committed, to the aims of the organization in which they work, they will be **self-directing** (see **self-directed work group**).
- **Job satisfaction** is the key to involving and engaging individual employees and ensuring their commitment.
- An average individual, if given the opportunity and encouragement, will naturally seek responsibility.
- In ensuring commitment and responsibility, employees will be able to use their imagination, ingenuity and creativity to solve work problems with less direct supervision.

Managements which follow Theory Y are often considered to be soft management systems and recognize that the intellectual potential of their employees is vital to the success of the business. In many cases, it is argued, businesses ignore the Theory Y benefits and under-utilize their employees.

McGregor saw his two theories as being very separate attitudes. He believed that it was difficult to use Theory Y for large-scale operations, particularly those involved in mass production. It was an ideal choice for the management of professionals. For McGregor, Theory Y was essential in helping to encourage participative problem solving and the development of effective management.

McGregor, Douglas, *The Human Side of Enterprise*. New York: McGraw-Hill Education, 1985 (25th anniversary printing).

Measured day work

Measured day work is a remuneration system where pay is fixed at a higher rate than the normal hourly rate, provided an employee attains a certain level of performance or output. Other measured day work schemes require a specified output in return for a fixed daily wage. There are also more complex schemes which allow employees to step up to higher rates if they consistently perform at a particular level of output, which, theoretically, has no limit.

Mediation

The term 'mediation' refers to an attempted means of **dispute resolution**. A third party will be brought in to listen to the views of each side of the dispute and will then feedback the feelings and requirements to the other side. The third party will be independent of the two sides of the dispute.

Medical evaluation

In certain employment situations the employer may require job **applicants** to provide a statement or a signature on a pre-prepared statement which testifies to their health and number of days taken off due to illness over a specified period of time. In other cases a medical evaluation will literally involve a physical examination, either by the organization's medical staff, or by an assigned general practitioner.

Mentor and mentor programme

A mentor is usually an experienced and relatively highly placed individual within an organization, who is responsible for assisting the career development of another, less experienced, member of staff. In effect, the mentor operates as a coach, a sponsor and an advocate for that individual.

The ways in which mentors provide guidance, support and knowledge to their protégés differ according to the way in which the mentoring programme has been framed. Some mentoring programmes are formal and prescriptive in respect of the time, effort and involvement which the mentor is expected to make or devote. A mentoring programme can be seen as a grooming exercise, based on the assumption that the protégé is destined for a key post in the organization at some point in the medium to long term. This grooming form of mentoring tends to be centred on a one-to-one basis, whereas a network mentoring programme relies on the expertise and involvement of a number of mentors who all provide support and share information aimed at improving the career potential of a protégé.

Normally there are four recognized stages in setting up a mentoring system; these are:

1 The mentor and the protégé are introduced to one another informally and spend some time getting acquainted with one another, learning of each other's interests, values and goals, in order to give the relationship a degree of substance.

2 The mentor and protégé now discuss their initial expectations of one another and agree a set of procedures, which will normally involve the frequency and length of time that they will meet.

3 This stage focuses on fulfilling the needs and objectives related to

M

professional growth. As new situations develop, objectives are set to match these. This is the longest stage of the process and may continue for a number of months.

4 Throughout the whole process the mentor and the protégé continually redefine their relationships with one another and with the rest of the organization.

Hegstad, Christine D., 'Formal Mentoring as a Strategy for Human Resource Development: a Review of Research', *Human Resource Development Quarterly* (Winter 1999).

Merit raise

A merit raise is a means by which employees' remuneration can be enhanced as a direct reflection of their performance. Merit raises tend to derive from a manager's or supervisor's recommendation, rather than an identification by the human resources department, or a specific request to carry out an evaluation of performance by an employee. Merit raises normally occur outside the regular pay negotiation timetable.

Minimum wage

See **(National) Minimum Wage Regulations 1998** *and* **Fair Labour Standards Act 1996.**

Mission statement

In many cases indications of a human resource management's fundamental policy will be contained within a mission statement. A mission statement essentially describes, as succinctly as possible, the organization's business vision. This would include their fundamental values and the essential purpose of the organization. It will also make allusions as to its future or its pursuit for the future, as mission statements tend to be a statement of where a businesses wishes to be rather than a description of where they are at the current time. In this respect, mission statements, although the fundamental ethos may remain the same, are subject to periodic change. A business may choose to incorporate within its mission statement a vision of how it wishes its employees and systems to respond, react and fulfil the needs of its customers or clients. The human resources department will, therefore, seek to match these aspirations by instituting employee development programmes and associated training, in order to fulfil the espoused desires and commitments made in the mission statement.

Mixed interview

A mixed interview is a means of describing variations in the types of questions which may be asked of a potential employee during a job **interview**. Typically, a mixed interview format will consist of a number of different types of questions, including structured and unstructured questions.

Moonlighters

The term 'moonlighter' refers to individual employees who work for more than one employer simultaneously. In most cases the different employers of the moonlighter will be unaware that the employee is working for somebody else at the same time as they are working for them.

Motivation

Motivation implies the instilling in employees of a drive to take action. In human resource terms this means inducing or providing an incentive to employees to perform to the best of their abilities. The subject of motivation has been at the heart of a large number of theories over a number of years, including those of **Maslow** and **Hertzberg**. Both theorists recognized that there were a series of actions or circumstances which could be initiated by an employer in order to achieve a degree of motivation. Both recognized too that simply providing pay and a degree of security were insufficient in the long term to motivate employees. Motivation needed to be longer lasting and reinforced by concrete rewards and praise. At its most basic, motivation needs to be sustained by employers in order not only to ensure continued high performance and productivity, but also to create a situation where employees have a positive attitude towards work, a commitment to the organization and, above all, a belief that their individual roles are not only valued but of crucial interest to the organization.

M

Multi-skilling

The term 'multi-skilling' relates to incorporating a higher level of flexibility into the job roles across an organization, usually in those activities requiring unskilled to skilled or technical expertise. This flexibility often crosses boundaries which have historically or traditionally been set, and it requires the willingness of employees if it is to succeed. The newly multi-skilled employees would also have to be prepared to work at their newly acquired skills and follow training or retraining programmes in order to do so. Commonly, trained employees will assist with the retraining of those going through the multi-skilling process.

There are some advantages and disadvantages to multi-skilling, including those shown in Table 20.

Table 20   An evaluation of multi-skilling

Advantages	Disadvantages
An organization can introduce new equipment and working methods quickly.	**Labour turnover** can increase as employees become more skilled.
The employees improve their overall level of skills and knowledge.	The costs of training and retraining programmes can be high.
All of the organization's resources are used to their full potential.	Because individuals can move from one group to another, there could be resultant shortages in particular groups. This can affect the way the group performs in the longer term as there is a constant risk that one member of the group or team will be missing.
The employees can contribute more effectively, and to their full potential, to the meeting of the organization's objectives.	Managers tend not to be involved in the multi-skilling process and often remain rigid in their views of the tasks they should perform.
	Employees do not always enjoy job satisfaction, particularly if they are not involved in tasks they were initially trained to do.

M

The introduction of multi-skilling can affect employees in more than their work situation and may spill over into their domestic life, particularly if their extended roles involve irregular work hours. However, employees could find that their **job satisfaction** is increased because they are no longer so strictly supervised or controlled.

Myers–Briggs Type Indicator (MBTI)

The Myers–Briggs Type Indicator®, or MBTI®, is based on the teachings of Carl Gustav Jung, and identifies four behaviour preferences.

- extroversion versus introversion;
- sensing versus intuition;
- thinking versus feeling;
- judgement versus perception.

The combination of these four preferences produces a personality type, such as EIFP or ISTJ. The model can be used for a variety of different applications, including interpersonal skills development, self-awareness, career **counselling** and **team work**.

The MTR-I (Management Team Roles Indicator) system is an extension to the Myers–Briggs Type Indicator, as it can assign team roles based on a questionnaire. The Myers–Briggs system is amongst a wide variety of different **psychometric tests**, including the Keirsey Temperament Sorter and the Careers Values Inventory.

www.mrt-i.com

M

(National) Minimum Wage Regulations 1998 (UK)

The national minimum wage aimed to provide employees with decent minimum standards and fairness in the workplace. It applies to most employees and sets hourly rates below which pay must not be allowed to fall.

It helps businesses by ensuring that competition is on the basis of the quality of the goods and services they provide and not on low prices relying predominantly on low rates of pay. The rates set are based on the recommendations of the independent Low Pay Commission.

www.dti.gov.uk/er/nmwr/annex1.htm
www.hmso.gov.uk/acts/acts1998/19980039.htm

Needs assessment

Needs assessment is a form of **training needs analysis** which seeks to identify either an employee's or an organization's current or future problems which could be addressed through employee development and training.

Negligence

The definition of the term 'negligence' is a failure to exercise the correct amount of care that an average, reasonable person would expect to exercise in any given situation. Negligence can be a legally actionable act, but there has to be a 'duty of care' in existence and it has to be proved that the individual involved was in breach of their duty of care and that their actions caused damage. The terms 'duty of care' and 'negligence' are most often pertinent to the medical and childcare professions.

Negotiation

Negotiation is a vital communication skill required by both managers and human resources personnel. Negotiation has a great deal to do with the relative power of the negotiators. Negotiations can occur either at an individual level or between employees' representatives, such as between **trade unions** and another group of individuals who represent the business. Equally, negotiation can take place at local, national or even international levels, between employee representatives and representatives of employer groups and/or governments.

French and Raven suggested eight key areas which largely determine the basis of negotiations and how they may be expected to progress. These eight considerations are summarized in Table 21.

French, John R. P. and Raven, Bertram, 'Basis of Social Power', in Dorwin Cartwright (ed.), *Studies in Social Power*. Ann Arbor, MI: University of Michigan, 1959.

Table 21   Requirements for successful negotiations

Consideration	Description
Positional power	This type of power derives from an individual's position within the organization relative to other individuals. This form of power is particularly in evidence when negotiations occur between managers and their direct employees.
Information power	This type of power derives from differences between people in terms of their access to important information. An individual who lacks access to information can be controlled by another individual who has that information. In other words, some individuals find themselves dependent upon those who have already acquired the information, possibly by virtue of their position within the organization.
Control of rewards	Those individuals in managerial or supervisory positions within an organization have the ability to dispense rewards to less senior members of staff, making their subordinates dependent on them.
Coercive power	This type of power is related to the ability of a manager or supervisor to punish less senior employees. Once again, the less senior employees are dependent upon their supervisor or manager.
Alliances and networks	This type of power is derived from both an individual's access to information and his or her relative position to members of stronger alliances and networks, and they can use this to exercise power and authority.

$\Rightarrow$

Table 21 Requirements for successful negotiations (*continued*)

Consideration	Description
Access to and control of agendas	The setting of the ground rules or topics to be discussed within a negotiation process is obviously a determining factor in the outcome of the negotiations. If an individual can set the agenda, or in other words, determine what will be discussed, then the negotiation process has already been somewhat undermined before it even begins.
Control of meaning and symbols	This is particularly relevant to a jargon-ridden organization, where the use of language can radically affect the negotiation process. Access to these symbols and their meaning can strongly determine the effectiveness of negotiators who are not conversant with the jargon.
Personal power	The adoption of the characteristics of an effective role model, or the use of these characteristics by a dominant personality, can determine the effectiveness of a negotiator.

Neuro-linguistic programming (NLP)

Neuro-linguistic programming (NLP) involves the study of how individuals perform well. It then goes on to suggest how this can be enhanced and taught to others. NLP relies on the investigation of results, identifying what has been achieved and the processes which led to that achievement. In this way it is believed that individuals can develop the tools and technique to enable them to achieve in exactly the same way as those upon whom the models have been based. NLP has been increasingly applied to various aspects of business skills, including **teamwork and team building**, **negotiation**, leadership, presentation and goal setting. Exponents of NLP believe that this is an entirely revolutionary means by which individuals can hone their skills, achieve their goals and communicate more effectively.

NLP trains individuals to process the information which comes at them from various different sources, including the senses. It recognizes that some of these stimuli are ignored; others are distorted (as a result of experience), whilst others are generalized. NLP also recognizes that some individuals address situations from the perspective of all the things that could go wrong. Others believe, from socialization, that they will never make a correct decision. NLP seeks to address these issues, to reinforce the positive and to dispel negative influences or thought process that could adversely affect an individual's ability to learn.

O'Connor, John and Seymour, John, *Introducing NLP: Neuro-Linguistic Programming*. London: HarperCollins, 1993.

Noise at Work Regulations 1989 (UK)

These regulations require employers to ensure that their employees are protected from hearing damage as a result of their work. A new EU Directive on the minimum health and safety requirements regarding exposure of workers to the risks arising from physical agents (noise), which will repeal Directive 86/188/EEC, was adopted in early December 2002. It came into force on 15 February 2003.

www.hmso.gov.uk/si/si1989/Uksi_19891790_en_1.htm

Non-financial incentives

Employers offer non-financial incentives to their employees in the knowledge that pay alone is not a long-term motivator. Typically, non-financial incentives will include **job enlargement**, **job enrichment**, **job rotation** and **appraisal**. All of these aspects seek to identify and improve the overall quality of the work which each employee experiences. Other employers may offer alternative incentives, which may include the provision of canteen facilities, rest areas, training, flexible working hours, **mentoring** and enhanced employee support when dealing with problems or issues which may affect their lives.

N

Observation

Observation is an approach used by human resources management in order to collect information regarding job and job-related performance. The process involves direct observation by a human resource specialist, usually employing check lists and performance-based measuring tools to assess the overall effectiveness and performance of a particular job holder.

Occupational Safety and Health Act (OSH) 1970 (US)

The Occupational Safety and Health Act of 1970 requires US employers to provide workplaces free from serious recognized hazards and to comply with occupational safety and health standards.

www.dol.gov/dol/compliance/comp-osha.htm

Office of Federal Contract Compliance Programs (OFCCP) (US)

The role of the Office of Federal Contract Compliance Programs (OFCCP) is to ensure that businesses working with the Federal government comply with their contractual obligations. Specifically, the OFCCP monitors equal employment opportunity and encourages positive programmes to recruit, hire and promote workers who traditionally have been discriminated against (including minorities, women, the disabled and veterans).

www.dol.gov/esa/regs/compliance/ofccp/fs503.htm

Office of Labor-Management Standards (OLMS) (US)

The Office of Labor-Management Standards enforces provisions of the **Labor-Management Reporting and Disclosure Act (LMRDA)** and related laws. The OLMS seeks to establish basic standards of responsibility for unions representing employees in private industry, Federal government employees, and Postal Service employees.

OLMS also administers the election of union officers and the safe-guarding of union funds and assets amongst other union-related concerns.

www.dol.gov/esa/olms_org.htm

Office of the Assistant Secretary for Administration and Management (OASAM) (US)

The Assistant Secretary for Administration and Management exists to provide leadership and policy guidance to the Secretary of Labor. OASAM is particularly involved in the areas of budgets, human resources, information technology, safety and health, facilities management and administration.

OASAM also aims to ensure compliance with non-discrimination statutes that apply to Department of Labor employees and/or applicants for employment, and DOL financial assistance programmes.

www.dol.gov/oasam

Office of Workers' Compensation Programs (US)

The Office of Workers' Compensation Programs administers four disability compensation programmes:

- Energy Employees' Occupational Illness Compensation Program;
- Division of Federal Employees' Compensation;
- Division of Coal Mine Workers' Compensation;
- Division of Longshore and Harbor Workers' Compensation.

These provide for wage replacement benefits, medical treatment, vocational rehabilitation and other benefits to workers or their dependants who have experienced work-related injury or occupational disease.

www.dol.gov/esa/owcp_org.htm

O

Offices, Shops and Railway Premises Act 1963 (UK)

This Act concentrates on shops and offices and provides a number of clear guidelines to the employer on the provision of facilities to employees, including temperature, fresh air supply, toilet and washing facilities, lighting, and area of working space. Specifically, the Act requires employers to:

- provide a minimum of 40 square feet of space per person working in the office;

- ensure offices are adequately heated, lit, have clean air, available fresh drinking water and toilets;
- provide sedentary employees with adequate seating;
- provide a staff room for meals;
- keep floors, passages and stairs in good order;
- ensure dangerous office machinery is guarded.

www.hse.gov.uk

Off-the-job training

Off-the-job training, usually in business time, is often provided through employee attendance at training colleges and other external training agencies. Either suitable and relevant training programmes will be identified by human resources management pro-actively (in the sense that all employees of a particular grade or level are sent on specific training courses), or an employee will approach the human resources department (usually with the endorsement of the line manager), and the department will then decide on the relevance of the training to the employee's current role and possible roles in the future.

On-the-job training

On-the-job training is training undertaken at the business's premises. Trainees or individuals in particular grades will undergo on-the-job training (OJT) under the supervision of an experienced and qualified trainer in order to acquire the skills needed for the job. The trainees' performance (under actual working conditions) is continually monitored and recorded in a training logbook.

The key associated advantages and disadvantages can be seen in Table 22.

Sisson, Gary R., *Hands-on Training: A Simple and Effective Method for On-the-job Training.* New York: McGraw-Hill Education, 2001.

Open-door policy

An open-door policy is essentially a senior management approach to interaction with employees. An organization which adopts an open-door policy encourages employees to approach senior management with problems and concerns about their own work or the business in general.

Table 22 An evaluation of on-the-job training

Advantages	Disadvantages
Training employees in their own working environment can help them gain direct experience to a standard approved by the employer.	Requires skills and knowledge from a potential trainer who may not be apparent or available in the business among the existing members of staff.
Employees will have more confidence to use equipment if supervised and guided.	Insufficient time to train is a concern as it may be felt that the trainee is competent enough to cope; equally, the training may be frequently interrupted by day-to-day matters.
It is easy to assess improvement and progress, allowing intervention to resolve problems.	Bad habits will be passed on to the trainees.
Employees are still working whilst training and as they gain confidence they become increasingly productive.	Limited time may mean that the trainee is overconfident and may need additional training at a later date.
Employees have an opportunity to get to know staff and be more at ease if trained by staff that they already know.	External trainers brought into the business may not be fully conversant with policies and procedures.
It is a cost-effective means of training.	Space needs to be allocated for the training as it will usually involve both practical and theoretical elements.

Organization development (OD)

Organization development is a planned process of change. Organization development is about performance improvement, in which a business will seek to align more closely to the environment and markets in which it operates in order to achieve its strategies efficiently and effectively. OD can involve developing organizations in terms of culture, values, people, structures, processes and resources.

OD is an issue often specific in terms of process, timing and those involved. There are, however, some overarching processes and elements that can be identified as being common to many OD situations. OD tends to begin with research into the current situation to assess all the issues. This research will inevitably involve the following aspects:

- clarifying the impact of obligations, which have to be honoured;
- the availability of appropriate resources such as skills, facilities and finances;
- the desires and career aspirations of those who will be affected;
- the proposed plan's overall fit with future business strategy.

Once the research process is completed, the organization should have a better view of how the OD will work in practice. This begins with planning the change programme, which may involve the design of a new organizational structure, **job descriptions** and **job evaluation**, salary and benefits provision, physical resources, phasing in of the overall project, and the management of impacts on existing employees.

Throughout the process, the organization needs to ensure that it conducts communication, development and **counselling** events to assist the establishment of the new organizational structure. It may also be necessary to reshape or reprofile certain areas of the organization with the intention of improving **employee retention** and the best use of skills and expertise in order to make the intended developments in efficiency.

Hamlin, Bob, Keep, Jane and Ash, Ken (eds), *Organizational Change and Development: A Reflective Guide for Managers, Trainers and Developers*. Harlow, Essex: Financial Times/Prentice-Hall, 2000.

Mello, Jeffrey, *Strategic Human Resource Management*. Mason, OH: South Western College Publishing, 2001.

Organizational culture

There are a number of ways in which an organization's culture can be classified. The main classifications were suggested by a number of researchers, including Roger Harrison, **Charles Handy**, Terrence Deal and Allen Kennedy, and R. E. Quinn and M. R. McGrath. As years have passed, so these classifications have become more developed, making it possible only to approach them in broad terms.

In 1972 Roger Harrison suggested four main categories of organizational culture – power, role, task and person. Charles Handy reworked Harrison's theory and identified the categories as described in Table 23.

During the 1980s Terrence Deal and Allen Kennedy developed their own set of theories about organizational culture and the way in which it affected how managements made decisions and formed their strategies. Their conclusions are shown in Table 24.

R. E. Quinn and M. R. McGrath also identified four different organizational cultures, as shown in Table 25.

It should be remembered that no one organization fits neatly into any

Table 23   Categories of organizational culture according to Handy

Culture	Description
Power	This type of culture is based on trust and good personal communication. There is little need for rigid bureaucratic procedures since power and authority is based on only a few individuals. The power culture is dynamic in that change can take place quickly but is dependent on a small number of key, powerful individuals. This culture tends to be tough on employees because the key focus is the success of the organization, often resulting in high **labour turnover**.
Role	This type of culture tends to be bureaucratic in nature, thus requiring logical, coordinated and rational processes with heavy emphasis on rules and procedures. Control lies with a small number of employees who have high degrees of authority. The organizations tend to be stable, operating in a predictable environment with products and services that have a long lifespan. Not considered to be innovative organizations, they can adapt to gradual, minor change, but not to radical ones.
Task	This type of organizational culture relies on employee expertise. The matrix structure tends to prevail in these organizations, with teams of individuals specializing. They need, and tend, to be flexible organizations with individual employees working with **autonomy** allowing fast reaction to changes in the external environment and having set procedures in place to address this aspect.
Person	This type of culture relies on collective decision-making, often associated with partnerships. Compromise is important and individuals will tend to work within their own specialist area, coordinating all aspects and working with autonomy without the need to report to other employees.

O

one of the categories mentioned and the majority are too complex to be categorized generally. The classifications should be regarded only as a reference point for comparison of extremes.

Deal, Terrence and Kennedy, Allen, *Corporate Cultures: The Rights and Rituals of Corporate Life*. New York: Addison-Wesley, 1982.

Handy, C. B., *Understanding Organizations*. Harmondsworth: Penguin, 1985.

Quinn, R. E. and McGrath, M. R., T*he Transformation of Organizational Cultures: A Competing Values Perspective in Organizational Culture*, edited by C. C. Lundberg and J. Martin. London: Sage Publications, 1985.

Scholz, C., *Organizational Culture and Leadership*. San Francisco, CA: Jossey Bass, 1985.

Table 24 Organizational culture according to Deal and Kennedy

Culture	Description
Macho	The management in these types of organizations have to make decisions quickly and adopt a tough attitude towards their employees and fellow managers. There is a high degree of internal competition and the operations tend to be high risk. The majority of these organizations do not form strategies or plan for the long term but are considered short termist, with a low level of cooperation within the organization itself. There is a high **labour turnover** resulting in a weak organizational culture.
Work hard/play hard	This type of culture tends to be associated with sales. The majority of individual employees are sales orientated but the level of risk is low. It is the employees' ability to accumulate sales that is important and the culture tends to encourage team building and social activities for employees. The organization encourages competition and offers rewards for success, but does not necessarily rate quality as highly as volume.
Company	These types of organization are often in high-risk areas and operate on the basis that decisions take a long time to come to fruition. Decision making takes place at the top of this hierarchical organization and the overall approach can often be old-fashioned. Each new invention or technical breakthrough will pose a threat to the business.
Process	This type of culture operates in a low-risk, slow feedback environment where employees are encouraged to focus on how they do things rather than what they do. They tend to be systems- and procedures-based, requiring employees to work in an orderly and detailed fashion, attending meetings and work groups. There will be rigid levels of management in the hierarchical structure, but because the organization operates in a predictable environment, reactions from management are often slow.

O

Orientation follow-up

Orientation follow-ups are procedures and checks undertaken by human resources after an **orientation programme** to make an assessment as to whether the information and related orientation activities were effective and the new employees are more cognizant of the policies, procedures and other related aspects contained within the orientation programme and training package.

Table 25   Organizational culture according to Quinn and McGrath

Culture	Description
Rational	The rational culture is firmly based on the needs of a market. The organization places emphasis on productivity and efficiency and encourages management to be goal-orientated and decisive. All activities are focused on tangible performance and employees are rewarded on achievement.
Adhocracy	This type of culture is an adaptive, creative and autonomous one where authority is largely based on the abilities and charismatic nature of leaders. These organizations tend to be risk-orientated and emphasis is placed on employees' adherence to the values of the organization itself.
Consensual	These types of organization are often concerned with equality, integrity and fairness and much of the authority is based on informal acceptance of power. Decisions are made by **collective agreements** or consensus, and dominant leaders are not often present. Morale is important, as is cooperation and support between employees in order to reach organizational objectives. Employee loyalty is high.
Hierarchical	This type of culture relies on stability and control through the setting of rigid regulations and procedures. Decisions are made logically on facts alone with the management tending to be cautious and conservative. The employees are strictly controlled, with management expecting obedience.

Orientation programme

Orientation programmes are used by an organization and usually run by, or organized by, a human resources department in order to familiarize new employees with the organization which they have recently joined. A typical orientation programme will include general information and training on the policies and procedures of the organization, the roles and functions of other employees and departments within the organization, as well as specific information related to their own role in the business.

Normally, orientation programmes, or **induction**, take place soon after the new employee has joined the organization; however, it is not always practical to run these programmes immediately and it is generally the case that an organization will routinely run the programmes at fixed times in the year in order to provide this information and training to all new employees who have joined over the period immediately preceding this date. In cases where the organization has mass recruitment it may be possible to run the orientation programme for all new employees as part of the overall recruitment and induction process. Orientation programmes are often assessed by **orientation follow-up**.

Smalley, Larry R., *On-the-job Orientation and Training*. Indianapolis, IN: Pfeiffer Wiley, 1994.

Ouchi, William

See **theory z**.

Outplacement

Outplacement is a human resources responsibility that involves finding alternative employment for employees with other businesses. Outplacement may be an integral part of any downsizing operation and may require human resources to undertake any or all of the following services to employees who are no longer required by the organization:

- career assessment (options and opportunities);
- résumé writing/review (résumé review and re-writing when appropriate);
- checking letters of application (providing templates and advice);
- career counselling (face-to-face or phone counselling and career coaching for a set period or until the employee finds a new position);
- interview counselling (techniques and tips);
- mock interviews (prior to an interview with a new prospective employer).

Lord, David A., Meyer, John L. and Shadle, Carolyn C., *The Changing Outplacement Process: New Methods and Opportunities for Transition Management*. Westport, CT: Greenwood Press, 1994.

Output-based appraisals

Focus on job products is the primary criterion. The most commonly used output-based appraisal is **management by objectives** (MBO). MBO specifies the performance goals that an individual can hope to attain within an appropriate length of time. The objectives that each manager sets are derived from the overall goals and objectives of the organization. Implementing an MBO appraisal system comprises four basic stages, shown in Figure 22.

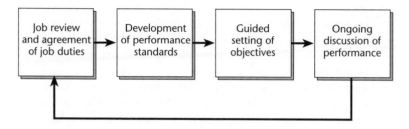

Figure 22   Implementing an MBO appraisal

Landy, F. J. and Farr, J. L., *The Measurement of Work Performance: Methods, Theory and Applications.* New York: Academic Press, 1983.

Outside authority approach

The outside authority approach is a human resource audit methodology which uses an external consultant or independently researched and published material as a **benchmark** or set of standards by which the human resource programmes can be compared.

Outsourcing

The outsourcing of human resources is gradually gaining ground as a primary means by which the functions related to employees are handled by a business. There have been significant changes in policy where a shift has been in progress from providing human resources in-house to using external organizations. In effect, outsourcing is the use of another organization or an agency for some, or all, of the human resource functions.

Outsourcing is not merely restricted to the smaller business: notably, a business which has grown significantly over recent years has a greater tendency to consider outsourcing, particularly if it prefers to focus on the operations of the core business and there is a culture of outsourcing which has enhanced its growth.

In the US, the human resource industry as a whole was worth an estimated $13.9 billion in 1999 and according to research businesses such as Dataquest, it is expected to have reached $37.7 billion in 2003.

Outsourcing human resources falls into four broad categories:

O

- Professional Employer Organizations (PEO) takes on all of the responsibilities of the human resource administration for a business, including the legal responsibilities, the hiring of employees, and dismissals. Typically, the relationship is cooperative, with the PEO handling human resources and the business itself dealing with all other aspects of operations. Not all PEOs take the full responsibility for human resources; some merely handle payroll and benefits systems.
- Business Process Outsourcing (BPO), although a general term used to describe outsourcing in the broadest sense, refers to human resources in respect of supporting the human resource functions with technology and software (including data warehousing and other services).
- Application Service Providers (ASPs) restrict their relationship with a business to providing either web-based or customized software to help manage human resource functions such as payroll and benefits.
- E-services can be either ASPs or BPOs, which again are restricted to web-based services such as recruitment, software and data warehousing, or other forms of data storage and access provision for human resources.

Incomes Data Services, *Outsourcing HR Administration*. London: Incomes Data, Services, 2000.

Vanson, Sally, *The Challenge of Outsourcing Human Resources*. Oxford: Chandos Publishing, 2001.

Overtime

Overtime occurs when an employer requires or permits an employee to work extra hours over and above their normal working day or week. Under normal circumstances, the employer will provide premium pay for such overtime work.

In the US, under the terms of the **Fair Labor Standards Act** (FLSA), overtime payments must be one and a half times the normal pay for hours worked in excess of 40 hours in a week. Not all overtime necessarily means the payment of additional wages as often overtime work is traded for other time off from work (usually at the 1.5 times rate). Human resources managers would be responsible for the monitoring, recording and payment of any such overtime work carried out by an employee.

Overworking

There has been an increasing trend for organizations to reduce the number of employees rather than reducing what they are expected to accomplish. Employees, therefore, fill the gap by investing more time working than they are contracted to do. Although, profit-wise, this is beneficial to the organization, it is vital to look at the consequences in the long term. The solutions to overworking can be complex, yet they need to be addressed by the human resources department and the organization as a whole, together with an approach by the individual employees and the teams in which they work. Possible solutions are summarized in Table 26.

Table 26 Possible solutions to the problem of overwork

Individual employees	Teams	Human resources and the organization
Set leave times and stick with the decision.	Consider and amend the ways in which work is managed.	Set policy guidelines which expressly state that employees should not work beyond a prescribed number of additional hours.
Eliminate work that is low in value and priority.	Simplify processes and systems to eliminate duplication and wasted effort.	Provide incentives to customers and suppliers if they give good notice of what is required of the business.
Question the purpose of tasks, the level and complexity of tasks, and the standards set.	Set priorities and recognize that it is acceptable not to undertake low-priority work.	Refuse to accept tight deadlines.
Recognize that the volume of work is not a personal problem but an organizational one.	Build a supportive system based on trust and open communications.	Discourage employees from taking work home with them and ensure that they take their statutory holidays and breaks.

O

Pp

Paired comparison method

Some organizations perform a scaled-down version of **job evaluation** in order to examine a few jobs; in some cases, an organization may only have a limited number of different jobs. In both cases, it may be desirable to simplify the process of job evaluation, and rather than using a standard point-factor methodology, the human resources department adopts what is known as a paired-comparison methodology.

The total value of the job is calculated on the basis of (usually) four criteria (skill, effort, responsibility, and working conditions), although the organization may choose to compare more than four criteria. The jobs are then ranked against one another (as opposed to using a predetermined relative scale). Weighting is an optional factor in this method (usually achieved by assigning 2 or 1.5 to illustrate more, or less, impact on the scores on each criterion or factor). This is done for each factor and the result will be to magnify the impact of the scores on factors with a greater weight over those in lower-weighted or non-weighted factors. If all factors are weighted in this way, the points are then tallied for the total weighted score for each job. The jobs are then compared with one another according to total value, and appropriate compensation is assigned.

Parental leave (UK)

Parental leave is the right to take time off work to look after a child or to make arrangements for the child's welfare, enshrined within law under the Children Act 1989, the Maternity and Parental Leave Regulations 1999, the Maternity and Parental Leave (Amendment) Regulations 2001 and the Maternity and Parental Leave (Amendment) Regulations 2002. It allows eligible employees (who have completed one year's qualifying service) to take a period of unpaid leave to care for each child born or adopted on or after 15 December 1994.

Parents can take parental leave as soon as the child is born or as soon as they have completed the required one year's qualifying service with their employer (whichever is later). Parents are entitled to take 13 weeks' parental leave for each child (or 18 weeks for each child entitled to a disability living allowance)

Employers and employees tend to agree on how the arrangements for parental leave will operate – across the workforce or through collective agreements, or in some cases individually. Employees do have the right to go to an employment tribunal in cases where the employer prevents or attempts to prevent them from taking parental leave. In addition, an employee on parental leave is protected from instances of victimization (including dismissal).

www.hmso.gov.uk/acts/acts1989/Ukpga_19890041_en_1.htm

www.legislation.hmso.gov.uk/si/si1999/19993312.htm

www.legislation.hmso.gov.uk/si/si2001/20014010.htm

www.legislation.hmso.gov.uk/si/si2002/20022789.htm

Parental leave (US)

The Family and Medical Leave Act (FMLA) in the US asserts that certain employees should be granted up to 12 weeks of unpaid, job-protected leave per year. FMLA applies to all public agencies, all public and private elementary and secondary schools, and organizations with 50 or more employees.

All employers within these categories must provide eligible employees with up to 12 weeks of unpaid leave each year for any of the following reasons:

- the birth and care of the newborn child of an employee;
- the placement with the employee of a child for adoption or foster care;
- the need to care for an immediate family member (spouse, child, or parent) with a serious health condition;
- medical leave when the employee is unable to work because of a serious health condition.

These rules apply provided that the employee has worked for the employer on the following basis:

- for at least 12 months;
- for at least 1,250 hours over the past 12 months;
- at a location where the company employs 50 or more employees within 75 miles.

The **Fair Labor Standards Act (FLSA)** determines whether the employee has matched any or all of the above criteria.

www.dol.gov/esa/whd/fmla

P

Participation

Employee participation is synonymous with concepts such as employee involvement, commitment, empowerment, participative management, quality circles, team-working and total quality management. Indeed the range of employee participation schemes is vast, but in many organizations they have become a permanent phenomenon.

Despite the criticisms of employee participation or employee involvement, neither of which are new concepts, the rise in human resources management has seen approaches which regard the employee as an asset that can be invested in (training and development) and included in decision making (leading to employee motivation, commitment and higher performance). Many businesses adopted participative management schemes during the early 1980s. At the same time businesses were responding to increased competition from various countries, which exposed weaknesses in working practices, output and productivity.

The first Employee Involvement (EI) schemes were quality circles (QCs), but after an initial interest in QCs, they were on the decline by the mid-1980s. The main reasons for the failures were managers not having the right training and leadership skills and that ultimately QCs did not have the decision-making power to maintain interest. **Teamwork and team building** became fashionable, with groups of workers taking responsibility for an entire unit of work, with the emphasis on problem solving. Again many attempts failed to succeed against a backdrop of the need for training and the absence of results-centred actions. The team-working fad failed to address the fact that imbedded culture cannot be changed without the presence of long-term strategies.

Total quality management (TQM) has proved to be equally unworkable in many organizations as they are too preoccupied with production orientations; equally they often neglect the other aspects of employee participation (often referred to as 'soft human resources management') such as true employee involvement and teamwork.

Unless there is a strong commitment to employee participation many of the attempts will inevitably fail; this is exacerbated by high management turnover. Each new wave of management introduces a new wave of participation and increasingly both government legislation and economic trends have resulted in the institution of new schemes. None the less, employees are seen to approve of participation schemes, which may in part be explained by higher levels of education and training. Equally, society has adapted legislation to protect employee rights, and steps to increase the democratization of society have begun to encourage organizations to treat employees fairly, and, above all, the expectation is to work for a business that supports democratic, participative and egalitarian principles.

There is an implied linkage between the complexity of decisions in business and the increasing need to involve employees with specialist knowledge of functional areas. However, as Nykodym noted, the management of such systems is problematic in itself. Managers are unwilling to lose decision-making powers and overall there is little evidence to suggest that participation is anything more than a very restrained process mainly aimed at the receiving of specialist information to help decision making.

Research seems to indicate that there are four main reasons why participation has been, overall, a failure or, at least, has not achieved what was expected:

- the lack of continuity of managers (caused by following individual career paths);
- the lack of middle management support;
- wrong choice of EI strategy;
- employee scepticism.

Holden suggests that there are a number of key areas to address as far as the implementation of participation schemes is concerned:

- a willingness by management to concede some of their prerogatives;
- training managers (and supervisors) in participation initiatives;
- having a clear policy regarding the role and prerogatives of line managers in relation to senior management and the workforce under their supervision;
- training workers in group working skills such as presentation, leadership, assertiveness, problem solving, etc.;
- providing proper feedback mechanisms which clearly indicate that the workforce is being listened to;
- implementing group decisions to reinforce the view amongst the workforce that their contributions are valued;
- recognizing that conflicting views have a place in developing initiatives.

Employee participation remains at the very core of human resources management as it is clear that if the participation is effectively implemented then the benefits in terms of both empowerment and the ability to manage and control are greatly enhanced. Participation can still be seen as a continual power struggle between management and employees – often the root cause of its failure. Despite failures, many

P

organizations have reintroduced schemes, and gradually organizational culture is adapting to allow participation to become an integral element of business strategy.

Allender, H., 'Self-Directed Work Teams: How Far is Too Far?' *Total Quality Management*, September/October 1993, pp. 13–15.

Holden, L., 'Employee Communications on the Increase', *Involvement and Participation*, November 1991, pp. 5–8.

Kanter, R., *The Change Masters: Innovations for Productivity in the American Corporation*. New York: Simon and Schuster, 1983.

Lawler, E. and Mohrman, S., 'Quality Circles After the Fad', *Harvard Business Review*, January–February 1985, pp. 65–71.

Nykodym, Nick, Simonetti, Jack L., Nielson, Warren R., and Welling, Barbara, 'Employee Empowerment', *Empowerments in Organization*, 2(3) (1994), pp. 45–55.

Peters, J. and Waterman, H., *In Search of Excellence: Lessons from America's Best-run Companies*. New York: Harper & Row, 1985.

Smith, C. and Brannick, M., 'A Role and Expectancy Model of Participative Decision-making: A Replication and Theoretical Extension', *Journal of Organizational Behaviour*, 11(2) (1990), pp. 331–40.

Participative goal-setting

Participative goal-setting is a means by which the creation and development of a new or existing team can be achieved. Participative goal-setting involves team members in the personal and professional success of one another. These activities contribute to the development of trust and productive working relationships between and amongst the team.

The principal foundations of goal-setting are that it helps people to know:

- what is to be done and what is not to be done;
- how much needs to be done;
- who will have the responsibility of doing certain tasks.

Goal-setting is most effective when:

- goals are specific;
- goals are difficult, but not impossible;
- when feedback is provided about goals.

In organizations, goal-setting is applied through **management by objectives** (MBO) programmes (note that MBO insists on participative goal-setting), which have four basic ingredients:

- goal specificity;
- participative decision making (both manager and subordinate deciding goals and agreeing the objectives);

- explicit time periods;
- performance feedback (letting people know how well they did).

Locke, E. A. and Latham, G. P., *A Theory of Goal-Setting and Task Performance.* London: Prentice-Hall International (UK), 1990.

Part-time workers

Over 7 million (one in four of the workforce) are part-time staff in the UK, second only to the Netherlands (as a proportion) in the EU. Businesses are becoming ever more reliant upon their part-time workers to provide the flexibility they need. Part-time workers can provide vital cover over busy periods and assist the business in being able to offer 24-hour cover. There are various working patterns involved and, increasingly, businesses will offer their part-time workers a range of employee benefits on a pro rata basis.

Part-time workers are those who provide their services for a working day which is shorter than normal or for a limited number of days per week (or per month). Part-time work is generally preferred by people who need to combine work with other activities (e.g. family commitments). This may be part of the reason that the majority of individuals who fall into this group are women and young people (in this latter case study may be the other commitment).

Under recent legislation, both in the US and in the EU, part-time workers enjoy the same rights as full-time workers; their pay and their social security rights and obligations are calculated on a pro rata basis.

Part-time workers (PLFT) Regulations 2000 (UK)

These regulations provide part-time workers with the right not to be treated less favourably than comparable full-time workers (unless it is objectively justifiable). The Part-time Workers (Prevention of Less Favourable Treatment) Regulations 2000 give the terms and conditions of employment that part-time workers are entitled to by law compared with full-time workers. A part-time worker may make a complaint to an employment tribunal if he thinks his employment rights have not been met, and the tribunal will enforce those rights if necessary.

The Part-time Workers (Prevention of Less Favourable Treatment) Regulations 2000 (Supplementary) Regulations 2001 give workers making a claim under the Part-time Workers (Prevention of Less Favourable Treatment) Regulations 2000 greater capacity to reach agreement and settle the dispute without recourse to an employment tribunal.

Pay equity

Pay equity is often referred to as either 'the wage gap' or 'pay parity'. Fair pay or equitable pay practices have become important for two main reasons:

- As more women have entered the workforce, the wage gap between men and women has attracted attention. Recent surveys of working women have identified fair pay as their priority issue.
- As the market for skilled workers has become more competitive, businesses have found it necessary to ensure that all their employees are compensated fairly, in order to attract and retain their staff.

Three terms have come to be used interchangeably: fair pay, pay equity, and comparable worth. Many women work in occupations such as clerical, nursing and service work. These occupations are traditionally underpaid although in comparison with occupations held by men, they still require similar levels of skill, effort, responsibility and knowledge.

The US National Committee on Pay Equity reported that, while the gap in wages has narrowed, employed women still earned, on average, only 74 per cent of men's average weekly income (1997). Pay equity or fair pay practices can be seen as moves towards non-discrimination. The US Equal Pay Act of 1963 requires that employees doing the same job must be paid the same salary; pay equity goes further and demands that employers examine their pay practices to ensure that certain jobs associated with 'women's work' are not underpaid, but this requires a comparison of dissimilar jobs.

Again in the US, Federal Law, Title VII of the Civil Rights Act, requires employers with at least 15 employees to:

- pay women equally for work similar to that performed by men in the same company;
- provide training opportunities for women equal to those offered to men;
- give women the same consideration for promotion as is given to men;
- pay 'women's jobs' the same as 'men's jobs' if they require the same level of skill, effort, responsibility and working conditions.

There are some key aspects which have led to long-standing differentials in pay, including the following:

- the designs of the pay systems of businesses are historical;
- most employees think it is unfair if some employees, through no fault of their own, suffer a drop in pay due to restructuring;

P

- employees demand parity with higher paid workers in the same job;
- employees feeling unrewarded for their own contribution;
- employees resent narrowing differentials;
- there is a need to understand the impact of the introduction of the minimum wage.

Currently, the UK is considering the Equality Bill which states that it will:

> Make provision making it unlawful to discriminate on the grounds of age, gender reassignment, religion or belief or sexual orientation; to make new provision with respect to discrimination on the grounds of disability, race or sex; to make provision making it unlawful to harass or victimise another person on any of those grounds; to make provision facilitating progress towards the achievement of equality as between persons of certain descriptions; to establish and provide for the functions of the Equality Commission for Great Britain; and for connected purposes.
>
> www.parliament.the-stationery-office.co.uk/pa/ld200203/ldbills/019/03019–a.htm

Enshrined within the bill is the assumption that pay equity will become an inherent requirement of employers. Across the EU, despite moves to close the pay equity gap, there are still many glaring differences:

Gender pay gap developments in the EU – current trends:

Increasing gap	Austria, Portugal, Sweden
Stable gap	Denmark, Finland
Narrowing gap	Belgium, Germany, Greece, Ireland, Luxembourg, Netherlands, Spain

Source: European Foundation for the Improvement of Living and Working Conditions.

The pay gap continues between women and men in all EU Member States. Across the EU as a whole, women doing the same work as men are paid 76% of the gross hourly wage men earn (employment rate for women 51.2% compared with 70.8% for men, women accounting for some 83% of part-time workers).

P

Dickinson, Julie, 'The Role of Beliefs about the Fairness of Wage Settlements in Wage Setting', *People Management*, November 1995.

Rhoads, Steven E., *Incomparable Worth: Pay Equity Meets the Market*. Cambridge: Cambridge University Press, 1993

Hegewisch, Ariane, Gregory, Jeanne and Sales, Rosemary, *Women, Work and Inequality: The Challenge of Equal Pay in a Deregulated Labour Market*. Basingstoke: Palgrave Macmillan, 1999.

Pay secrecy

The question of pay secrecy is a key concern and talking point in human resources management. The policy of secrecy is something of a norm in most organizations as the compensation employees receive is privileged information to both the parties.

Employees are keen to keep their pay details a secret, and pay secrecy diminishes the opportunity for comparison among employees and the organization's possible exposure to accusations of inequality. Pay differences in themselves are difficult to explain, particularly to those who are doing the same job, but equally, pay secrecy shields those who are underpaid as a result of their under-performance.

Open pay policies, on the other hand can make perfect sense for the following reasons:

- They open communication and build trust.
- The business is perceived as a fair and equitable employer
- An employee's right to privacy needs to be balanced against his/her right to know.
- An open pay system illustrates the management's desire to be open.
- it ensures instant measures to deal with inequalities;
- It takes the power and control from the managers and compels them not to reward favourites, but to base pay on merit.
- In maximizing motivation, it lets employees see how performance is defined and measured and finally rewarded.

Payment by results (PBR)

Payment by results is a remuneration system by which pay is not directly related to the amount of time actually worked (such as time-based pay). Remuneration is determined by the employee's measurable performance, specifically in terms of the quantity and quality of work completed.

PBR has a considerable flaw in as much as it is notoriously difficult to calculate the amount to be paid in a fair and objective manner. The most common forms of PBR are **piece-work** and **incentive** bonus systems.

Peer-group diagnosis

Peer diagnosis can be used either in performance appraisals or in assessing the general effectiveness and fit of an individual employee in a number of different situations.

Peer diagnosis demonstrates the importance of interaction in involving a learner in diagnosis. The system allows for all of the participants to communicate with one another, to show mutual commitment and to contribute. Each member of the peer group can attempt to justify his or her beliefs, and challenge the beliefs of others (expressing degrees of agreement or disagreement). This allows the group to gradually establish the validity of the assessment they have given to their peers.

Each question raises new discussion topics which allow the group to clarify issues and support their claims with facts. Simultaneously, all members of the group will give and receive feedback on their claims through the interaction.

Greer, J. E., McCalla, G. I., Collins, J. A., Kumar, V. S., Meagher, P. and Vassileva, J. I., 'Supporting Peer Help and Collaboration in Distributed Workplace Environments', *International Journal of Artificial Intelligence in Education*, 9 (1998).

Pension schemes

A pension is a contributory or in some cases non-contributory scheme which aims to provide an income based on the working-life earnings of an employee. Most businesses have their own pension schemes, usually administered via the human resources department, or ensure that individual employees have their own portable pension schemes. Company or individual pensions are seen as being in addition to any state aided or funded pension scheme derived from funds taken in the form of taxation or insurance contributions.

Performance appraisal

See **appraisal.**

Performance Management

Performance Management can be seen as a systematic and data-oriented approach to managing employees based on positive reinforcement as the primary driver to maximize their performance. Performance Management assumes that there will be a disparity between what employees are currently achieving (on the basis that they have to do this work and perform to this standard) and the possibility that they desire to perform better (based on the assumption that they have desires to perform more effectively if given the opportunity and the encouragement). In many respects, the concept behind Performance Management is a recognition of this potential gap between actual performance and desired performance. This can be illustrated using the graph in Figure 23, which identifies the discretionary effort of an individual. This discretionary effort is applied according to circumstances and is variable. Performance Management seeks to identify the gap between 'having to' and 'wanting to' and push the performance up to the 'want to' level.

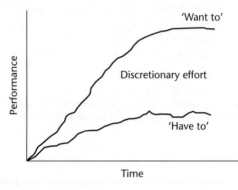

Figure 23 Discretionary effort

Source: www.p-management.com

Performance Management has been used in its various forms since the mid-1970s and it is believed to be applicable to almost every area of a business. Its primary focus is, of course, employees. The first major step in implementing a Performance Management system is to move away from negative reinforcement of standards, which seeks to punish individuals for not performing to (often) unspoken levels of performance. Performance Management uses positive reinforcement to generate effort beyond what is normally (minimally) exhibited by the employees. In this way, the discretionary effort is encouraged and the organization as a whole can move towards a maximization of performance.

Kotter, John P. and Heskett, James L., *Corporate Culture and Performance*. New York: Free Press, 1992.

Porter, Michael, *The Competitive Advantage: Creating and Sustaining Superior Performance*. New York: Simon & Schuster, 1998.

Performance measures

Performance appraisals are the most common form of performance measurement, but the concept also incorporates employee feedback, development and compensation. Overwhelmingly, however, the majority of employees are dissatisfied with performance management systems (the Society of Human Resource Management quotes a 90% figure).

Framing an effective performance management system can be fraught with difficulties. However, the following aspects are seen to be integral in the creation of such a scheme:

- A clear definition and measurement of performance is vital.
- Content and measurement should derive from internal and external customers.
- There should be a formal process of investigating and correcting situational influences and constraints on performance.

Above all, accurate and fair performance management needs to assess employees in relation to the factors listed in Table 27.

Table 27   Assessment of employees

Communication, coordination and support	Equipment and environment
Amount and relevance of training received.	Equipment and tools necessary to do the job.
Information, instructions, and specifications needed to do the job.	Process for obtaining and retaining raw materials, parts and supplies.
Coordination of work activities.	Dependability of equipment.
Cooperation, communication, and relations between co-workers.	Conditions in which job is performed.
Financial resources available and time allowed to produce quantity and quality of work.	

Soltani, Ebrahim, Gennard, John, Meer, Robert van der and Williams, Terry, *Content Issues of HR-Related Performance Measurement: A Total Quality Management Approach.* University of Strathclyde Report, 2002.

Performance-related pay

Performance-related pay (PRP) is used by employers to reward employees on an individual or a team basis. As a remuneration system, it is widely used as it is perceived as a means by which incentives can be awarded to employees who are performing well without the requirement to progress them further up the pay scale.

In effect, PRP rewards individuals differently for carrying out the same job role and, as such, there is an inherent inequality in the system. It is therefore imperative that a transparent system is designed using the following criteria:

- Objectives need to be set and these need to be communicated to employees to ensure understanding.
- There should be some consideration of mitigating factors which may affect performance.
- The evaluation of performance needs to be translated into a form of performance rating.
- The link can therefore be made between the rating and the pay which will be awarded.
- There should be an in-built appeals procedure.

The framing of a PRP should also incorporate the following concepts:

- It should be recognized that bias may creep into the performance assessment.
- Performance criteria should be quantitative rather than qualitative or subjective.
- There should be no differentials built in that may penalize women or minority groups.
- If the scheme is perceived to be unfair, then there is a likelihood that the system will fail.
- There should be no deployment of 'hidden criteria' in awarding pay.
- Whilst long service should be considered desirable, this should be rewarded in a different way, without including it as a consideration in PRP.
- The distribution of appraisal ratings and PRP should be monitored by gender, ethnic group, job level and length of service.
- Managers and employees should have access to this monitoring data.
- Managers need regular training to update them on techniques of appraisal, the setting of objectives and the elimination of bias in performance evaluations.
- Formal appeals should be outside the normal grievance procedures.
- Appeals should be monitored for obvious signs of bias.
- Comprehensive reviews of the payroll records need to be carried out.
- Employee attitude studies need to be carried out to assess the current levels of confidence in the system.

● These attitude studies need to be made available to all employees and managers.

Brown, Duncan and Armstrong, Michael, *Paying for Contribution: New Performance-related Pay Strategies*. London: Kogan Page, 1998.
Chingos, Peter T., *Paying for Performance: A Guide to Compensation Management*. Chichester: John Wiley, 2002.

Performance standards

Performance standards are set in a number of different functions within an organization. The term could relate to the quantity or quality of work that individual employees produce during the course of their job, or alternatively, these standards could be used to assess an employee for **appraisal** or training purposes. In other words, they are the **benchmarks** against which standards are measured.

Typically, a performance standard would be set to measure the quantity of output, but it should be borne in mind that the quality of that output is also of prime importance. Assessment of standards of performance is easier to implement in a manual or production-output situation than in managerial or administrative jobs. Often this problem is overcome by selecting particular tasks within the variety completed as part of the job and ensuring their satisfactory completion. Imperative managerial targets can easily be monitored, like sales figures or customer contact numbers, but there is less scope for the setting of a performance standard for the whole job.

Performance tests

Employee performance tests are also known as Job Performance Measure (JPM). Usually performance tests are used during job application and recruitment exercises as part of the screening process. In the case of JPM, tests are carried out involving existing employees in order to assess their continued suitability for the post and to identify areas which may later require training and education. An identification of these areas may also assist the human resources department to prioritize spending on training and education based on a **training needs analysis**.

Cizek, Gregory L. (ed.), *Setting Performance Standards: Concepts, Methods, and Perspectives*. Hillside, NJ: Lawrence Erlbaum Associates, 2001.

Person specification

A person specification highlights the main characteristics which will be required from the individual who is to undertake a job role. Depending on the requirements of the job, these characteristics may include:

- physical attributes;
- current attainments;
- intelligence levels;
- aptitudes;
- interests;
- disposition;
- circumstances.

The person specification is used in relation to the **job specification**, from which the **job description** is written.

Personal Protective Equipment Regulations (PPR) 1992 (UK)

These regulations require employers to ensure that their employees have the appropriate protective clothing and equipment for their work. Personal Protective Equipment at Work Regulations (1992) form part of a series of health and safety regulations that implement European Directives. Personal Protective Equipment (PPE) is to be supplied wherever there are risks to health and safety that cannot be adequately controlled in other ways.

www.hmso.gov.uk/si/si1992/Uksi_19922966_en_1.htm

Personality test

Applicant or employee personality tests are said to be able to provide both the business and the individual with useful information on how they are likely to respond in various situations as well as revealing their underlying traits and behaviours.

Personality tests are claimed to be:

- supported by extensive research in relation to applications, reliability, and validity;
- able to contribute to an insight into the person undertaking the test;
- a factor which can encourage personal development and growth;
- an aid to professional and organizational development through coaching, career planning, and team-related behaviours which have been identified in the tests.

Some of the most widely used versions of personality tests include:

- Myers–Briggs Type Indicator®, which explores four basic questions that lead to a four-letter type. The four-letter type is a code for a dynamic balance between preferences of perception and judgement.

- Strong Interest Inventory®, which is a career-planning tool. Using answers to questions on occupations, activities, school subjects, leisure activities, types of people, personality qualities, and 'world of work' preferences, a report is generated on relative similar interests in 6 occupational areas, 22 basic interest scales, 211 occupations, and 4 personal styles.
- FIRO-B®, which asks questions about expressed and wanted behaviours in interactions, with regard to inclusion, control, and affection. This provides data regarding the frequency and kind of behaviours related to interacting with others, directing the conversation, and becoming involved in supportive behaviours.
- Spectrum CPI 260™, which covers eighteen scales related to interpersonal and leadership effectiveness. A report is generated graphically, presenting results on more than two dozen scales in five areas.

Barrett, Jim, *Test Yourself: Test your Aptitude, Personality and Motivation and Plan your Career*. London: Kogan Page, 2000.

Peters, Tom

Although Tom Peters has written extensively on broader issues regarding the success of businesses, his central message is about the use of leadership, or rather the habits of leaders. He prefers to use the term 'leadership' rather than 'management' as he suggests that managers should focus on leadership qualities, specifically motivating and facilitating their employees. He therefore places leadership, as can be seen in the diagram in Figure 24, at the centre of all aspects of the business, including creating new ideas through innovation, satisfying customers and, above all, deploying people (employees) in the most effective manner.

Although Tom Peters is probably best known for his theories on customer orientation, having identified 12 attributes or traits of the most successful US businesses, many of these have human resource implications, as can be seen in Table 28.

See also **management by walking about (MBWA).**

Peters, Tom and Waterman, Robert H., *In Search of Excellence: Lessons from America's Best-running Companies*. Profile Business, 1995.

P

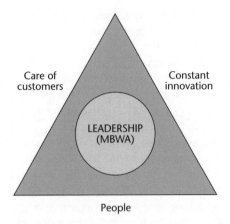

Care of customers

Constant innovation

LEADERSHIP (MBWA)

People

Figure 24   Tom Peters' theory of leadership

Table 28   Qualities needed for a successful business

Trait or quality	Description
Quality obsession	Given the assumption that quality is of paramount importance, leaders should tackle quality issues the moment they arise.
Passionate systems	The drive for quality should not just be a system; it should be an ideology with a system.
Measurement of quality	Everyone in the organization should understand how quality is measured.
Quality rewards	Incentives should be given to those who consistently provide quality.
Quality training	All employees should receive quality training on quality.
Multi-function teams	**Quality circles** should be established, with the power to drive change.
Small improvements	Any improvement in quality, however small, should be celebrated and rewarded.
Continuous **Hawthorne Effect**	Employees should always be given new goals, and leaders should be seen to be seen.
Quality teams and structures	A structure of quality teams should be established to closely examine all aspects and processes of the business.

$\Rightarrow$

P

Table 28 Qualities needed for a successful business (*continued*)

Trait or quality	Description
Total involvement	Suppliers and distributors should be included in any quality drive or vision.
Quality and cost	There is a direct relationship between quality (which reduces wastage, etc.) and profitability. All employees should be aware of this.
Quality utopia	Having achieved specific quality goals, new ones should be set to strive towards.

Phased retirement

Phased retirement, or phased retirement pension plans, allow employees to cash-in their pension fund in stages. It is normally available to employees between the ages of 50 and 75.

In terms of work commitments, a phased retirement means a gradual reduction in hours and pay, supported by a gradual reliance on the pension benefits accrued over the years. The process of gradually accessing pension benefits is also known as 'draw-down'.

Piece-work

Piece-work means that employees are not paid according to the hours that they work but instead are paid by the number of items produced. A worker should, theoretically, not get less than the minimum wage if paid on a piece-work basis.

Many factories pay staff a flat rate per hour plus 'piece' work (so much extra per piece of work), which allows experienced staff the opportunity to increase their wages.

Point system

Point systems are a form of job evaluation which assesses the relative importance of a job's key factors in order to compare them with other job roles in the business. A common set of criteria, to assess the value, effort, responsibility and efficiency of each of the factors, is deployed in order to assess clearly the comparative data which is collected.

Having allocated points to each of the jobs, the human resources department is then able to make meaningful comparisons in order to create a fair and equitable pay structure for all employees.

Positive discrimination

Positive discrimination is a now outdated way of describing **affirmative action**.

Preventive discipline

Preventive discipline is action taken either by management or by human resources departments prior to any breaches in employee discipline. The proactive approach is adopted in order to ensure that employees follow the prescribed codes of behaviour before there is any breach of that code. In many cases, this action is taken because it is assumed that current behaviour may be moving in a direction that could mean a breach in the near future.

Proactive human resources management

Proactive human resources management (HRM) aims to have high flexibility and a high strategic focus. Human resources managers will be closely involved in business strategy formulation and the management of change. As the approach is a flexible one, human resources management is forward thinking, operating on the principles involved in the organization of learning. In these cases, human resources management is seen as one of the main drivers of direction and not simply a means by which to process employees.

In comparison, there are three other associated modes of approach for the management of human resources – these are:

- *Restrictive HRM* with low flexibility and strategy focus. Human resources departments have firmly established procedures which are reactive to events, and there is little forward planning.
- *Reactive HRM* is practised with high flexibility, but a low strategy focus. Procedures are flexible and available, but mainly reactive. Human resources management is responsive, but mainly defined by established procedures and there are few long-term strategic planning initiatives.
- *Planned HRM* has low flexibility, but a high strategy focus. Human resources management is effectively planned and there is a clear strategic focus. Once the procedures are set in place, human resources departments are not willing to change them without very good reason.

The relationships between the different forms of human resource management can be seen in the diagram in Figure 25.

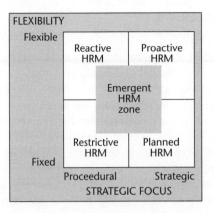

Figure 25   Approaches to human resources management

Bruce, Willa M., *Problem Employee Management: Proactive Strategies for Human Resource Managers*. Westport, CT: Greenwood Press, 1990.

Production bonus

A production bonus is a supplementary component of pay usually provided for in industry-wide agreements. Despite the implications of the term, the production bonus has no specific connection with the attainment of output targets by the employees.

Productivity

Productivity is a measure of an organization's outputs divided by its inputs. In other words a comparison of the value of products and services produced and offered by the business, and the costs of employees, capital and materials, and other associated costs.

See **productivity bargaining** *and* **productivity audit**.

Productivity audit

A productivity audit, in relation to human resources, will investigate a number of issues including labour costs, absenteeism and levels of wastage. These investigations will be related directly to the productivity of the organization and, in the past, more strictly related to production itself. Productivity audits have broadened their scope to include factors which are not directly related to production (i.e. indirect costs are now brought into the equation as opposed to the investigations simply considering direct costs).

A full productivity audit would therefore consider the following issues:

- an identification and quantifying of specific and immediate opportunities for cost reduction and productivity improvements;
- a measurement of the true value delivered to the business by individual projects, employees, teams and services;
- an accurate, value-based comparison between different groups and departments;
- scale ranking productivity by the value of activities and services;
- a matching process which links customer satisfaction with the cost of providing the service and with the value of that service;
- a benchmarking process judging internal operating costs against those of industry leaders.

Productivity bargaining

Productivity bargaining, as a concept and process, was probably coined some forty years ago when trade unions and employers considered the question of pay increases in relation to productivity. Productivity bargaining saw trade unions conceding changes in working practices, staffing levels and organization of work in exchange for pay settlements.

The underlying concept is that pay increases should be self-financing in the sense that the concessions fund the increases in pay. Productivity bargaining was a widely used formula during the 1960s, but since then (as a term at least) the process has been superseded by other forms of pay negotiation. Clearly, productivity bargaining required the full cooperation and endorsement of the trade unions in the form of collective bargaining as the concessions made would be applied either across the whole business or, in some cases, across the whole industry.

Productivity bargaining is now probably better known as an efficiency agreement or a flexibility agreement, but both concepts have many of the characteristics of productivity bargaining as they both rely on the employees or their representatives making concessions on issues such as working conditions and levels of staffing in order to secure the pay increases. In many respects, these new agreements aim to be self-financing just as productivity bargaining was intended to be.

See **productivity** *and* **productivity audit.**

Professional development

Professional development has become an integral part of the human resources function, which is achieved by a variety of different means including:

- workshops;
- membership of professional organizations;
- certification arising out of studies;
- conference attendance and delivery of papers;
- job shadowing;
- after-action reviews and in-process reviews;
- informal counselling;
- report-writing assignments;
- cross-training;
- buddy assignments;
- on-the-job training;
- assignment to teams/committees;
- committee leadership;
- mentoring.

There are five major functions of professional development, or employee development, which are:

1 Expanding the knowledge base – helping to develop new information and conceptual understandings related to the changing goals and expectations of the business and the industry.
2 Learning from practice – learning from others how to put new concepts, ideas and models into practice.
3 Developing new attitudes and beliefs – changing attitudes and beliefs are among the most difficult aspects of any profession. This means offering opportunities to exchange ideas with those who share similar realities, responsibilities, and challenges/problems and are willing to share strategies.
4 Opportunities for self-renewal – an individually-oriented approach to professional development provides opportunities for improvement for employees at all levels.
5 Collaborating with and contributing to the growth of others – taking advantage of the expertise of others, and being recognized for one's own successes, can be an incentive for continued study and development.

Marczely, B., 'Staff Development for a Healthy Self-concept', *Journal of Staff Development*, 11(1) (1990), pp. 40–2.

Sparks, D. and Loucks-Horsley, S., 'Five Models of Staff Development for Teachers', *Journal of Staff Development*, 10(4) (1989), pp. 40–57.

P

Profit sharing

This is a term which is applied to a number of schemes offered by employers which aim to give the employees a stake in the business; many were prompted in the UK by the Finance Acts (1978, 1980 and 1984).

Around 20 per cent of UK business has some form of employee share ownership and the move is seen as being a form of employee participation and industrial democracy. In reality, however, the level of share ownership is low and the employees have little or no real control over the business (mainly as the shares tend to have non-voting rights).

The three most common forms of profit sharing are:

- *Employee Share Ownership Plans (ESOP)*, which were brought to the UK from the US and provide a means by which employees can gain equity in the business. A trust is formed and the dividends on the preference shares pay off the loans used to purchase the shares on behalf of the employees. The shares are held in trust, but employees have the right to sell them.
- *Profit Sharing Schemes (PSS)* usually take the form of Approved Profit Sharing (APS) schemes, which involve the distribution of shares to employees free of charge. Shares are purchased through a trust which is financed from the profits of the business. Alternatively, employees can become involved in **SAYE** (Save As You Earn), whereby employees sign a savings contract with the option to purchase shares at the end of a contract period at a predetermined price. Both of these methods are more popular as they have tax benefits attached to them.
- *Profit-related Pay (PRP)* schemes are present in around 20 per cent of private sector business and are, essentially, an element in the total employee pay package. Profit-related pay is variable according to the profits made by the business, making a direct link between the activities of the employees, their productivity, and the extra pay that they ultimately receive in the form of PRP.

Profit sharing is seen as being an effective means by which a business can encourage individual performance and motivation. Employees have a direct interest in the success of the business and therefore greater commitment and profit-consciousness.

The obvious downside as far as employees are concerned is that they are tying both their jobs and their savings to the success or failure of the business. As far as the business is concerned there is also a worry that increasing staff involvement (particularly in share ownership) may mean that the employees will make increasing demands that they be given a

P

greater role in the decision making. Management may be unwilling to make concessions in the strategic decision making which can affect profitability and employee pay, as they may be considering longer-term issues.

Progressive discipline

This is a form of discipline or disciplinary procedure which introduces stronger penalties for employees who persistently breach the rules and regulations of the organization. Repeat offenders, under a progressive discipline regime, would be moved on further up the disciplinary procedures for offences similar to those that they had committed in the past.

Protection from Harassment Act 1997 (UK)

The Protection from Harassment Act 1997 created a new means by which victims of harassment in the workplace can obtain compensation. Under the terms of this Act, for example, an employer would be vicariously liable under the Protection from Harassment Act 1997 for damages arising from any harassment by a senior staff member towards a junior staff member.

www.legislation.hmso.gov.uk/acts/acts1997/1997040.htm

Provision and Use of Work Equipment Regulations (PUWER) 1992 (UK)

These regulations aim to ensure that all equipment, including machinery, used by employees is safe and meets guaranteed minimum standards.

These Regulations tidied up the laws governing equipment used at work. They place general duties on employers and list minimum requirements for work equipment, to deal with selected hazards in all industry.

www.hmso.gov.uk/si/si1998/19982306.htm

P

Psychometric testing

A psychometric test can be used to judge an individual's intelligence, their personality and attitudes, levels of motivation, and general psychological make-up. Typically, psychometric tests involve individuals in completing a questionnaire requiring them to express their preferences, highlight their desired outcomes to given situations or describe their own opinions of their personality. Organizations use a variety of different established and respected methods of psychometric testing, including:

- the **Myers–Briggs Type Indicator** – which categorizes individuals under four main headings;
- the 16 PF test – which claims the existence of as many as 16 different categories, or clusters, of human behaviour;
- the DISC test – which identifies aspects of an individual's behaviour by identifying their degrees of dominance and influence over others, or tendencies for submission and compliance;
- the Eysenck personality inventory – which requires individuals to answer a series of 'yes or no' questions in order to establish whether they can be categorized as introvert or extrovert and stable or neurotic.

Psychometric testing is a relatively low-cost exercise and can be carried out with a number of individuals at the same time. This testing process allows the organization to highlight required behavioural traits amongst **applicants** with similar qualifications and experience.

Public Interest Disclosure Act 1998 (UK)

Known as the Whistle Blowing Act, the Public Interest Disclosure Act 1998 protects workers from detrimental treatment or victimization from their employer if, in the public interest, they blow the whistle on wrongdoing. The Act protects most workers in the public, private and voluntary sectors. The Act does not apply to self-employed professionals (other than in the NHS), voluntary workers, police officers or the intelligence services.

www.legislation.hmso.gov.uk/acts/acts1998/19980023.htm

P

Quality circle

A quality circle is a discussion group which meets on a regular basis to identify quality problems, investigate solutions and make recommendations as to the most suitable solution. The members of quality circles are employees and may include individuals with specific skills or expertise, such as engineers, quality inspectors or salespersons. Quality circles were first created in the 1950s in the Toyota motor company. In the 1980s this Japanese form of **employee participation** and consultation was adopted on a large scale in both Europe and the US. Quality circles aim to use untapped knowledge from employees, as well as providing them with the opportunity to show their knowledge and talents in terms of their problem-solving skills.

Quality of work life (QWL)

Quality of work life has become a key aspect of human resources, largely as a result of increasing legislation on the humanization of the workplace. In Europe, Article 13 of the Working Time Directive specifically states:

> Member States shall take the measures necessary to ensure that an employer who intends to organise work according to a certain pattern takes account of the general principle of adapting work to the worker, with a view, in particular, to alleviating monotonous work and work at a pre-determined work-rate, depending on the type of activity, and of safety and health requirements, especially as regards breaks during work time.

See also **Working Time Regulations 1998 (UK); Working Time Regulations 1999;** *and* **Working Time (Amendment) Regulations 2002.**

Quinn, R. E.

See **organizational culture.**

Rr

Race Relations Act 1976 (UK)

The Race Relations Act 1976 (RRA) addresses discrimination on grounds of race, colour, nationality or ethnic or national origin and has considerable implications with regard to human resources.

The Act covers direct discrimination, indirect discrimination (such as excluding areas of high settlement of minority ethnic groups or insisting on British qualifications) and victimization. Allied to this, the Asylum and Immigration Act 1996 (Section 8) deals with illegal working, making it a criminal offence to employ an individual who is not entitled to live or work in the United Kingdom (employers are obliged to check the applicant's status).

This factor has caused a degree of concern, as noted by the Commission for Racial Equality, in that changes in recruitment and selection procedures in order to comply with the Asylum and Immigration Act may put employers in breach of the RRA. Human resources personnel, therefore, need to ensure that documentation checks are carried out at the same time and in the same way for all applicants without bias, regardless of their race, colour or ethnic background.

www.homeoffice.gov.uk/raceact/racerel1.htm

Race Relations (Amendment) Act 2000 (UK)

The Race Relations (Amendment) Act 2000 amended the Race Relations Act 1976 in order to implement the EC Article 13 Race Directive. The 2000 Act outlaws race discrimination in public authority functions not previously covered by the 1976 Act. The Act also places a general duty on public authorities to work towards the elimination of unlawful discrimination and promote equality of opportunity and good relations between persons of different racial groups.

www.legislation.hmso.gov.uk/acts/acts2000/20000034.htm

Ranking method

Essentially, the ranking method is a means by which an employer can evaluate or appraise individual employees on the basis of their best and worst traits. In identifying areas of excellence, employers can ensure that employees receive praise, and perhaps, if these good points sufficiently outweigh their negative traits, then this may form a basis for enhanced pay or a financial incentive. Negative traits can be focused upon in order to identify training requirements to resolve these issues.

Rating scale

Essentially a rating scale is not dissimilar to a **job ranking** system, in as much as it seeks to make an evaluation of an employee's performance, based on a set of criteria. Rating scales are usually associated with a subjective evaluation by the individual carrying out the assessment.

Reactive human resources management

Reactive human resources management adopts the contrary position to **proactive human resources management**. A reactive human resources stance relies on the ability to respond to problems and make rapid decisions about them as they arise. Adopting this approach means that human resources managers can concentrate on current issues rather than attempting to put in place policies and procedures that can effectively anticipate and deal with future or presumed issues.

Realistic job preview

Many organizations, under the direction of human resources departments, will offer job **applicants**, primarily those who have been short-listed, the opportunity to experience, or at least see, the realities of actually working for the organization. This process may involve showing the potential candidates around the premises, where they can make a personal assessment of the **working conditions**, equipment available, facilities and general demeanour of the rest of the workforce. These tours around the organization often take place on the day on which the **interviews** are being held and candidates are given the opportunity to meet individuals who may become their colleagues.

A natural extension of this, although not widely practised, is offering short-listed candidates the opportunity to have a taster period, perhaps shadowing an existing employee who is engaged in work similar to that which they have applied for.

R

Record analysis

A record analysis involves a review of the organization's past **human resource audit**. The review would seek to assess the effectiveness of these audits and to ascertain whether there are specific trends or recurring issues which may need to be addressed. Equally, a record analysis can be used in preparation for a future human resource audit in order to identify areas of concern or interest that should become the focus of that audit, or a major part of it.

Recruiter habits

The term 'recruiter habits' can be applied both to the human resources department of an organization and to any external recruiter who works on behalf of the organization. The habits of recruiters can be identified in terms of their preferred methods and systems, or behaviours prevalent in any of their recruitment drives or campaigns. Recruiters will tend to use tried and trusted systems of attracting potential **applicants** and will seek to learn by mistakes they have found in the past, by eliminating them from future recruitment campaigns.

Recruitment

The exact nature of a recruitment procedure will tend to be based on exactly what the preferred methodology may be and whether the recruitment is occurring internally, externally or via an external recruiter. Typically, recruitment procedures will inevitably begin with the recognition that a specific post, either existing or newly created, exists as a vacancy. Exactly how the organization chooses to fill this vacancy may be based on previous experience, taking into account any successes or failures that may have been encountered in the past.

Having drawn up a **job description**, **job specification** and **person specification** from a **job design**, the organization then proceeds to create related documents upon which decisions related to the recruitment will be based. Whether **internal recruitment** or **external recruitment** is used, the organization now needs to advertise the post and attempt to attract suitable candidates. In the case of internal recruitment, this may simply mean a suitable advertisement in the organization's newsletter or a document posted on a notice-board.

In the case of external recruitment, the organization may choose to place an advertisement in a local or national newspaper, in a trade magazine, or on the internet (**e-recruiting**). Alternatively, at this stage they may decide to enlist the services of either a government agency or

R

an **employment agency** to attract and perhaps short-list candidates on their behalf. Assuming that the organization wishes to carry out the recruitment themselves, through their own human resources department, there will now be a requirement to respond to inquiries, based on the criteria which have been outlined in the job advertisement. This may, of course, involve dealing with CVs or **résumés**, letters of application and application forms. A process then needs to be established in order to assess the various applications that may have arrived by the date determined in the advertisement. At this stage the organization has the choice of whether to pursue **employment references** or whether to postpone this aspect until the candidates have been short-listed.

The short-listing process aims to identify the most suitable candidates to fill the post, using the information primarily provided by the candidates themselves. A series of checks may be made prior to the confirmation of the short-list, perhaps using external agencies to carry out background checks on a limited number of individuals.

The **interview** process may require the short-listed candidates to answer a number of questions related to their past working experience, reasons for applying for the post, aspirations and other more personal issues. If nothing else, the interview process allows those on the interview panel to make a direct comparison between what they have read and what they now see. As part of this process, candidates may also be required to undergo a **medical evaluation**, or consent to taking a **personality test**. At the end of the interviewing process a decision needs to be made as to the most suitable candidate.

Prudent organizations will offer the most suitable candidate the opportunity to confirm that they wish to take up the job offer before informing those who were not chosen that, on this occasion, they have been unsuccessful. This means that should the most suitable candidate have changed his or her mind, then the next most suitable candidate can now be offered the post. Unsuccessful candidates are often grateful for objective comments about their performance and a short statement as to why they were not suitable for the advertised post, although there is no legal obligation to provide this.

Once the suitable candidate has accepted the job offer, the next stage in the recruitment process is to draw up a **contract of employment** and agree a start date. The new employee will normally begin a working relationship with the organization by undertaking an **induction** programme, which can be seen as an integral part of the recruitment process as it serves to orientate the individual into the organization itself.

Wood, Robert and Payne, Tim, *Competency-based Recruitment and Selection: A Practical Guide*. Chichester: John Wiley, 1998.

Red-circled rate

A red-circled rate is most commonly put into place following a **job evaluation** exercise. As a result of the job evaluation, some of the posts held may have been downgraded. The individuals currently completing the tasks required of the job will be maintained at their current salary (red-circled) until they have been replaced. Those inheriting the job will automatically be placed on the newly downgraded rate of pay for the job.

Redundancy

Employee protection legislation makes it clear that an employee is redundant when the whole or main reason for dismissal is that the employer's need for them to continue to work in their job role has ceased. This could be as the result of an organization choosing **downsizing** in order to streamline its activities. There are two main forms of redundancy, voluntary or compulsory.

In *voluntary redundancy* the employer collectively informs the department or entire staff of the intention to make redundancies, and initially leaves the option open for staff to volunteer for redundancy. This could prove costly to the employer, as those staff with longer service often take advantage of their higher redundancy-payments entitlement. The company has to consider its needs and balance them with the perceived value of those employees volunteering. Voluntary redundancy is only an offer and the employer is under no legal obligation to accept the employee's offer to take redundancy, and neither does the organization have to justify its criteria for offering this option.

In *compulsory redundancy* the employer decides who is to be made redundant. In making this decision the employer would have to follow certain procedures and considerations, as well as showing the employee certain obligations. Firstly, all dismissal procedures are subject to:

- legislation;
- **contracts of employment**;
- employee association and **trade union** agreements.

In all cases of redundancy, good employment practice recognizes that:

- the employee is given as much warning as possible;
- alternative employment is offered, where possible, which the employee is not obliged to accept;
- fair and objective criteria will be used to determine who is chosen for redundancy;

- communication between the employer and employees, or their representatives, remains open;
- employees, who have worked for the organization for more than two years, are entitled to take paid time off work in order to seek a new job.

The employer needs to ensure that the criteria used for selection are agreed with the employees' representatives and that they are clearly defined. These criteria must be applied fairly and consistently to all employees within the organization. The criteria may include:

- length of service;
- last in, first out;
- measure of applicable skills;
- experience;
- aptitude;
- performance, attendance and disciplinary record.

Criteria that an organization would not be wise to consider for purposes of redundancy are given below. Should any of these be proved to be amongst their criteria, then the employee(s) could have grounds to claim **unfair dismissal**:

- sex or race;
- maternity or disability;
- trade union affiliation reasons;
- carrying out representative activities on behalf of employees.

Many employers prefer to place redundant employees on **garden leave**.

See also **collective redundancy** *and* **Trade Union Reform and Employment Rights Act 1993**.

Reference

See **employment reference**.

Rehabilitation Act (Section 503) 1973 (US)

Section 503 of the Rehabilitation Act and the **Americans with Disabilities Act** seek to cover all individuals who have a range of impairments. The Acts recognize that individuals who have recovered from their disabilities may face job **discrimination** because of their past medical records. Provided the individuals have the necessary education, skills or other job-related requirements, then the employer must make reasonable accommodation to accept them as potential or existing employees. In effect this means that employers should make adjustments or modifications in the work, job application process, work environment, job structure, equipment, employment practices or the way that job duties are performed so that an individual can perform the essential functions of the job.

www.dol.gov/dol/compliance/comp-rehab.htm

Rehabilitation of Offenders Act 1974 (UK)

The Rehabilitation of Offenders Act 1974 enables certain criminal convictions to become 'spent' (or otherwise ignored), provided a 'rehabilitation period' has elapsed.

The period is a set length of time (from the date of conviction), after which the ex-offender is not (normally) obliged to mention the conviction. This is of particular significance in the case of job interviews and applications.

www.homeoffice.gov.uk/cpd/sou/rehabcon.htm

Reinstatement or re-engagement

Reinstatement and re-engagement refer to situations which may occur as a result of the final deliberation of an employment tribunal. Provided it has been proved that **unfair dismissal** took place, then three situations may occur, two of which involve the re-employment of the applicant by the employer. Reinstatement means that an employee is to be given back the job which was lost, and treated in all respects by the employer as if the dismissal had not occurred. Re-engagement involves the re-employment of the employee, but not necessarily in the same job or under the same terms and conditions of employment as before. Both reinstatement and re-engagement will normally entail an award being granted to the employee for **compensation** for the loss of earnings suffered up until the time the employment tribunal delivered its verdict on the case.

The other possibility arising out of a successful verdict against unfair dismissal is that reinstatement or re-engagement does not occur and that compensation is paid to the employee.

A tribunal will consider and take into account whether the employee wishes to be reinstated or re-engaged. The tribunal will normally take into account the practicalities of the employee returning to work; in cases where there was partial blame attached to the employee, it is usually not the case that reinstatement or re-engagement will be ordered.

www.acas.org.uk

Relocation

In certain instances it may be unavoidable that employees are asked to continue to work for the organization, but in an alternative location. There may be many reasons why relocation has been considered and approved by the business. Typically, the closure or merging of branches or offices within an organization, or location changes as a result of an acquisition, may entail the redeployment of staff to alternative premises. Under most circumstances the employer, at the first instance, will offer relocation to most, if not all, employees, assuming of course that this will not mean duplication or over-manning at the new location. It is certainly the case that specific employees will be approached and offered a relocation package as they continue to be considered vital to the long-term prospects of the business.

Relocation programmes and associated assistance becomes a considerable task for human resources departments, in as much as they may have to be simultaneously dealing with employees who have been offered, and have accepted, relocation packages and others who have not been offered this assistance, or have chosen not to accept it.

Replacement chart

Human resources managers may use a job replacement chart as a visual representation which identifies named individuals who can assume the responsibilities of other employees in their absence. Replacement charts can be used both for short-term absences, such as illness, **compassionate leave** or holidays, and for potentially longer-term absences or permanent absences in the event of **retirement**. Human resources departments use the replacement chart in order to visualize contingencies which may, in the longer term, need a more permanent solution.

Reporting of Injuries, Diseases and Dangerous Occurrences Regulations (RIDDOR) 1992 (UK)

A revised version of these regulations came into force in 1996, requiring employers to notify the Health and Safety Executive of occupational injuries, diseases and dangerous events in the workplace.

www.hmso.gov.uk/si/si1995/Uksi_19953163_en_1.htm

Restructuring

Just the mention of the word 'restructuring' brings enormous dread and negative images to both an organization and its employees.

Restructuring is recognition of the fact that as the organization is currently structured there are severe deficiencies in its operations. Inevitably, for employees and human resources management, any restructuring exercise will involve an enormous degree of upheaval. Restructuring tends to occur either when a business is teetering on the brink of disaster, or as a pre-requisite demanded by a financial institution as a priority issue before funds will be released to the organization.

For human resources, restructuring can mean not only dealing with a potentially large percentage of the employees as casualties of the process, but also that those who remain may have their jobs entirely redesigned or realigned, to match a new structure which aims to be more efficient and productive.

Résumé

The word 'résumé' refers to the US version of the curriculum vitae (CV). In a similar way to the CV, as used in the UK, a résumé will detail an individual's name, address and date of birth, relevant education, qualifications and experience. It will be submitted to an organization that is currently undergoing a **recruitment** drive, for assessment by the human resources department to identify whether the individual should be called in for **interview**.

Retirement

Although each country may specifically state the generally accepted age of retirement, many employees are not only prepared to continue beyond the normal retirement age, but they are positively encouraged to do so by their employers. Although many individuals approaching retirement age are at the top end of any pay scale, they also invariably represent individuals who have had the most experience of dealing with a variety of situations – a resource which is invaluable to the employer.

Increasingly, however, employers are offering their employees flexible retirements, which could take the form either of a **phased retirement** or of a process whereby the retirement-aged individual is retained well beyond normal retirement age for a fixed period of time. This is so that they can pass on their skills and expertise to those who will eventually replace them. With a flexible retirement scheme, employers face the problem of not knowing precisely when an individual may or may not choose to go into full retirement; this presents difficulties for managing human resources, as it is difficult to judge when a replacement is needed.

Fixed retirement is still perhaps the most common form, and, depending upon the prevailing national legislation, employees can plan to step down gradually from their job over a period of time. It is incumbent upon human resources management to ensure that all is in place for the individual's retirement; this will involve the preparation of any benefits, lump sums or other payments, as well as setting into motion the payment (if applicable) of the company's pension to the individual.

In retaining employees beyond retirement age a business runs the risk of blocking the promotion prospects of younger individuals who may feel frustrated in not being given the opportunity for promotion when it was expected and may well choose to seek employment elsewhere.

Ringi-sie

Ringi-sie, or, more commonly, *Ringi*, is a Japanese management term which literally means reverential inquiry. It is, in fact, a bottom–up system which consists of circulating documents at the lowest levels of management, or supervision, so that each individual can endorse the document with their signature, signifying that they have read and digested the contents.

There is an inference that whilst the process involves active **participation**, there is not the implication that the document will necessarily be changed. It is simply circulated and endorsed. The concept is based on the premise that the upper tiers of management merely act as facilitators to those in lower management positions; in other words their role is to enable these managers to carry out their tasks.

Role playing

Role playing can be used as an element of a training programme in order to expose the trainees to simulations of real situations. Trainees or facilitators are required to adopt different roles in order to simulate specific situations, which will then enable the other trainees to react within the parameters of policies and procedures which may have already been relayed to them earlier in the programme.

Role playing is also used to illustrate how it may feel to be another individual in a specific circumstance, in other words to provide an opportunity for the trainees to empathize with others.

Rotter, Julian

See **locus of control**.

R

Ss

Safety and health audit

A safety and health audit, or a health and safety audit, involves the investigation and recognition of all health and safety issues which have occurred in the past. The audit also includes an assessment of any current dangers and seeks to implement immediate remedies to eliminate the danger.

> *See also* **Health and Safety at Work Act 1974** *and* **health and safety for employees regulations.**

Salary spine

A salary spine is usually taken to imply a unified structure of pay throughout an organization. Salary spines are typically used in organizations which have a degree of commonality throughout a broad range of job titles. Specifically, these are often used in teaching, the armed forces and the civil service.

The salary spines are usually rigid structures, hence the name, which relates to the fact that employees are placed on a specific level of the salary spine and progression is usually automatic, depending upon length of service, rather than individual performance in any given year.

SAYE

SAYE is an acronym for Save As You Earn. In most cases SAYE schemes are set up by employers, giving employees the right to purchase a number of shares in the organization at a fixed price. SAYEs are also known as share saves, where a fixed monthly sum is deducted from an employee's pay by the employer for between 3 and 7 years, at the end of which the employee receives a bonus. The bonus payment is derived from a calculation of the total amount of savings over the 3- to 7-year period. In the UK, upwards of 1.75 million employees are involved in SAYE schemes in over 1,000 organizations.

Schein, Edgar H.

Schein created a questionnaire-based system by which individuals could identify their career motivators or career anchors. Schein believed that there were eight such anchors and that each individual would have a distinct preference towards one of them. A summary of the eight career anchors can be found in Table 29.

Table 29   Schein's career motivators

Career anchor/ competence	Description
Technical/functional	Individuals who define their career through challenges and the work they are undertaking.
Managerial	Problem solvers who like to lead and control.
Independence	Individuals who value freedom above all.
Security	Those who desire stability.
Entrepreneurial creativity	Those with innovative ideas and practical skills.
Service	Those who value being able to help others.
Challenge	Those who seek solutions or ways around problems.
Lifestyle	Work is subservient to domestic and social life and just a means to fund it.

Schein, Edgar H., *Career Anchors: Discovering Your Real Values – Instrument and Trainers Manual*. Indianapolis, IN: Pfeiffer Wiley, 1996.

Secondment

Secondment involves individuals temporarily leaving their place of employment in order to work for another organization. Typically, individuals who have predominantly theoretically-based roles within an organization will seek practical experience linked to their job by working in a related aspect for another organization.

Selection process

See **recruitment.**

S

Selection ratio

A selection ratio may be used by human resources departments in order to calculate the number of individuals employed at the end of a recruitment campaign, compared with the total number of applicants for the position.

Self and peer assessment (SAPA)

Self and peer assessment (SAPA) is a variation of the **appraisal** system which requires individual employees to make personal appraisals, which are then cross-referenced with similar assessment of them by their colleagues, as opposed to their managers.

Self-development group

Self-development groups, under the direction and assistance of human resources managers, are allocated time and resources in order to identify, deliver or buy-in training to match their specific and identified needs. Human resources departments will facilitate the provision of any external training or will arrange **in-house training** where required.

Self-directed work group/team

In many respects a self-directed work group or team is the ultimate form of **delegation**. It has been a system used in a variety of different sets of circumstances both in manufacturing and in the office environment. In terms of manufacturing, it can be likened to a cell-structure form of production, where the employees themselves decide how the work will be allocated, in what order, and what the overall objectives are (within guidelines). The employees are considered all to be on an equal basis and democratically reach their decisions.

Seniority

Seniority is one of the various measures that may be used by human resources departments in order to identify individuals within the organization who are eligible for promotion, or, perhaps, **redundancy**. Seniority does not necessarily imply age, but is a measure of the length of time the individual has been in continuous employment with the current employer.

An alternative explanation of the term 'seniority' could refer to the current position of authority which an individual holds in the **chain of command**.

Severance pay

Severance pay is an alternative term used to describe the total package payable to an employee when he or she leaves the employment of the current organization. Severance pay will include all outstanding entitlements, including holidays, possibly a period of notice and any other payments due in relation to the nature of the employee's departure.

Sex Discrimination Act 1975 (UK)

The Sex Discrimination Act 1975 (SDA) makes it unlawful to discriminate on grounds of sex or marital status in recruitment, promotion and training. Specifically, the SDA covers the following areas, of direct significance to human resources:

- The SDA defines direct sex discrimination in situations where a person of one sex is treated less favourably than a person of the other sex would have been treated in the same circumstances.
- The SDA defines indirect sex discrimination as being cases where the majority of the workers are of one sex, and they are being discriminated against. A prime example of this is the case of part-time workers (traditionally predominantly women in the UK). If it can be shown that part-time workers are being discriminated against and the majority of those workers are women, then this is a case of indirect discrimination.
- Discrimination may also occur in cases where a worker is victimized on the grounds of their gender.

www.pfc.org.uk/legal/sda.htm

Sexual harassment

This is the harassment of employees on the basis of their gender.

See also **harassment** *and* **Sex Discrimination Act 1975.**

Share option

See **SAYE** *and* **Employee Share Schemes Act 2002.**

Shared responsibility model

A shared responsibility model is primarily related to situations where both the employer and the employees cooperate in ensuring that the workplace remains a safe and healthy environment. Both parties take active steps to identify and eliminate potential dangers as and when they occur.

Shift work

Shift work is a pattern of work in which one employee replaces another on the same job within a 24-hour period. Shift workers normally work in groups that make up a separate shift team. In some shift systems, each group of shift workers will regularly change its hours of work and rotate morning, afternoon, and night shifts.

The continuous shift work system provides cover for 24 hours, seven days a week. A non-continuous or discontinuous shift system provides cover for less than the total hours available in a week, typically a total of 5 × 24-hour periods in 7 days, or 12 hours out of 24.

Shift work is widespread throughout Europe, typically in industries in which equipment, services or manufacturing processes must continue on a 24-hour cycle. Examples of this type of industry range from newspaper production and public utilities, to hospitals and the emergency services. A development in more recent years has been the spread of shift working to industries such as **tele-work** and banking. The main reasons for developing a system of shift work are:

- Economic – because the pace of change has quickened, together with the rate at which machinery and equipment become obsolete, shift work enables employers to make maximum use of machinery and equipment to reduce production costs and increase output.
- Social – changes in living and working patterns have created a demand for products and services outside the more traditional working hours. Retail outlets are now commonly open every day of the week and some are open 24 hours a day.

The **Working Time Regulations** (1998, 1999 and 2002) govern the hours people can work, and prescribe special health provisions for night workers.

Sickness

See **statutory sick pay.**

Situational interview

A situational interview is a face-to-face meeting usually held during the recruitment and selection process. This employment interview will direct questions to the **applicant** that aim to extract a response to a number of likely situations that could occur within the advertised job role. The potential new employees will then be assessed on the quality of the answers given regarding how they would handle these specific incidents.

See also **interviews.**

Skill-/knowledge-based pay

This is a remuneration system that, unlike the majority of pay systems which link remuneration to a job title, links the actual skills and knowledge of the employees to their wage or salary.

Skills analysis/skills assessment

An important function of human resources is to determine the skills available in the current workforce and to identify skills which are needed to carry out jobs within the organization. The analysis will help to identify where skills do not match, particularly in cases where jobs are changing. A starting point is often the **job description** which would contain information about the manual and mental skills required to carry out the job. Ultimately this should assist human resources managers to identify the correct mix of employees to do particular jobs.

SMART

SMART is an acronym for Specific, Measurable, Achievable, Results-orientated and Time-constrained. It is a term which can be applied equally to human resources management and to many other areas of business activity. Its use seeks to ensure that any activity is quantifiable and objective-related.

Social Chapter

Social policy is an integral part of EU plans to achieve economic integration. The promise of legislation to back the Social Chapter was unwelcome in the UK as it was thought that this would add costs to businesses and have a negative effect on job creation.

The Conservative government in power at the time, negotiated an opt-out from the Social Chapter of the Maastricht Treaty, on the basis that the forthcoming and existing European employment directives would damage the flexibility of the UK labour market. Following the

S

Labour victory in May 1997, the government signed up to the Social Chapter with the proviso that there was a transitional phase to aid adjustments.

The major concerns of the Social Chapter in relation to human resources are:

- protection of rights of workers who move within the EU;
- fair pay for employment;
- improvement of conditions of employment (including working hours);
- Social Security provision for low-income groups and the unemployed;
- freedom of association and the right to collective bargaining;
- vocational training;
- equal treatment for men and women;
- health and safety at work;
- employment opportunities for young people, the disabled and people over the age of compulsory retirement.

www.europa.eu.int

Social expectations

Social expectations are a more formal way of describing **quality of work life (QWL)**. Social expectations encompass the general desires of employees, specifically their aspirations with regard to **working conditions**, pay, and a challenging job role.

Society for Human Resource Management (US and worldwide)

The Society for Human Resource Management (SHRM) is the world's largest professional human resource organization, with over 170,000 members. The society was founded in 1948 and has 500 affiliated chapters operating in some 120 countries around the world.

See also **Chartered Institute of Personnel and Development.**

www.shrm.org/

Socio-technical system

Socio-technical systems refer to instances in which the introduction of technology affects work groups and relationships between employees that effectively restructure the way in which work is carried out.

Soft management

Soft management, as the term suggests, places an emphasis on employees and motivation as a means by which productivity and performance may be achieved. The system relies on the proactive use of human resources to develop, encourage and support employees.

See also **hard management**.

Span of control

The span of control is the number of subordinates for whom a manager has direct responsibility. The ideal number frequently quoted is between 5 and 9 individuals under the control of one manager. Beyond this it becomes increasingly difficult to react or respond to their specific needs. Span of control, therefore, implies that additional levels of hierarchy need to be inserted, both above and below each manager, in order to reduce the span of control to a manageable level.

Staff authority

Staff authority is distinguished from **line authority** as these individuals have the power to advise, not to direct employees. Typically, human resources managers would be considered to have staff authority towards all members of staff, but only line authority within the human resources department itself.

Staff development

See **professional development**.

Staff welfare

Staff welfare describes all of the ancillary, but necessary, functions and responsibilities of human resources departments in relation to employees. The provision of staff welfare differs from organization to organization. However, it will usually involve various supportive measures or facilities aimed to enhance the employees' time at work; for example, staff canteen facilities and rest areas. It will also include any **counselling** or advisory services to assist employees in dealing with any situations outside of the workplace which are affecting their ability to sustain performance.

S

Staffing table

Staffing tables are used by human resources departments as a means by which a prediction or tally of potential employees can be logged. Human resources managers will list the job title of anticipated employee leavers, as well as predicted or planned future needs for additional employees, by each job title. In this way, human resources managers can organize and be aware of the fact that specific recruitment drives will have to be launched at specific times in the short and medium terms.

Start-up cost (employee)

In terms of human resources, the term 'start-up cost' has an entirely different set of connotations from those associated with the costs involved in beginning a new business. When associated with employees, start-up costs refer to the comparative lack of productivity of new employees in the first stages of their employment with the organization. It is recognized that new employees are significantly less efficient and productive than experienced employees. Although their individual performance may be adequate, they are less likely to be able to appreciate the implications of their work and to prioritize their tasks effectively. Equally, it is also recognized that new employees require considerably more supervision by experienced staff, thereby reducing the supervisor's contribution in terms of productivity over these initial periods of time.

Statutory sick pay

In the majority of countries employees are entitled to be paid statutory sick pay when they are absent from work through illness. Notable exceptions may be those who remain in work after the state **retirement** age. A different system is in place in the case of pregnancy, in which case **maternity benefits** apply.

The period covering statutory sick pay is largely dependent on the length of service which the individual has accumulated. In many cases, provided the minimum employment period has been reached, statutory sick pay covers some six months, after which time an alternative payment, such as an incapacity benefit, may be due.

Storey, Walter

Walter Storey (1929–83) was an industrial psychologist who launched a management training programme, Interpersonal Communications Workshop (ICW), at the General Electric Company. The programme was initially designed for internal training, but was later accepted as being so effective that it became the blueprint for many interpersonal communication training programmes. Storey believed not only that the education of adults was based on the deepening of self-awareness and the expansion of interpersonal skills, but also that through experiential learning, individuals could hone their leadership skills. The fundamental concept behind the programme was that the training would provide the individuals with a new set of skills which had been learned through class participation. They could then directly apply these skills to real situations in the workplace. In the formal sessions, trainees focused on teamwork, feedback and personal development, all key features in effective leadership and management. Around 10,000 individuals participated in Storey's programmes and, by and large, they proved to be more productive upon their return to the workplace.

Strategic human resource development

Strategic human resource development is a holistic approach to human resources, which emphasizes skills and the management of employees, in relation to the corporate strategy of the organization.

Stress management

'Stress management' is an increasingly common term, which most employees consider is relevant to their job role. Research has shown that the majority of individuals consider that their job is stressful. However, in-depth research by an organization into the considered levels of stress within the workforce could have an adverse effect on productivity. Research surveys have discovered that 70% of managers know that their employees are suffering from stress; 60% of **absenteeism** is stress-related; 100 million working days are lost annually, resulting in costs throughout the UK of in excess of £1.5m. Continued stressful situations that are not dealt with can lead to **burnout**.

There are innumerable reasons why stress can occur, including:

- meeting deadlines and targets that have been set to a tight schedule;
- inadequate or uninterested management;
- inadequate resources;
- a conflict of values, either within **groups** or with management and colleagues;
- frustration;
- change within the organization.

S

Stress management has become an increasingly important area for the management of human resources. **Employee assistance programmes**, which provide the employee with a counselling and mentoring service, have been in existence in the US for a number of years. Many UK organizations are now also adopting these programmes, although research carried out by Marie McHugh has identified six issues that managers still need to address:

1 Stress is costly to an organization.
2 Stress-related costs have to be reduced.
3 Often they are not aware of employee stress levels.
4 Often they have no solution to managing stress.
5 Often they under-value employees and do not see the need for counselling and support.
6 They do not see the link between employee stress and organizational success.

McHugh and Brennan concluded that the concept of a cross-organizational *total stress management* approach should be considered, as shown in the diagram in Figure 26.

Figure 26 Cross-organizational total stress management

All individuals have differing stress thresholds, which represent how they cope and when they reach the stage where they are unable to cope. Several researchers have discovered that the majority of individuals fit into one of two different categories, either *Type A* or *Type B*, as shown in Table 30.

Table 30   Stress thresholds

Type A characteristics	Type B characteristics
Subject to pressures of time and responsibility.	Do not find pressure in time and responsibility.
Work hard and are competitive, but can appear aggressive and impatient.	Work hard but are calm in their approach, with little need to be self-praising.
Subject to physical stress symptoms.	Do not show signs of stress, either in their approach, or physically.
Extrovert and neurotic.	Introvert and calm.

Friedman, M. and Rosenman, R., *Type A Behaviour and Your Heart*. New York: Alfred A. Knopf, 1974.

Newstrom, W. and Davies, Keith, *Organizational Behaviour: Human Behaviour at Work*, 9th edn. New York: McGraw-Hill, 1993.

Stressors

Stressors are conditions, situations or factors which may cause stress to an employee. Human resources will attempt to identify and eliminate stressors as a proactive policy which may include spreading work loads more equitably, ensuring that adequate training has been provided, or ensuring that long-term absences are covered by temporary or contract staff. By adopting a proactive stance, human resources managers can reduce possible **employee retention** problems and long-term sickness or **absenteeism**.

See also **stress management**.

Structured interview

Structured interviews may take place both in the **recruitment** procedure and during **appraisals**, **disciplinary procedures** or **grievance procedures**. Structured interviews are typified by a series of questions from a predetermined checklist, which are asked of all employees or potential employees in these given situations.

Succession plan

Succession planning involves human resources management taking a longer-term view of possible human resources needs. Typically, this would involve taking into account future retirements and the possibility of specific individuals leaving the organization for a variety of reasons. Policies and procedures would be set in motion in order to identify possible internal replacements for key jobs, specifically in the event of a known and planned retirement. If suitable internal candidates are not available to fill these future vacant posts, then human resources departments can begin a longer-term campaign to identify potential candidates from rival organizations, perhaps using the services of **head hunting** agencies.

Suggestion scheme

Many organizations find the honest and constructive suggestions made by employees as to the efficiency of the organization's processes and procedures to be invaluable. So much so, that they provide the employees with a straightforward way of presenting these suggestions by the

Table 31 An evaluation of suggestion schemes

Advantages	Disadvantages
An improvement in procedures and methods for the organization and the employees.	Interest in the scheme may deteriorate if the management do not encourage employee participation.
A safer working environment.	Maintaining the scheme can be expensive in terms of both money and time.
Increased and widened channels of communication because the employees feel able to express their opinions.	
Innovative and creative employees can be encouraged, often by receiving a reward for a successfully implemented suggestion.	
Increased employee job satisfaction.	
Benefits to the organization, through the suggestion scheme, that eliminate the cost and time considerations.	

use of a suggestion scheme. A committee of managers would filter through the suggestions and select those considered to be appropriate, having investigated the implications and possibilities attached to each.

Suggestion schemes have a number of advantages and disadvantages, as can be seen in Table 31.

Support group

A support group has direct associations with both **self-development groups** and **self-directed work group or teams** in as much as the employees within the group provide one another with practical assistance in achieving personal and group objectives. Support groups may also be applied to employees who share the same ethnic or racial background within an organization, who provide one another with emotional support relating to problems or challenges that individual members have encountered.

Systemic discrimination

Although **discrimination** may not be a policy or, indeed, intentional, the term 'systemic discrimination' refers to practices or actions carried out by an organization which have a discriminatory effect.

S

Taylor, Frederick Winslow

At the start of his research, Taylor (1856–1915) assumed that employees only work for money. He developed a series of work study techniques which he considered would enable employees to reduce the amount of time it would take to carry out different tasks, leaving the planning and organization of tasks for the managers and supervisors. He believed that encouragement to work harder and the promise of additional benefits, such as money, as a reward for this would make employees sufficiently motivated to work harder.

Taylor, however, was proved wrong. He discovered that employees would only work harder when they were being supervised, but would return to their normal pace of work once the supervision was removed.

Since Taylor's writing on 'scientific management', much emphasis has been placed on **job design**. Henry Ford developed Taylor's principles into what has become known as **Fordism**.

Bratton, John and Gold, Jeffrey, *Human Resource Management: Theory and Practice*. Basingstoke: Palgrave Macmillan, 2003.

Kanigel, Robert, *The One Best Way: Frederick Winslow Taylor and the Enigma of Efficiency*. Boston, MA: Little, Brown, 1997.

Taylor, Frederick Winslow, *Principles of Scientific Management*. New York: W. W. Norton, 1967.

Summary of Taylor's work at www.accel-team.com/scientific/scientific_02.html

Teamwork and team building

Many organizations have gradually come to the realization that teams represent a proven means by which productivity and performance can be assured. Various industry surveys, particularly in the manufacturing sector, seem to suggest that over two-thirds of all organizations actively encourage teams. The actual nature of the team is of prime importance and their creation is of particular relevance to the management of human resources. Essentially there are three different types of team, all of which have a degree of authority, **autonomy** or **empowerment**.

Empowered teams are usually given the authority to plan and implement improvements. Self-directed teams are virtually autonomous and are mainly responsible for supervisory issues. Cross-functional teams are more complex as they involve various individuals from different departments, who are working towards a common end.

Training needs to be provided to teams both before and during their creation in order to assist the members in establishing their relationships with one another and understanding their new responsibilities. It is also essential that teams are given clear instructions and, above all, support from the management in order to carry out their tasks. Once a team has been established and a degree of authority delegated to them, management and human resources personnel need to step back and allow the team to develop, and learn how their new working practices will operate.

The team itself, management and the human resources department retain the responsibility for monitoring and motivating the teams and their members. This requires effective communication skills and a feedback system which enables teams to request additional assistance should it be required.

Telecommuting

Telecommuting has become a viable option for many organizations with the enormous leaps in information technology standards. From an employer's point of view, telecommuting offers considerable advantages, including less pressure on office space and increases in employee morale and effectiveness. In essence, telecommuting means that employees can work in a remote location away from the office in familiar surroundings and manage their own day. In reality, however, telecommuting is far more prescriptive as there are now means by which employers can accurately monitor precisely on what, and when, an employee is working. Telecommuting can be seen as having slightly different connotations from those of tele-working, as a telecommuter may be required to balance the working week between periods of attendance at the employer's premises and periods of work at home.

In the US, nearly 40 per cent of organizations positively encourage telecommuting and the trends worldwide seem to suggest that businesses are moving towards having smaller central offices and larger numbers of remote telecommuting employees.

The human resource implications are considerable, as it becomes difficult to liaise with employees, added to which there are difficulties regarding safety at home and home office **ergonomics**.

See also **tele-work.**

Tele-work

Tele-working permits employees to spend all, or an agreed part, of their working week at a location remote from their employers' workplace. Working from home, or home-working, is one obvious form of tele-working but there are several different categories:

- Traditional mobile workers – this category would include sales representatives and delivery drivers. They receive instructions and information via telephones, computers or fax machines at home or in their vehicles.
- Managerial and professional staff who spend working days away from their office base and also communicate via telephones, computers or fax machines from their home, car or other remote location.
- Specialists or office support staff who carry out a range of duties from home or other remote locations and communicate via telephones, fax machines and computers.
- Other workers who operate from local centres with computer and telecommunications facilities. These tele-workers are sometimes also referred to as tele-cottagers.

Tele-working can reduce costs by providing savings on office space and other facilities. It can improve productivity as people are not interrupted by the day-to-day distractions of office life and politics. The employees involved in tele-work have more freedom and options as to where they live, how they organize their work and when they carry it out. Additionally, those who have domestic or care commitments can benefit from the additional skills and expertise of workers who may not be available to attend the workplace. Tele-working can also reduce or eliminate the amount of time spent on travelling for the employee, and organizations can reduce their levels of **absenteeism** and **labour turnover**.

There are, however, some disadvantages to tele-work. Providing suitable technology can be expensive for the organization and some employees may feel socially isolated. Despite improvements in technology, managers may find it difficult to communicate with and manage remote workers. Career development and training may suffer and **health and safety** issues and the recording of working time may also be problematic.

The introduction of a tele-working system within an organization would need careful planning to ensure that the following issues are clear to all:

- Changes to an employee's contract of employment may have to be agreed.
- Employees must be self-motivated, self-disciplined, competent and able to work with little supervision.
- Employees' homes or other available premises must be suitable for tele-working.
- Health and safety issues need to be considered.
- The organization's property that might be used at the tele-workers' premises must be secure and safe.
- If the tele-work involves computer use, then a reliable password or code system will be required to ensure appropriate access to information.
- Any restrictions to working times should be agreed.
- If the tele-worker's home is being used, then consideration should be given to an allowance to cover extra heating and lighting costs.
- Tele-workers may need to inform insurance companies, landlords or mortgage companies, or the Inland Revenue, about their changed circumstances.
- Arrangements should be made for effective management, development and communication through, for example, regular contact, clear targets, appraisals and access to training.

Temporary contracts

A temporary worker is someone employed for a limited period of time. The job is usually expected by both sides to last for only a short time. Temporary workers may be employed directly by the employer or by **employment agencies**, which will recruit, select and sometimes train temporary workers and hire them out to employers.

Contracts may be agreed which end on the completion of a particular task rather than on a specific date. Temporary workers are sometimes hired on **fixed-term contracts**, although whatever their contractual status, they receive the same rights to notice of termination as those employed by the organization on a permanent basis. UK employment law makes no distinction between permanent and temporary employees. To qualify for various employment rights, however, employees must have served a minimum period of continuous employment with their employer. Most temporary workers will have insufficient service but they may have accrued enough **continuous employment** to qualify, even if they have had short breaks in their employment with the organization.

Temporary workers can provide an organization with greater flexibility because the numbers employed can be varied according to changes

T

in demand for manpower. Temporary workers can also provide cover for permanent staff on holiday, **maternity leave** or sick leave, as well as additional support during peak times. They might also be employed to provide the specialist skills needed by an organization in order to carry out specific projects. Organizations sometimes use temporary workers as a screening device for potential permanent recruitment, although some organizations find that temporary workers may lack the **motivation** and commitment of permanent employees.

Theory X and theory Y

See **McGregor, Douglas.**

Theory Z

William Ouchi suggested an approach to human resource management that has been adopted in Japan. Ouchi's Theory Z began with the development of three management strategies:

- the development of a commitment to life-long employment;
- encouraging employees to feel a sense of belonging to the organization by projecting to them the philosophy and objectives of the organization;
- attention to detail in the selection and recruitment process and ensuring that new recruits are accepted into the organization's values and social environment.

As can be seen in Table 32, Ouchi came up with six techniques which would assist in the implementation of the strategies.

Three-hundred-and-sixty-degree performance appraisal

See **360-degree performance appraisal (p. 281).**

Ticket to Work and Work Incentives Improvement Act 1999 (US)

Aimed at facilitating work for individuals with disabilities, Title I of the Act provides access to employment training and placement services, and Title II of the Act provides health care supports for working individuals with disabilities.

www.cms.hhs.gov/twwiia

www.ssa.gov/work/Ticket/ticket_info.html

Table 32   Implementation of Ouchi's management strategies

Technique	Implementation method
Seniority-based promotion systems	Make new recruits feel they can spend the rest of their career with the organization by allowing them to gain experience through **job rotation**. Make progress through management levels steady and slow so that the employees gain generalist as opposed to specialist skills.
Continuous development	Ensure that employees are continually updated by means of training and appraisal. Encourage long-term career plans to allow a sense of job security.
Groups and teams	Encourage group-based tasks rather than individual-based tasks to help develop the socialization process.
Communication	Communication has to be open and easily accessible through all levels of the workforce. There is no distinction in dress code between managers and employees and all use the same facilities, such as canteens.
Employee participation	Encourage discussion and participation, particularly regarding areas of anticipated change.
Production-centred systems	The focus is on productivity, although a high concern for employees' welfare and satisfaction is always shown.

Time studies

Effectively, time studies owe much to time and motion studies which were developed by **Frank and Lillian Gilbreth**. Time studies involve the identification and measurement in time of each of the sub-elements of a particular job in order to discover how long the whole job takes to be completed. Often, time studies can be used as a means by which productivity payments and other forms of **performance-related pay** are determined.

Trade unions

Trade unions protect the interests of their members in areas relating to wages and salaries, working conditions, job security and welfare benefits. They negotiate with the management of organizations on behalf of members of the trade union who work for the business. The national committee of the trade union is an elected group of permanent employees who implement the policies of the members. Regional and district committees are formed around the country, with branches in the larger towns, and union members are attached to one of these. Trade union representatives negotiate with the management of an organization during the documenting and implementation of **collective agreements**, **collective bargaining**, and **dispute resolution**. They would also be entitled to attend disciplinary and grievance **interviews**, as well as being involved in discussions regarding **dismissal**.

See also **craft union; industrial union;** *and* **Trade Union Reform and Employment Rights Act 1993 (UK).**

Trades Union Congress (TUC) (UK)

The TUC is an overarching organizational body which has 69 affiliated unions in the UK, with a total membership of some 7 million. The TUC's role is to negotiate on behalf of these unions at European level, liaise and negotiate with political parties and businesses, as well as disseminating information to the general public.

Specifically, the TUC is responsible for the following activities:

- the drawing up of common policies;
- the lobbying of national and European governments;
- highlighting economic and social issues;
- the representation of employees on public bodies;
- representation of their membership in Europe and with the International Labour Organization;
- research on employment-related issues;
- training and education;
- service development for members;
- conflict resolution between unions;
- broadening the network of alliances and agreements between unions worldwide.

The Congress itself is the decision-making body of the TUC and is held annually (in September). The decisions of the Congress frame the work and priorities of the TUC for the coming year. The General Council takes over the policy-making role between each Congress and directs the progress of policy. The General Council appoints individuals to an Executive Committee, which meets on a monthly basis to manage the financial affairs of the TUC and deal with urgent issues.

www.tuc.org.uk/

Trade Union Reform and Employment Rights Act 1993 (UK)

The Trade Union Reform and Employment Rights Act contained measures to continue the government's programme of reforming industrial relations and employment law.

The Act gives employees the following rights:

- to receive a written statement of their main conditions of employment, including pay, hours and holidays;
- a minimum of 14 weeks' maternity leave, and protection against dismissal on maternity-related grounds;
- protection against dismissal or other adverse treatment on grounds related to health and safety;
- protection against being unfairly dismissed for exercising any statutory employment protection right.

With regard to trade union members, the Act covers the following aspects:

- freedom to decide which union they join;
- a postal ballot before a strike;
- protection against fraud and abuse in trade union elections and finances;
- the right not to have union subscriptions deducted from their pay without their consent.

Controversially, the Act also addressed unions and competitiveness:

- requiring unions to give employers at least seven days' notice of industrial action;
- protecting businesses against the damage that strikes can cause;
- providing customers who are deprived of goods or services as a result of unlawful industrial action the right to take legal proceedings;
- abolishing the Wages Councils;
- introducing a new Careers Services.

www.legislation.hmso.gov.uk/acts/acts1993/Ukpga_19930019_en_1.htm

Training

See **training needs analysis; teamwork and team building; buddy system; Learning and Skills Act 2000; learning organization; multi-skilling; on-the-job training; off-the-job training; role playing;** *and* **self-development group.**

Training needs analysis (TNA)

Training needs analysis seeks to provide a systematic series of check-lists and guidelines in order to identify specific training requirements within the organization. Human resources managers would be expected to fully investigate the exact nature of training requirements, detailing issues such as the age, gender, skills and experience of those who require the training. In addition to this they would need to address specific issues regarding the nature of training, including its location, and the availability of the trainers, materials and support required. Ideally training needs analysis not only involves this potentially immense data collection exercise, but also addresses the benefits and suitability of the training. Many organizations will actually measure, as a part of TNA, the return on investment of the proposed learning programme.

www.trainingneedsanalysis.co.uk

Transactional analysis

See **Hay, Julie.**

Transfer of undertakings

The term 'transfer of undertakings' applies to situations where a business effectively relinquishes its control over its own business and passes on all of the rights and responsibilities to another business. In human resources terms this clearly means that part of the resources and assets of the original business consist of its employees, to whom the new owner of the business now has a responsibility. Usually written into the **contract of employment** is a clause which specifically states that an outgoing employer will seek to assure employees that in the event of a merger, takeover or acquisition, the fundamental principles of the contract of employment will be honoured. At a later date the new business may seek to renegotiate the contract of employment, but at the point of transfer of ownership, a transfer of undertaking, or acceptance of employees' existing contracts, is agreed by the new owner.

Transference and transferable skills

In many respects these two terms are interchangeable as they both refer to situations which imply the ability of an employee to apply their current skills, experience and training to another job role which may not have been necessarily related to the work already being undertaken.

Basic skills, such as communication and numeracy, may be applicable and therefore transferable to the majority of jobs. More specific skills may not necessarily be transferable but they could be amended through training to be useful in different roles. The term 'transference' takes the concept one stage further and specifically refers to situations where individuals have undergone training and now are evaluated by their ability or willingness to use that training in their job for the benefit of the organization.

Allied to these two concepts is 'cascading', which refers to situations where employees have gained training or have existing skills and are willing to impart their knowledge to other employees in the organization.

Tuckman, Bruce

Bruce Tuckman's model, developed in the 1960s, refers to the development and behaviour of teams. Tuckman suggested that there were four stages of progression which describe the maturing of relationships, style and eventual leadership of teams, as can be seen in Figure 27.

The four elements of Tuckman's model are summarized in Table 33.

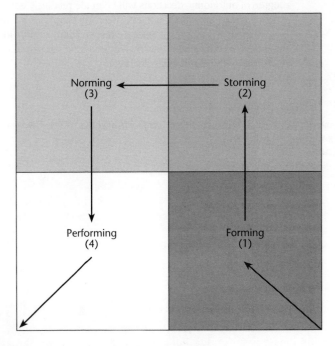

Figure 27 Tuckman's model of team behaviour

Table 33 Elements of Tuckman's model of team behaviour

Phase	Description
Forming	This stage of a team's existence requires leadership, as roles and responsibilities are unclear and the leader must take the responsibility of explaining the team's purpose, objectives and relationships outside the team.
Storming	Team members attempt to assess their relationship to one another and challenge decisions which may result in the creation of factions within the team. The team needs to be refocused on its goals and encouraged to accept compromises.
Norming	Finally a degree of consensus has been reached. Team members are clear about their roles and responsibilities and major decisions will be made by the team as a whole. The team is now unified and has a commitment to one another, and it is at this stage the team will begin to develop the way in which it will work and share decisions.
Performing	The team now knows exactly what is expected of it and will attempt to exceed expectations. Assuming the team has a degree of autonomy, decisions will be made relatively easily and disagreements dealt with effectively by processes already established. The team will delegate responsibility to individual members and the leader may be required to assist particular members with personal development.

Montebello, A. R. and Buzzotta, V. R., 'Work Teams that Work', *Training and Development*, March 1993.

T

Under-utilization

The term 'under-utilization' refers to a situation that exists when a department of an organization, or the organization as a whole, employs a smaller proportion of protected ethnic or other minority groups than those which are found on a regular basis within the organization's labour market as a whole.

Unfair dismissal

As **dismissal** and the law is quite a complex issue, suffice to say that an employee has the right not to be unfairly dismissed from a job. Generally speaking, however, individual employees have the right to make a claim for unfair dismissal if they have:

- been dismissed on grounds contrary to the terms of their **contract of employment**;
- been dismissed on the grounds of either direct or indirect **discrimination**;
- been dismissed for an automatically unfair reason, such as a health and safety issue;
- been dismissed because of pregnancy;
- been dismissed because of their assertion of a statutory right;
- been dismissed because of **trade union** membership;
- been dismissed because of an organization's merger or takeover by another business;
- been dismissed because of a spent conviction.

Before any claim for unfair dismissal can be made the following questions should be addressed:

1 How long has the employee worked for the organization? Employees with less than one year's service do not qualify for claims of unfair dismissal.
2 Has the employee been involved in an act of **gross misconduct**?

If so, was a proper investigation carried out according to the organization's **disciplinary procedure**? If so, is dismissal the ultimate
sanction?

3 Has the employee had repeated **absenteeism** due to illness? If so,
could a doctor be called to give a statement? Did the organization
offer the employee alternative employment in order to eliminate the
need for so much absence?

There are certain individuals and groups who are exempt from claiming
for unfair dismissal, including police officers, those on **fixed-term
contracts**, and members of the armed forces.

In cases of dispute between the employer and employee, **ACAS** will
attempt to resolve the issue.

Unstructured interview

An unstructured interview is one that is not as planned as a **structured
interview** from the point of view of the questions to be posed. In an
unstructured interview, few questions will be prepared in advance, thus
giving the interviewer the opportunity to wait until the interviewee has
made a response before deciding on a follow-up question. This allows
the interviewer to pursue a more in-depth response from individual
interviewees.

U

Variable pay

Variable pay is essentially a performance-linked remuneration system. It includes piece rates, wage incentives, **profit sharing**, **bonuses** or the awarding of lump sums based on merit. For the most part the remuneration is actually linked to the profitability of the business and in most countries between 4 per cent and 10 per cent of businesses have an element of variable pay as part of their remuneration package. One of the most common forms of variable pay is a commission on sales made, allowing sales representatives to receive a higher revenue, commensurate with their performance and ability to sell. Variable pay has become more common as it does not guarantee more than the base salary offered to employees, and therefore the onus is upon the employees to assist the management in producing a profit.

Vertical communication

Vertical communication is distinguished from **horizontal communication** in referring to communications which occur up and down the organizational structure. Vertical communication should incorporate both upward communications from the employees to the management and downward communications from the management to the workforce, as typified in instructions, policies, procedures and regulations. A sophisticated organization which seeks to involve its employees will encourage vertical communication, both upward and downward.

Vesting

'Vesting' is a term related to pensions and **retirement** plans and specifically refers to situations where there is a provision in an employer retirement plan that accords the right to an employee to receive a pension after having completed a specified number of years of employment for the organization.

Vietnam Era Veterans' Readjustment Assistance Act (VEVRAA) 1974 (US)

This Act protects the employment rights of disabled military veterans and states employer obligations with regards to National Guard members and Reservists who may be called to active duty.

Virtual organization

In literal terms, a virtual organization does not exist. However, the term is used to describe an organization which does not have a physical presence or central organizational structure and relies on a network of remote employees engaged in a variety of **telecommuting** and **telework** activities. It may also refer to an organization which employs outworkers, paid on a piece rate system. The virtual organization acts as a provider of work and a fulfilment service or intermediary between the outworkers and the customer.

Vocational training

Vocational training or qualifications are those which are directly related to the job being undertaken by the employee. As far as human resources are concerned, vocational training can occur both in-house and via external training providers. The key aspect of vocational training is that whatever is learned on the training programmes is directly applicable and usable by the employee in the work situation.

Vroom, Victor

Vroom, together with Edward E. Lawler and Lyman W. Porter, put forward his theory to suggest that the relationship between people's behaviour at work and their goals was not as simple as was first imagined. Vroom realized that an employee's performance is based on his or her personality, skills, knowledge, experience and abilities. This being the case, it was apparent that some employees would be more suited to their **job role** than others and that some would understand instruction more readily than others. The theory proposed that:

- Each individual has a different set of goals.
- They will only try to achieve their goals if they think they have a chance to attain them.
- The value of the goal, in personal terms, affects motivation and behaviour.

V

Vroom's expectancy theory is one of the most popular motivation theories. It basically depends upon the following three factors:

- *Valence* – this is the depth of want that the employee feels for either extrinsic rewards (money, promotion, time off, benefits) or intrinsic rewards (satisfaction). Management needs to discover what the employees want by offering a variety of rewards so they select something they would value.

- *Expectancy* – everyone has different expectations and different levels of confidence about what they are capable of doing. If employees have fulfilled their valence wants, but are asked to do something that they feel unable to do, then they will not be motivated enough to do it. Despite the fact that there may be a promise of an additional desired reward, an employee who is not motivated will not fulfil. Management would need to discover the employee's resource, training or additional supervision needs in order to improve their opportunity to succeed and remove their chances of failure.

- *Instrumentality* – this is all centred around employees' expectations about whether they will get what they want, even if it has been promised them by an employer. Managers should ensure that promises of rewards are fulfilled and ensure the employee is aware of what relevant rewards are linked to improved performance.

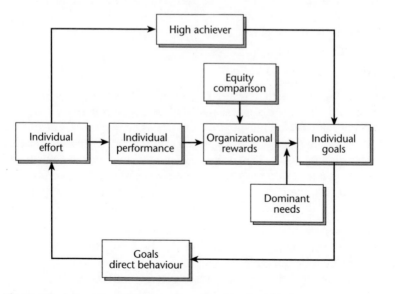

Figure 28 Integration of contemporary theories of motivation

Using Vroom's theory, summarized in Figure 28, a business could identify the characteristics of the job that would allow the employee some of the following, to encourage motivation:

- self-development opportunities;
- satisfaction opportunities;
- recognition opportunities;
- a degree of independence in deciding how tasks should be handled;
- a varied range of tasks;
- a variety of surroundings;
- opportunity for interaction with others;
- challenging and varied, but clearly stated, goals with an indication as to the expected performance.

Porter, Lyman W. and Lawler, Edward E., *Managerial Attitudes and Performance*. Homewood, IL: Irwin-Dorsey, 1968.

Porter, Lyman W. and Lawler, Edward E., *Behavior in Organizations*. New York: McGraw-Hill, 1975.

Vroom, Victor H., *Managing People, Not Personnel: Motivation and Performance Appraisal*. Cambridge, MA: Harvard Business School Press, 1990.

Vroom, Victor H., *Work and Motivation*. Indianapolis, IN: Jossey-Bass Wiley, 1994.

V

Wage and Hour Division (US)

The Wage and Hour Division administers the wage, hour and child labor provisions of the **Fair Labor Standards Act**. In addition, the division is involved in several other programmes covering wages for government contracts, farm labour, family and medical leave, immigration and polygraph testing.

> www.dol.gov/esa/whd

Wage and salary survey

In many respects a wage and salary survey can be seen as an adjunct to a **labour market analysis** as it specifically involves the investigation of current trends in remuneration paid by other organizations within the business's own labour market. The analysis of the data can enable the organization to ensure that its wage and salary structure has **external equity**, which will, in turn, help assist in achieving **employee retention**.

Weber, Max

Max Weber (1864–1920) based his conclusions about bureaucracy on his studies of such disparate organizations as the Catholic Church, the Prussian army and the empire of the Egyptians. He concluded that employees frequently suffer from inequity in most areas of work, from selection to promotion. His key points can be summarized as in Table 34.

> Verstehen: Max Weber's HomePage is at www.faculty.rsu.edu/~felwell/Theorists/ Weber/Whome.htm

Weighted checklist

Weighted checklists can be used during **appraisals**, using a predetermined set of statements or words to describe an individual employee's performance or characteristics. The system requires that each statement or word be assigned a different value or weight, which can then be tallied to give a total score as a measure of the employee's current standing and level of performance.

Table 34 Bureaucratic inequity

Principle of bureaucracy	Description
Division of labour	The workforce is split into specialized areas according to expertise.
Chain of command	There is a pyramid-shaped organizational structure, which defines the hierarchy and the authority of the organization.
Rules and regulations	There are formalized rules which govern the running of the organization, which assists the organization in dealing with the potential disruption caused by changes in management.
Impersonality	Management is detached from the workforce to ensure that sentimentality or familiarity does not impede decision making.
Selection and promotion	Selection of employees and their subsequent opportunities for advancement in the organization are strictly governed by their utility as far as the organization is concerned. Friendship plays no part in the advancement, which usually based on seniority and express achievements.
Documentation	There is a meticulous system of document creation, completion and storage, to chart all activities for the purposes of monitoring and evaluating those activities.
Centralization	All decision making comes from the upper strata of the organization, where individuals reside who have seniority and clearly recognizable achievements over a period of time.

W

Work–life balance

Increasing pressure on employees to commit to longer working hours and sublimate their home life for work has become a considerable concern in many countries over the past few years.

In March 2000, for example, the British government launched a scheme through the Department of Trade and Industry with the following objectives:

> Its aim is twofold: to convince employers of the economic benefits of work–life balance, by presenting real-life case studies; and to convince employers of the need for change. The campaign focuses on three areas:
>
> 1 tackling the long-hours culture
> 2 targeting sectors with acute work–life balance problems
> 3 providing support and guidance
>
> The Work–Life Balance campaign is situated within the Department for Trade and Industry (DTI), where it sits alongside policy and legislation on employment rights. This includes maternity rights, paternity and adoption leave, time off for emergencies, parental leave and part-time work.
>
> www.dti.gov.uk/work-lifebalance/

More recently, the campaign has gained additional support amongst certain employers, leading to the formation of the Employer's Work–Life Balance part of the Work Foundation.

> www.employersforwork-lifebalance.org.uk/index.htm

Work measurement

Work measurement should be seen as a precursor to the beginning of an **appraisal** programme. Rather than evaluating each employee's performance on an individual basis, work measurement seeks to identify the essential performance criteria related to a specific **job role**. These common standards can then be tested as an integral part of the performance appraisal.

Work options

The term 'work options' refers to the wide variety of different work modes which can be differentiated, as variations from a standard working week. In this respect they include flexible working practices such as the **compressed working week, flexitime, job sharing, part-time workers** and other non-standard modes of attendance, including **telecommuting** and **tele-working**.

Work practices

Work practices are best described as the standard or preferred ways in which work is carried out within an organization. Many organizations will have clearly stated working practices, which may extend to issues such as a clear desk policy, response rate to telephone calls, defined attendance requirements, and dress code.

Work sampling

Work sampling is a **work-study technique** which extends the investigation into a particular job and its elements to a series of observations over a given period of time. This process is notably different in the sense that it seeks to accommodate the fact that not all times and circumstances may necessarily allow specific employees to carry out their work with maximum efficiency. An aggregate time is calculated based on the series of observations, which should, theoretically lead to a more equitable decision as to the standard time which is required to carry out the element of that job.

Work-study techniques

Work-study techniques are most closely associated with scientific management theorists, such as **F. W. Taylor** and **Frank and Lillian Gilbreth**. The technique involves examining exactly what is done and how it is done within a job, then analysing the elements, resources and relationships which may affect the efficiency of the task itself.

Worker directors

Worker directors are employees elected by **works councils** to represent employees on the board of a business. Although there is a growing requirement under **European Employment Strategy** and EU Directives related to **European Works Councils** to require businesses to have employee representation on boards, there has been considerable opposition for a number of different reasons. Most notably, worker directors are reluctant to make decisions without referring back to their peer groups, thus slowing down the decision-making process.

Businesses are also very apprehensive on the question of confidentiality, particularly when worker directors have access to information which may have a negative impact with those who placed them on the board in the first place. **Trade unions** have, in the past, also been suspicious of worker directors as they feel that their presence simply confuses the issue, as the unions may end up having to fight one of their own members in the role of a member of the board.

Workflow

Workflow simply describes the sequence of operations related to an organization's activities. Workflow identifies how products, services or tasks proceed through the organization, who is involved, and how long each stage of the operation needs in order to fulfil its part of the whole process.

Workforce Investment Act 1998 (US)

The Workforce Investment Act effectively created a workforce development system in the US:

> The Workforce Investment Act of 1998 provides the framework for a unique national workforce preparation and employment system designed to meet the needs of the nation's business and the needs of job seekers and those who want to further their careers. (US Department of Labor, Overview, 1998)

The key features of the Workforce Investment Act are:

- *Consolidated funding streams.* Several large Federal grant programmes have been consolidated through WIA.
- *Workforce Investment Boards.* The Workforce Investment Act establishes Workforce Investment Boards at the State and local levels.
- *One Stop Shops.* The system is based around the concept of One Stop Shops – unified service providers to the unemployed, the employed and employers.
- *Eligibility for Services.* WIA establishes three types of service: (a) core services for all adults aged 18 years and older; (b) intensive services for unemployed individuals who have been unable to obtain jobs through core services; and (c) training services for those who are eligible for intensive services but are still unable to find employment.
- *Individual Training Accounts.* WIA aims to be demand-led. Individuals are empowered to make choices about the particular

W

type of training or the particular provider they wish to use. They are given a sum of money to purchase that training.

- *Accountability*. Achieved through output measures rather than inputs, with financial penalties for states that fail to meet the pre-established performance marks, but rewards for those that exceed them.
- *Approved providers*. Only approved providers can receive a training voucher (from an Individual Training Account).

www.wia-workforceinvestmentact.net
www.doleta.gov/

Working conditions

Working conditions are a primary concern of both management and human resources departments in the sense that employees' working environments can often determine their performance, and their productivity. Poor working conditions, which may include physical aspects such as cramped conditions, inadequate equipment or furniture and lack of facilities, are coupled with aspects which may cause unnecessary stresses and strains to the employees. The managing of working conditions has increasingly become a vital aspect of human resources management as many of the issues have relatively simple solutions. Yet until human resources departments began to appreciate the negative impacts of poor working conditions, little was done to address these issues.

Working Time Regulations 1998 (UK)

This is a very detailed set of regulations which apply to 'adult workers' (over 18) and to 'young workers' (over compulsory school age). The regulations cover working hours, night work, daily rest periods, weekly rest periods and annual leave. The regulations can be summarized In Table 35.

www.hmso.gov.uk/si/si1998/19981833.htm

Working Time Regulations 1999

Statutory Instrument 1999 No. 3372 was an amendment to the Working Time Regulations 1998. The most significant changes were the removal of the need for employers to keep records of the hours worked by individuals who have opted out of the 48-hour week, and the extension of the scope of the 'unmeasured working time' exemption.

www.hmso.gov.uk/si/si1999/19993372.htm

Table 35   Working Time Regulations 1998

Regulation coverage	Summarised details
Working hours	A worker's working time, including overtime, must not exceed an average of 48 hours in each 7 days. If the worker claims this right not to exceed the 48 hours, then he must not suffer any detriment because of it. A worker can agree to work longer than 48 hours per week, but this agreement should be made in writing with the employer. Employers are obliged to keep records of the hours worked.
Night work	Normal hours of work, for night workers, shall not exceed an *average* of 8 hours for each 24 hours. If the night work involves 'special hazards' or heavy physical or mental strain, then this limit is reduced to 8 hours worked in any 24-hour period.
Daily rest periods	Adult workers are entitled to a rest period of not less than 11 consecutive hours in each 24-hour period worked (12 for young workers). This rest period may be interrupted for certain types of work where the activities are split up over the day (or are of short duration). Where an adult worker's daily working time is more than 6 hours, they are entitled to a rest break (at least 20 minutes, 30 for young workers, for every 4.5 hours).
Weekly rest periods	Adult workers are entitled to at least 24 hours uninterrupted rest in each 7-day working period or two rest periods of 24 hours in each 14-day period worked, *or* one 48-hour rest period in each 14-day period (young workers 48 hours rest each 7 days).
Annual leave	Workers are entitled to at least 3 weeks' leave per year (4 weeks from 23 November 1998). Workers should be paid at the rate of a week's pay for each week of leave.

W

Working Time (Amendment) Regulations 2002

These Regulations amend the Working Time Regulations 1998 to implement the Young Workers Directive, protecting workers aged 16 and 17.

www.legislation.hmso.gov.uk/si/si2002/20023128.htm

Workplace bullying

In England and Wales alone, it has been estimated that around a million violent incidents occur in the workplace each year. A full quarter of these incidents involve a physical assault. High-risk occupations include social work, probation officers, teachers, security guards, health service professionals, police officers and bar staff. It has been further estimated that the compensation costs alone amount to some £0.25 billion each year.

In the National Health Service, there are some 65,000 incidents each year, with over 60 per cent of these incidents involving nurses. Violence in schools has hit the headlines on both sides of the Atlantic, notably the fatal stabbing of headmaster Philip Lawrence and the shootings at Columbine High School in the US.

Between January 1996 and May 2003 the UK National Workplace Bullying Advice Line logged the feedback from visitors to its websites from across the world and produced the statistics summarized in Tables 36 to 38. Work specific bullying and harassment revealed the data given in Table 37.

Table 36 Most bullied occupations

Most bullied professions and sectors	
Teachers, lecturers and administrative staff in schools and colleges	20%
Health care professionals	12%
Social services and caring professions	10%
Voluntary and non-profit organizations	6–8%
Civil servants	5%
Public sector employees: total	65%
Private sector employees: total	30%
Students and the retired	5%

W

Table 37 Sources of bullying

Source of bullying at work	
Management	90%
Peer to peer	8%
Subordinates	2%
Females	50%
Serial bullies	90%

The reasons for workplace bullying are vague in many cases, but the information given in Table 38 was gleaned from respondents with regard to actions or circumstances arising out of the incidents.

Table 38 Reasons for bullying, and results

Reasons for bullying and reaction/redress	
Racial, sexual and disability bullying	5%
Victim considers suicide	10%
Attempted suicides	1%
Legal action taken or under consideration	20%
Legal action in court	2%
Successful in court (as a percentage of above figure)	50%
Claims for personal injuries	10%

www.bullyinginstitute.org/
www.bullyonline.org/workbully/index.htm

Workplace diversity

Workplace diversity recognizes that employees within an organization have a range of different values, perceptions and behaviours. In **managing diversity**, human resources managers seek to address these issues in the knowledge that not all employees will necessarily have the same perceptions or interpretations of policies and procedures, nor will they necessarily respond in the same manner.

Workplace (Health, Safety and Welfare) Regulations 1992 (UK)

These regulations cover a wide range of health, safety and welfare issues, including heating, lighting, seating and ventilation, welfare and work stations. The Workplace (Health, Safety and Welfare) Regulations 1992 completed a series of six sets of health and safety regulations to implement EC Directives (replacing a number of old and detailed laws).

Under the terms of the Regulations, employers have to ensure that workplaces meet the health, safety and welfare needs of all members of a workforce, including people with disabilities. Several of the Regulations require things to be 'suitable'. Regulation 2(3) clearly states that things should be suitable for anyone (including people with disabilities).

Work-related upper limb disorders (WRULD)

The term 'WRULD' is somewhat synonymous with Repetitive Strain Injury, or Cumulative Trauma Disorder, etc. It covers a large variety of conditions and symptoms including carpal tunnel syndrome, de Quervain's syndrome, tendonitis, tenosynovitis, tennis elbow and thoracic outlet syndrome.

www.hmso.gov.uk/si/si1992/Uksi_19923004_en_1.htm

Works council

W

Although works councils are not legally required in organizations of a certain size in the UK until 2005, they are required by legislation in many other European countries. The involvement of employees within works councils varies very much, depending on the nature of the organization, its size and its location internationally. However, the scope of the discussion and decision making can range from recruitment procedures through to the council's legal right to delay complex issues, such as merger or takeover discussions.

The introduction of works councils has freed management from a number of issues, including the need to gain acceptance, or go through sometimes lengthy negotiation talks, with **trade union** representatives on issues relating to working conditions. Works councils have the power to execute decisions on issues such as overtime and promotion and have proved a positive step in encouraging management to accept ideas and suggestions from employees. This allows change to be introduced within an organization more easily and the works council members are also able to brief management regarding any issues that may be occurring which could result in some form of conflict within the organization.

There are some disadvantages, however, in that the decision-making process can be slower, the running of works councils can be costly and if not compiled from like-minded individuals, meetings can become hostile and eliminate some of the negotiation elements required.

See also **European Works Councils.**

Write-ins and walk-ins

These are two ways of describing the senders of unsolicited requests from those seeking employment that can be received by a human resource department. Write-ins are individuals who send their CV or **résumé**, along with a covering letter asking to be placed on a waiting list or to be considered for future vacancies. A walk-in is a job seeker who personally visits the organization in order to inquire as to whether there are any, or likely to be any, vacancies in the organization in the near future.

Wrongful dismissal

See **unfair dismissal.**

W

Zz

Zero-hour contracts

Zero-hour contracts are arrangements between an employer and an employee who has agreed to be available for work as and when required, therefore no particular number of hours or times of work are specified. Zero-hour contracts may suit some people who want occasional earnings, but they do run the risk of being misused, for instance when employees are asked to stop work during quiet periods but remain on the premises in case they are needed.

Under the **National Minimum Wage Regulations (1998)**, workers operating under a zero-hour contract on stand-by time, on-call time and downtime must be paid the national minimum wage, provided they are at their place of work and required to be there by the organization they work for. Similarly, this amount of time on premises is likely to count as working time under the **Working Time Regulations (1998, 1999** and **2002)** provided the worker is required to be on-call at the place of work.

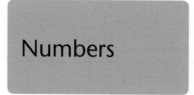

Numbers

360-degree performance appraisal

360-degree appraisal has rapidly become an integral part of performance management. A standard 360-degree appraisal system requires face-to-face feedback sessions, where employees are given an opportunity both to ask their own questions and to listen to feedback.

Many businesses have instituted a more sophisticated system in which employees are evaluated by a number of individuals, including senior staff and colleagues. The quality of the data which is collected is high and this data becomes the primary focus and driving force behind training programmes. In order to ensure that the system works to its best potential, there are six steps which need to be considered. These are summarized in Table 39.

Table 39   Requirements for 360–degree appraisal

Steps	Description
Open mind	Those undergoing the appraisal need to have commitment, vision and often the courage to face how they are viewed, as well as a willingness to implement any suggestions. As drawbacks are highlighted, an objective and open-minded view needs to be taken towards criticism.
Self-evaluation	A clear and honest listing of current competences is essential. The gaps in competences should be highlighted and prioritized, as this gives a clear message to those providing feedback that the individuals are prepared to discuss critical areas of their abilities.
Plan of action	There needs to be a clearly established set of performance categories. Normally feedback will be provided by managers and peers, both direct and indirect colleagues. The ideal number should not exceed 6–8 individuals.

$\Rightarrow$

Table 39 Requirements for 360–degree appraisal (*continued*)

Steps	Description
Mental preparation	Self-evaluation techniques require an individual not to be defensive and to be prepared to receive feedback. Whatever is said needs to be listened to and accepted.
Action	During the interviews those providing feedback are delivering the information for a positive purpose. Advice, suggestions and assistance should be sought, as well as clarification. The interview should be frank and honest.
Analysis	In essence, the feedback needs to be analysed in terms of strengths and weaknesses that have been identified. The strengths and weaknesses need to be categorized in order to identify areas of improvement or, perhaps, clarification. Specific areas may need specific actions.

After these six steps, a development plan needs to be agreed in order to identify specific steps and intended outcomes. There also needs to be a genuine commitment by the business to provide resources and other support in order for these outcomes to be met.

DeNisi, A. S. and Kluger, A. N., 'Feedback Effectiveness: Can 360-degree Appraisals be Improved?', *Academy of Management Executive*, 14 (1) (2000), pp. 129–39.
Ghorpade, J., 'Managing Five Paradoxes of 360-degree Feedback', *Academy of Management Executive*, 14 (1) (2000), pp. 140–50.

Index

Note: page numbers in **bold** indicate **definitions**. Most references are to the UK, except where otherwise specified.